LOSING THE SIGNAL

LOSING
THE
SIGNAL

THE SPECTACULAR
RISE AND FALL
OF BLACKBERRY

JACQUIE McNISH / / / SEAN SILCOFF

HarperCollins*Publishers*Ltd

Losing the Signal

Copyright © 2015 by Jacquie McNish and Sean Silcoff.

All rights reserved.

Published by HarperCollins Publishers Ltd

First published in Canada by HarperCollins Publishers Ltd in a hardcover edition: 2015

This trade paperback edition: 2016

HarperCollins books may be purchased for educational, business, or sales promotional use through our Special Markets Department.

HarperCollins Publishers Ltd
2 Bloor Street East, 20th Floor
Toronto, Ontario, Canada
M4W 1A8

www.harpercollins.ca

Library and Archives Canada Cataloguing in Publication information is available upon request

ISBN 978-1-44343-619-9

Designed by Anna Gorovoy

Printed and bound in the United States
RRD 9 8 7 6 5 4 3 2 1

FOR STEPHEN

—JACQUIE McNISH

FOR ERIN, CLARA, BEN, AND JACK

—SEAN SILCOFF

/ / / CONTENTS

Jim Balsillie fidgeted with his phone as his Dassault Falcon jet touched down at Dubai's international airport. It had been several hours since the co-chief executive and relentless global pitchman for Research In Motion Ltd. (RIM) powered off his BlackBerry when the plane left the company's Canadian hometown in Waterloo, Ontario. The man who convinced the world it could not operate without BlackBerry phones was itching to read his e-mails.

A restless forty-nine-year-old who kept in shape biking more than one hundred miles a week, Balsillie faced an uphill cycle in Dubai. After peaking two years earlier in 2009 as the world's biggest seller of smartphones and falling just shy of $20 billion in revenues, BlackBerry's sales were tumbling; its stock price was down more than 50 percent. Rivals Apple and Samsung had moved into the lead with a new generation of smartphones that expanded demand for wireless devices beyond the professional classes to fun-seeking consumers. The once addictive lure of BlackBerry's miniature keyboard and secure e-mail and message services was now being eclipsed by touch-screen iPhones and Androids that put Angry Birds games and YouTube videos into people's palms.

Nearly 1 billion people—one in seven people on earth—owned smart-phones, devices that hadn't existed a decade earlier. Not since the advent of network television in the late 1940s had a new technology been embraced so quickly by consumers. The race for market dominance was rapid and brut-ish. A few industry sovereigns, Motorola and Nokia, had already toppled. Some figured RIM would be the next casualty. The latest sign was a botched launch of a PlayBook tablet to compete with Apple's spectacularly successful iPad. The PlayBook had a tiny fraction of the apps that made the iPad popular and, in its rush to market, RIM had introduced the tablet without its trademark e-mail service.

Balsillie was in Dubai to deliver the keynote speech at the Persian Gulf's premier consumer electronics trade show. He knew he had to project confidence if he was going to reshape the industry narrative that RIM had lost its way. Offstage he faced an even bigger challenge. He had days of back-to-back meetings lined up with RIM's top local customers: ultrawealthy Middle East clients and telecom executives obsessed with BlackBerry's secure instant messaging service, BBM. He had to convince them that RIM's planned launch of the second generation of BlackBerry smartphones, already delayed by several months, would be better than Steve Jobs' iPhones.

As his jet taxied along the steaming tarmac, passing large patches of bleached sand and desert scrub, a bead of ticklish sweat traced down Balsillie's temple. He stared with disbelief at the device that revolutionized communication. Seconds earlier, tiny white bars formed a digital staircase in the upper right-hand screen of his BlackBerry Bold, indicating the phone was receiving a strong signal from a local wireless carrier. Good, good. But where were the four white dots indicating a connection to the BlackBerry network? Or the red flashing light announcing the arrival of e-mails in his in-box? Balsillie clicked the envelope icon on his screen to see if his in-box was filling up. *Nothing.* No new e-mails? After so many hours? Impossible. He closed his eyes. Shortly before the most important sales pitch of the year, the turnaround moment the company needed to bounce back, the product he was championing wasn't working.

/ / /

Slough, a town twenty miles west of London, England, has been little more than a historical footnote since its founding. It first enjoyed celebrity with British aristocracy in the 1660s as a resting place on the road to the therapeutic waters in Bath. In the 1930s the landscape was so fouled by smokestack factories that poet John Betjeman called for bombs to blow the town to smithereens. The BBC satire *The Office* gave the town another image problem in the early 2000s, choosing Slough (rhymes with "now") as the setting for a fictional series about the comically dysfunctional branch of a paper merchant.

On that October day in 2011, Slough would become the location of another corporate mishap. The problem began inside a nondescript gray office building. The squat facility was one of a handful of RIM's network operating centers that directed e-mail and BBM traffic for 70 million BlackBerry users. The nerve center of the Slough operation was a windowless room that was kept refrigerator-cold. Inside this brightly lit room, rows of gray steel cabinets hummed, firing millions of electronic messages every minute for customers in Europe, the Middle East, and Africa. A sister center in Waterloo, Ontario, handled the Western Hemisphere. No other phone maker operated its own in-house network, a rapid, encrypted, and tightly sealed system ensuring reliable high-speed traffic. That's why President Barack Obama refused a Secret Service missive to yield his BlackBerry after he was elected in 2008. Kings and queens, sheiks and business chieftains, were equally addicted to their "CrackBerrys."

Hours before Balsillie landed, the world's safest, most dependable wireless network responded to what should have been a minor problem. A server crashed. Normally, crashes aren't a big issue. The machines, computerized systems that briefly warehouse large packets of data such as e-mails, are so crucial to BlackBerry's network that reserve servers are continually powered up for emergencies. Known as hot backups, these stand-in machines are a primed, well-fed pony express, ready and waiting to spring forth.

RIM's recovery protocol was going according to plan within seconds of the Slough crash. The disabled server was shut off and its stalled messages began switching over to the backup. Unfortunately one component failed to do its job. A single router refused to route. The size of a suitcase, routers are computerized Rolodexes that store a database of Internet Protocol addresses to identify where incoming e-mails should be sent. When a new server takes over, routers are *supposed* to send waiting e-mails. Instead of sending addresses to the new server, the router, infected by an undetected software bug, instructed the disabled computer to restart—again and again and again. Before RIM's engineers knew what was happening, the two powerful machines were locked in a dangerous shoving match. The faulty router kept hammering the restart button on the disabled server, while the healthy machine fought back, attempting to regain control. When the slugfest was over minutes later, the servers had both been kayoed. The router was now lifeless: not only had it stopped working, but its memory was wiped clean.

/ / /

It was two in the morning when Mike Lazaridis got the call. Research In Motion's founder was a quick draw on his BlackBerry, even when startled awake. This call was from an engineer from the control room of the Waterloo Network Operating Centre, known internally as the NOC (sounds like "knock"). After a short conversation, Lazaridis pulled himself from bed, explaining to his half-awake wife, Ophelia: "The NOC is down."

Lazaridis had been through enough outages to know the last place he needed to be was the NOC control room, located on the top floor of a low-rise RIM building. He knew from experience that stress levels rose the minute he stepped into the war room. The company's founder was an intimidating presence, and attending engineers had enough to worry about trying to resuscitate the damaged network. In his office he called into "the dial-up," an emergency conference call that customarily takes place during an outage. At the other end, Robin Bienfait, chief information officer, tried to explain what was happening. Something unusual, something bad, was going on in Slough. Nobody could explain why, but millions of e-mails had stopped moving through Slough's servers. Its systems had collapsed. Standard responses were making things worse. Stalled e-mails from Europe, the Middle East, and parts of Asia were rerouted to North America, but the cascading traffic was more than Waterloo could manage. North America was likely going down. If the situation didn't change, it looked like the entire global network would be knocked out.

Aware of the consequences, Lazaridis tapped out a two-word text message on his BlackBerry to Balsillie: "Call me." An e-mail devotee, Lazaridis rarely bothered with text messages. But with the network outage, short text messages, relayed outside RIM's network through local carriers' wireless signals, were his only option. When his phone rang later, Lazaridis was prepared.

"Jim, everything is okay, but you should know there is a problem. Our network is down. Nothing is getting through. It is a complete outage."

"Down? How is that possible?" Balsillie asked. He had stepped off the jet in Dubai and was still fiddling with his unresponsive BlackBerry.

"We don't know why. Everyone is trying to fix it. We will fix it. We just don't know when we are going to get it back up."

/ / /

As he hung up, Balsillie's instinct was to jet back home to help manage the crisis. But fleeing Dubai would make the situation worse, he realized. Black-

Berry users everywhere were going through angry withdrawal. While Lazaridis's team raced to revive the network, he had to reassure powerful corporate and government customers that a fix was on the way. He would have to tap what little reserves of energy he himself had after months of corporate defeats and this new, potentially ruinous network outage.

Between meetings he juggled calls from powerful wireless carriers and major RIM users, Fortune 500 companies, and powerful governments. Unless their service was back up soon, customers complained, their faith in the company would be irreparably damaged.

"Don't worry," Balsillie reassured everyone. "It's almost fixed, another hour or two, tops, and we'll be back up."

Hours later, he spoke to a full house at the Gulf Information Technology Exhibition, but nobody listened to his pitch on the latest Bold phone features. Everyone wanted to know how much longer they would be without e-mail and BBM messages. His private meetings were equally grueling. The region's powerful business leaders were desperate to get back on line. "When will my BlackBerry start working again?" they begged.

Balsillie told everyone the same thing: *Hang on, any minute now.* To further placate powerful, needy clients, he doled out special editions of the company's Bold phones. To the most powerful sheiks, he presented custom-made gold or white phones. The recipients were delighted, especially when Balsillie assured them they were one of two honorary recipients of the exclusive prize. The other phone, he confided, belonged to Mohammed bin Rashid Al Maktoum, constitutional monarch of Dubai and prime minister of the United Arab Emirates. When Balsillie left Dubai on October 13 he had handed out dozens of the "exclusive" phones. By then, however, the flashy devices were little more than paperweights, a gaudy symbol of his company's missteps in recent years. RIM's global network was still knocked out.

Until that October day, BlackBerry was an improbable success story, the winner of one of the wildest, most disruptive technology races of the past century. A pint-sized company from a small city in Mennonite country, led by two men with little in common but their outsized ambition, had changed the way the world communicated. Just as desktop computers unseated mainframes by simplifying and accelerating once laborious tasks, BlackBerrys cut through computer wires and phone lines to free workers from desks. E-mails and documents could be fired off from cars or sent before the check arrived at restaurants—all without anyone knowing the sender was out of the office.

BlackBerry changed more than the workplace. We were liberated from offices and homes. Employers, clients, family and friends too, could reach us wherever wireless radio signals traveled. Work was no longer nine to five; it never ended. The same was true of socializing—we never had to be alone with our thoughts. BlackBerrys made us fast and efficient, but a little neurotic. The handsets transformed legions of users into addicts. For three days in October 2011, RIM customers were forced to go cold turkey. No BlackBerry. Where did everybody go? Life seemed impossible. When the outage ended, users were as committed as ever to mobile messaging. For Research In Motion, however, it was a different story. RIM was losing the signal to the market it created.

PART ONE

IF AT FIRST, THE IDEA IS NOT ABSURD,
THEN THERE IS NO HOPE FOR IT.

—ALBERT EINSTEIN

1 / / / REACH FOR THE TOP

The students at Prince of Wales Public School had long since stopped paying attention to Reg Nicholls squeaking away on the blackboard. Every few minutes the math teacher frowned, erasing part of his work. Then: more numbers, a spiraling out-of-control formula, and that awful scraping of chalk on blackboard. Finally, the classroom fell silent. Poor Nicholls stood motionless. "Can anyone tell me where I went wrong?" he asked.

An answer came from the back of the room: "When you were born."

The room erupted. Nicholls raced to the back of the class, dragging his heckler into the hallway. The sputtering, mottle-faced instructor pinned twelve-year-old Jim Balsillie against a wall of lockers. Balsillie stared right back at Nicholls. Balsillie's real punishment came the next day when he was kicked out of math. He'd have to study on his own for the rest of term. See how far that gets you, his teacher said. Oh, and you're still going to have to join classmates for the compulsory provincewide math test in a couple of weeks.

Later that month, Balsillie rejoined his class for the big test at the Peterborough, Ontario, school. The smart-ass, it turns out, really *was* smart. Studying all on his own, the lippy twelve-year-old math castoff scored first in the grade 7 test, not just at Prince of Wales but in the entire province. A regional superintendent traveled to the school to bestow the 1974 math honor on him. When he raced home to tell his mom, Laurel, about winning the award, she just shook her head, laughing, repeating a line she often used to sum up her difficult middle child: "Jim, you always fall in shit and come up smelling like roses."

Getting in trouble was relatively easy in Peterborough's working-class west end, where houses were small and ambitions were oversized; where lawns doubled as parking lots and sports games frequently ended in fights. Young Jim, the middle of three children born within three years, fit right in with the time and territory. "I was always a troublemaker," he says, "mouthy and cocky." Growing up, Balsillie played a lot of hockey and lacrosse and loved watching Peterborough Petes junior hockey games at Memorial Centre with his father, who had seasons tickets. Many Petes players made it to the NHL—including Bob Gainey and Steve Yzerman—and Balsillie dreamed of one day following them and returning to his hometown with hockey's greatest trophy, the Stanley Cup.

Even more important to Balsillie than Petes players was the team's coach. "The leading figure in my eyes was Roger Neilson—an innovative coach in so many ways." Neilson was junior hockey's infamous trickster. When pulling his goalie for an extra attacker, Roger had his net-minder leave his stick across the mouth of the crease to stop long shots. When he was managing a local baseball team, Neilson had a catcher hide a pared apple in his equipment. When a runner for the other team dangled off third base, the catcher fired the apple over his third basemen's head. The jubilant runner then dashed home, smiling, only to be touched out with the real ball by Roger Neilson's catcher at home plate.

When he wasn't pulling a fast one, Neilson fought the rules. That's how he became known as "Rule Book Roger." The establishment—referees and umpires, who were league officials—hated Rule Book Roger. Not teenage Jim Balsillie: he loved the maverick as much as he loved the game. Neilson's skirmishes mirrored the deep-rooted conflicts with authority that defined Balsillie's teenage years. He was close to his mother and her parents, but he sparred frequently with his father; he was a bright student who alienated teachers with a razor-sharp tongue. Although suspicious of figures of power, Balsillie also aspired to join Canada's business establishment. Balsillie would struggle throughout his career to make peace with his warring two-headed demon: the positive force of ambition versus a deep-rooted distrust of authority.

Predictably, perhaps, Balsillie's trouble with those in charge first became manifest in dealings with his father, Ray Balsillie, a descendent of French Métis, Canadian aboriginals of mixed European and indigenous ancestry that trace their roots to the fur trade. The Balsillies were a complicated bunch. One wing of the family worked at Saskatchewan's fabled Cumberland House, a northern Hudson Bay Company trading post that once housed the ill-fated Franklin expedition to the Arctic—Scottish explorers who perished in the far north in the 1840s. The Balsillie clan shares both Scot and Métis blood. All of which explains Jim Balsillie's piercing blue eyes, sharp cheekbones, and olive skin.

Ray Balsillie whose family moved from Manitoba to a small town south of Waterloo when he was a boy, left the family home as a teenager to make a fresh start in Seaforth, Ontario, with the Royal Canadian Air Force. As an adult Ray Balsillie seldom spoke of his native heritage, and his two sons and daughter were discouraged from raising the subject. It was only when Jim traveled as an adult to Winnipeg that he learned that an aunt was one of that city's most notorious residents. Gladys Balsillie, who died in 1987, began her career as a pilot before opening a popular restaurant and music venue, the Swinging Gate. When the restaurant closed, she made her mark managing exotic dancers at Winnipeg hotels. At her peak, the "Queen of the Strippers" managed more than one hundred male and female performers. Ray may have tried to hide his family's colorful past under the lush blue-green carpet of Ontario cottage country, but there was a strain of restless adventure in Balsillie blood—a history of flesh and fur traders.

Jim was born in 1961 in Seaforth, a small town near Lake Huron. Shortly after, Ray began moving the family around, accepting positions as an electrical repairman with various Ontario companies. Eventually the Balsillies settled in Peterborough, a small, conservative city in the heart of Ontario that, apart from their neighborhood, was straight as an accountant's ruler. When Jim was growing up, Peterborough was a predominantly white, churchgoing community defined by Trent University, a handful of U.S. manufacturing branch plants, and the summer influx of affluent Toronto cottagers. According to Jim, Ray Balsillie viewed himself as an outsider in the upbeat town; he gradually adopted a forlorn, Willy Loman–like air of defeat. "He grappled with insecurities," Balsillie says of his father. He and his dad's relationship "wasn't all hugs and kisses."

As Ray Balsillie withdrew from social activity, devoting his spare time to storing found objects and oddities in the family house, Jim flew in the opposite direction, growing increasingly ambitious. He cut his teeth as a salesman at age seven, selling Christmas cards door-to-door as his mother supervised from the sidewalk. Soon there were multiple paper routes, a painting business, and a job manning the lift at a nearby ski hill.

"I wanted the independence. I wanted nice things. If you wanted books, records, a car, athletic gear, you had to go earn it," he says.

What Balsillie really wanted was to be someone. Upon reading Peter C. Newman's seminal 1975 study of Canada's cozy business aristocracy, *The Canadian Establishment,* the tradesman's son decided that he had to join the country's most inbred club. Tracing the education and early career paths of powerful corporate chieftains mapped out in Newman's book, Balsillie realized he needed to take three giant steps: first, be accepted by an elite undergraduate school; second, land an accounting job at the establishment firm of Clarkson Gordon; and third, graduate from Harvard Business School. Balsillie had been an indifferent student who, except for his grade 7 home run in math, earned only average marks. He threw himself into studies his final year of high school. Upon being accepted by the University of Toronto's prestigious Trinity College, Balsillie replaced his childhood dreams of professional hockey with a new yearning. "I remember deciding I was going to be the best student in the history of the University of Toronto, set every academic record imaginable, prepare for every assignment, get 100 percent on everything," Balsillie says. "I was pretty sure they were going to put up a statue of me."

/ / /

It was deafening, like having your head next to a row of whirring propellers in an airfield. Grade 12 students at W. F. Herman Secondary School, in Windsor, Ontario, were busy in shop class, revving machines under the watchful eye of their electrical shop teacher, John Micsinszki. Students attached wires to motors, generators, instruments, and electrical panels at worktables. A bigger racket came from the back where a closet-sized power supply fed electricity to worktables. Once everything was plugged in, kids measured load factors, testing the efficiency of power coursing through machines.

The roar also tested one's ability to think. Minutes after starting, a confused student crossed wires on a motor, causing a burst of sparks. Micsinszki flew to the back of the shop to shut everything down. In his haste, he forgot students were still running generators at workstations. Within minutes, the machines routed so much electricity back to the idled power supply that it overheated, belching plumes of acrid fire and curdling purple smoke.

Now no one could see or hear. Micsinszki shouted for everyone to get out, turned off the motors, and extinguished the fire. When the smoke cleared, he knew he was staring at a financial and physical mess. Unless he figured out how to fix the fried machine, it was going to be impossible to teach electronics.

The solution to the mess arrived minutes later when a tall, broad-shouldered student with a thick hedge of dark hair returned to the shop room. Most kids spying the wreckage of Micsinszki's shop class complained of a sulfurous smell. Not Mike Lazaridis. He went right to the problem, examining the machine's wounded electrical panel. Micsinszki felt that no student at W. F. Herman had a keener grasp of applied science. A polite student with an easy smile, he was always asking permission to reassemble boxes of unwanted equipment donated by local companies. At first Micsinszki insisted Lazaridis study manuals. Soon, though, the prodigy was taking apart and assembling machines, even early, primitive computer systems, on the fly.

"Think you can fix this, Mike?" his teacher asked, nodding to the smoldering mess. After squinting at its wounded organs, Lazaridis offered a confident smile. It took months of tinkering, but Lazaridis eventually succeeded in breathing life back into the charred machine. News of his wizardry spread. Soon teachers were driving Lazaridis to their homes to repair broken TVs and stereos. His most lucrative job came from performing a favor for the school's librarian, who also coached W. F. Herman's Reach for the Top team. In the 1970s, Canadian high schools competed for a chance to shine in a nationally televised academic quiz show hosted by a young, pre-*Jeopardy* Alex Trebek. The key to the contest was connecting agile, well-stocked minds to gunfighter-fast buzzer hands.

W. F. Herman's practice buzzer was always breaking down—ropes of electrical wire came loose from battered hand controls. Lazaridis grew so frustrated with repair requests that he rebuilt the contraption at home, creating a simpler network built around a single thick cable connecting a control console to eight buzzer boxes, each housing a small light and electrical circuit that automatically reset the device for the next answer. Soon other schools were clamoring for the more reliable devices. By the time he graduated from high school, Lazaridis had sold enough buzzers to pay for his first year of university tuition.

It would be too easy to call Mike Lazaridis a born innovator. Better to say he excelled at the family business, which was transformation, new opportunities, and, sometimes, wholesale reinvention. Much of Mike Lazaridis's drive, the airy confidence everyone commented on, was shaped by his family's remarkable history. Born in Istanbul in 1961, Mihal Lazaridis was the first of Nick and Dorothy Lazaridis's two children. Greek transplants in a bustling Turkish city, his parents operated a women's clothing store. Like many Christians in Turkey, they found conditions difficult. Discrimination against non-Muslims was on the rise and the prospect of a compulsory military training program in a Muslim-dominated army promised further hardship. In 1964, the family of three followed Nick's brother, Paul, to Germany, where the siblings began training as tool and die makers. Dorothy Lazaridis earned extra money assembling hats from their small apartment. Four-year-old Mihal kept out of the way by making his own creations. One was a record player made out of Lego blocks, a pin, rubber bands, and a revolving tray. The creation never pulled music from his parents' records, but it did produce enough sound to convince them that their son was unusually skilled.

In 1966, the family followed Nick's brother again, this time to Canada in search of a job in North America's expanding automotive sector. A 1965 bilateral agreement relaxed trade restrictions around auto manufacturing, allowing Detroit automakers to integrate production plants in Canada and the United States. Nearby Windsor was now home to factories producing duty-free car and parts factories for sales in both countries. Nick soon landed a coveted job at a Chrysler assembly plant. Dorothy took part-time jobs as a waitress and seamstress. They saved money, hoping to buy a house and allow Nick to return to his retail roots. When Mihal, now Mike, wanted a sled to negotiate his new homeland's winter, Nick taught his son how to make it out of spare parts.

The Lazaridises' journey instilled in their eldest son an enduring belief that the world was what you make it and Canada was a place where dreams could come true. "It takes a lot of guts to leave behind your country, your family, and my dad's business and move to a whole new country and learn a whole new language," Lazaridis says. "In a sense [my parents] were entrepreneurs; they were explorers. To me, [change] was an opportunity."

When Mike was eight, his family had finally saved enough for a house with a room for him and his baby sister, Cleopatra. The Lazaridises moved into a two-story, postwar brick home in an east-end Windsor neighborhood filled with European and South American immigrants. Mike's interest in science was now a passion. With his father's help, he set up a worktable in a basement room that became known as "Mike's laboratory." One of his first projects was a machine that might quicken the transformation from Mihal to Mike. After failing a spelling test at Ada C. Richards Public School, Lazaridis asked his father to purchase a cassette recorder. With a spelling book in front of him he sat in his lab reading hundreds of words out loud to the machine, pausing after each word before announcing the correct spelling. Night after night he turned the electronic teacher on to test himself. Before long, he was competing in school spelling bees.

Basement quests grew more sophisticated after Lazaridis received a secondhand copy of *The Boy Electrician,* a chatty how-to guide for understanding and building electrical machines, radios, and other equipment. Lazaridis still cherishes the worn book like an old friend, but his early adventures with *The Boy Electrician* were frustrating. When he was able to scrape together money for needed parts, he discovered Windsor stores didn't stock items he needed, probably because his guidebook was published in 1914. Rather than discouraging Lazaridis, the setbacks deepened his determination, instilling in him a lifelong attention to thrift. If he could not afford or find materials, he would make them. There was always another way if you were smart and resourceful.

Lazaridis's best friends shared his love of science. Ken Wood's mom was a science teacher who provided ingredients for backyard experiments involving gunpowder, iodine bombs, and handmade rockets. His second pal, Doug Fregin, was a slight, painfully shy boy with thick glasses and a lazy eye who escaped teasing by building model planes. After Wood's family moved, Fregin became Lazaridis's shadow. "They were always together," says Bob Oxford, a longtime school classmate. Although neither science whiz joined other boys in daily games of hockey and football, both were welcomed into the neighborhood.

"They were accepted because everyone liked Mike," Oxford explains.

While Lazaridis read every science book at the local library, Fregin applied model-making skills to soldering circuit boards and wiring equipment. The *Boy Electrician* projects became more complex. After a neighbor, a ham radio operator, gave them some used equipment, Lazaridis and Fregin hit the big time at a grade 7 science fair. Surrounded by tattered paper volcanoes and wobbly constellations, Lazaridis and Fregin's entry was a solar panel fashioned out of wood, tinfoil, light sensors, and a relay system attached to a small motor. A roaming TV crew showcased the impressive invention on the local news.

Celebrity ensued. The school's eighth-grade yearbook featured a caricature of Lazaridis as a mad scientist with thunderbolts bursting from his head.

At W. F. Herman, Lazaridis encountered his first roadblock, a segregated world divided into two castes. The building's second floor was home to the school's elite science, math, and business classes. The first floor was devoted to electrical and machine shops. Second-floor kids went on to university, first-floor grads went to manufacturing jobs. John Micsinszki's wife, Margaret, remembers that her university-educated husband and other tech teachers "had no great love for the guidance department at Herman, where good academic students were discouraged from taking technical courses, even if the student intended to study engineering at university."

All this was initially a challenge for Lazaridis, a kid with a foot on both floors of W. F. Herman. He got around the problem by ignoring boundaries. A devoted math and science student, Lazaridis wasn't about to give up the chance to apply years of basement experiments to well-stocked machine shops. At first he was disappointed with the presumptuous second-floor teachers. "I didn't like the way they looked down at us," he says. Eventually, those instructors realized Lazaridis's electrical prowess had classroom benefits. Students struggling with math turned to Lazaridis, who would explain how complex formulas could be applied to everyday use, such as electricity. In shop, it was "Laz" that the kids turned to for help operating machines. "He basically taught everyone how to use all the equipment. He had a way of explaining it so we understood," Oxford recalls.

The greatest lesson he learned in high school came off-campus. As an electronics teacher and president of a ham radio club, Micsinszki introduced both Lazaridis and Fregin to the world of transistors and cathode-ray tubes. Before long, Lazaridis and Fregin were dropping by the Micsinszki home to talk shop. Margaret Micsinszki, one of the city's first high school computer science teachers, introduced the boys to computing advances. Taking advantage of afterschool tutelage, Lazaridis built his own oscilloscope, Fregin perfected circuit making, and they each built computers. Margaret was convinced that computer science would lead the next wave of modern innovation. Her husband saw a bigger future. "Don't get too seduced by these computers," he warned. "The person who puts wireless communications and computers together is really going to build something special."

Lazaridis never had to write that down. "The day he said that," he says, "it never left us."

/ / /

The men's dining hall at Trinity College was in giddy, anarchic chaos. Dinner buns were flying, tables were being thumped, and jeers were rising to the timbered rafters. Solemn chancellors from the century-old University of Toronto college looked on from their oil portraits, as they might have at Hogwarts, as a peculiar ritual unfolded. A first-year student had committed some unpardonable act and was now being "poored out." Lying prone on one of the hall's long trestle tables, holding onto the edge for dear life with the help of a few friends, the young man on trial struggled to stay put as the rest of the dining hall attempted to yank the human centerpiece onto the floor.

"Out, out, out," shouted dozens of jubilant men dressed in floor-length robes. Overseeing this tug-of-war was an older student eyeing his wristwatch. If the boy on trial could hang on for a full minute, he was allowed to leave the dining hall of his own volition. If not, he would be dragged from the room, shamed and ridiculed. The clock ticked, food and shouts filled the air. Then finally . . .

"Done!" the student proctor exclaimed, "Balsillie may walk."

As friends cheered, the first-year student stood, breaking into a wide grin as he adjusted his disheveled robe and sauntered out of the wood-paneled hall. Few walked away once targeted in a pooring-out ritual that was as old as the dining hall's wood-paneled walls. Most were pulled from tables or chairs within seconds. The punishment was meant to discourage "poor" behavior by first-year students. At Trinity, where most students descended from political and business bluebloods, stepping out of line usually amounted to breaches of old-world British civility. Poor table manners or boasting could prompt a pooring out. The ritual would fall victim to political correctness in later years, but not soon enough for Balsillie, a frequent target in his first year at Trinity in 1980.

According to former classmates, his offense was, almost always, trying too hard. Shortly after arriving at the castle-like gray stone college to earn a commerce degree, Balsillie was elected president of his year, earned a spot on the school's lacrosse team, and began organizing hockey and football matches. "You always had the impression that he had something to prove," says Andrew Coyne, a Trinity student at the time who went on to be a leading Canadian political columnist with Toronto's *National Post*.

In his first weeks at university, Balsillie drove himself hard, closeting himself in his dorm room to study, allowing only fifteen-minute breaks every hour to check the score of televised hockey games. When friends dragged him out one night to a frat party, he got home late and in no mood to study for an exam the next day. He aced it anyway and emerged from the experience with a new mantra: "Work hard, party hard."

Few students were as devoted to academic and social success, a relentless all-hours ambition that earned him the nickname "Balls." Balsillie organized theme parties celebrating obscure brews, like Carling Cinci lager, or the films of his favorite character, James Bond. When asked to help organize formal affairs, he displayed a unique talent for stretching a student budget by visiting funeral homes late in the business day in search of free, slightly used flowers to decorate the college's party rooms for formal dinners and dances. His vintage Volkswagen Beetle was often so stuffed with used floral arrangements that he could only see by poking his head through a thicket of ferns. He gamely agreed to grow a beard and perform in a short film about the perils of technology made by fellow Trinity student and future Oscar-nominated filmmaker Atom Egoyan called *A Clockwork Trinity*.

Balsillie was equally creative about studying. After forging friendships in residence with ambitious students who, like him, arrived from small towns with few connections, he organized a study club so members could share and discuss homework. The group included Malcolm Gladwell, from Elmira, Ontario, who would become the author of several bestsellers, including *The Tipping Point, Blink,* and *Outliers*. Another study-clubber was Nigel Wright, from Ancaster, Ontario, who would go on to become one of Canada's leading financiers and chief of staff to Prime Minister Stephen Harper.

At Trinity, Wright says Balsillie was "a force of nature," juggling multiple challenges with unlimited energy. He threw the best parties, excelled in sports, and ensured homework club members were prepared for exams. Study sessions were usually held in his room and snacks were plentiful. As they swapped notes, members also shared their ambitions. In Balsillie, Wright saw someone who was determined to change a world he believed was stacked against people who shared his working-class background and lack of connections. "His basic position was that he was not going to accept the world as it was. He was determined and dogged about obtaining his objective," Wright says. In those heady days at Trinity, Wright believed Balsillie's ambition would take him to Wall Street or a Fortune 500 company.

Following the career path he had mapped out from Newman's elite business guide, *The Canadian Establishment*, Balsillie landed a job at the accounting firm Clarkson Gordon after graduating from Trinity. Unlike other ambitious new hires jockeying for positions on big corporate accounting teams, Balsillie opted to join a smaller group that represented entrepreneurial owners of rapidly growing companies. At Clarkson Gordon, Balsillie learned two lessons: first, he did not like accounting; second, new business computing tools were leverage in the hands of an adept junior manager. Balsillie's talent for managing data and financial analysis with early spreadsheet programs got him a seat at takeover tables with senior managers and clients who wanted quick financial breakdowns as negotiations and terms shifted.

"All of a sudden," Balsillie says, "[I was] a rock star, you're in all the partner meetings. They'd say, 'Just bring Jim in.'"

After two years of spreadsheets, Balsillie achieved his final academic objective—acceptance into the masters program at Harvard Business School. By now he was dating Heidi Henschel, a rehab therapist from southern Ontario, who followed him to Boston in 1987. The couple managed Harvard's staggering tuition costs with the help of a fellowship and Balsillie's part-time income from managing a student guidebook and advising for a small financial services firm in Boston. At Harvard, Balsillie found few Canadian small-town peers. Classes were filled with ambitious, privileged students from the United States and other countries—cultured keeners competing for grades that would land them blue-chip business jobs. In his class of ninety MBA students, Balsillie says, "I felt there were eighty-nine Nobel Prize winners and one fraud."

The Canadian outsider learned to overcome his insecurity with humor. The edgy barbs that landed him in boiling water in grade school had morphed into nuanced parodies of professors, many of them aging business chiefs. He became so good at mimicking teachers that classmates captured his act on video. In one he stuffed a pillow up his shirt and waved menthol cigarettes and a can of cream soda as he ummed and ahhed through a lecture. The skewered professor delighted his class in his final lecture by airing Balsillie's parody. "This was huge," Balsillie remembers. "All of a sudden your social cachet goes to the moon."

Just as promising were Balsillie's career choices. He interviewed with a number of prestigious Wall Street firms, including Goldman Sachs, but his master plan took an unexpected turn in his final year when he met a group of business chiefs from the Young Presidents' Organization at a campus cocktail party in early 1989. When Balsillie arrived at the event, one of his classmates steered him to a tall, lean businessman with penetrating blue eyes. A fellow Canadian, Rick Brock warmed immediately to the animated student, inviting his new friend to dinner with a group of other presidents. The young entrepreneurs shared stories, offering frank advice about corporate and personal challenges. Balsillie felt like a business insider for the first time. When it was his turn to talk, Balsillie revealed his humble roots and lofty ambitions.

"I was impressed," says Brock. So impressed, he ordered a limousine and ferried Balsillie to a series of Boston bars. Near the end of the evening, Brock slapped more than a drink on the table. "Why don't you come and learn to run a business?" he asked. The business was Sutherland-Schultz, a midsized electronic equipment maker based near Waterloo, Ontario. Brock could offer only half of what Balsillie could make on Wall Street, but he convinced the student that a senior job at his plant would teach him more about operating a company than he could ever learn as a banker. When Brock woke up the next morning with a screaming headache, he reached for the phone and dialed Balsillie's number. "Remember that offer I gave you last night?" Brock asked. "I was afraid you wouldn't," came a nervous reply.

Balsillie was on his way back to Ontario. His friends were stunned by his career choice. Wall Street was the number one destination of any aspiring finance grad. It was the nerve center of what was then the biggest corporate takeover binge in history. Junk bonds, buyout barbarians, and Michael Milken were such household names that Hollywood named a blockbuster movie *Wall Street*. Balsillie's Harvard peers had never heard of Waterloo and Canadian friends knew nothing of Sutherland-Schultz. "We were astonished. It didn't seem to fit Jim's game plan," said Wright.

What they failed to grasp was that Balsillie's career vision had shifted: new spreadsheet applications at Clarkson Gordon revealed to him the power of technology. Lining up for job interviews with Fortune 500 companies, he realized he would be competing for years to make his way to the senior ranks. That prospect didn't interest him. Balsillie even sabotaged an interview with influential strategy consultant McKinsey & Company, giving wiseacre answers and accusing an interviewer of asking "stupid" questions. Brock was willing to give him an executive title immediately in a company that was just starting to automate manufacturing systems with computers. "I realized the only way I was going to make it [fast] in this world is by rewriting business rules," Balsillie says, "and technology is an opportunity to rewrite business rules."

/ / /

Lazaridis could hardly believe what he was seeing. Standing face pressed against the glass wall of a narrow walkway, he peered down at a cavernous room that looked like a sci-fi movie set. Paneled in lurid red floor and wall tiles, the chamber was jammed with dozens of large, multicolored cabinets, flashing light consoles, and a few studious young men and women operating desktop computers. It was early 1979 and Lazaridis was feasting his eyes on the fabled Red Room at the University of Waterloo. The room housed an IBM 360 Model 75, Canada's largest, fastest computer. The Red Room was a testament to the vision of businessmen and scholars who, in 1957, founded a university in a Mennonite farming community an hour's drive west of Toronto. The need for engineers was so urgent in the postwar boom era that Waterloo founders set up a co-op program that dispatched students each term to semester-long jobs so they could apply their learning in a commercial environment.

The program bridged the academic and corporate divide, allowing for collaboration on such ambitious projects as the Red Room in the 1960s. IBM sold the machine to the University of Waterloo at a discount and the Ontario government subsidized the $3 million acquisition, an item so alien to purchasing categories that the computer was listed as "furnishings." Lazaridis did not see furniture when he visited the computer science department with his parents during his final year of high school. He saw the future. "I just looked down into the room," he recalls, "and I said 'This is where I am going.'"

Wireless technology and computing were traveling toward each other at warp speed when Lazaridis enrolled in electrical engineering at Waterloo. The sprawling computer in the Red Room that so dazzled him in 1979 was unplugged in late 1980 to make way for smaller, more powerful mainframes and the arrival of early desktop computers. These systems were connected through local networks knitted together with cables. Long before e-mail, Lazaridis and classmates were using the university's network to hand in assignments or dispatch messages over the pioneering Arpanet, the U.S. military's Advanced Research Projects Agency Network—the Internet's forerunner. "It was a whole new world. Everything was new," says Lazaridis. "It was like a fantasyland."

Just as he had divided studies at W. F. Herman, Lazaridis explored various disciplines at Waterloo. He supplemented core electrical engineering courses with computer science and physics classes. Of all his studies, it was quantum mechanics that made the greatest impact on him. Classical physics theories were being challenged in the early 1980s. Longstanding formulas that revealed how liquids were heated or why vehicles accelerated downhill had little application in the world of atoms and subatomic particles. One father of the emerging offshoot of classical physics was David Bohm, an American-born physicist whose dabbling in Marxism forced him to leave the country in the McCarthy era. The intuitive scientist continued his work abroad. Borrowing from religious, biological, psychological, and artistic influences, he theorized that atoms and particles were part of a deeper, intricate order in which they were influenced by the properties of other particles. While it would be decades before scientists would be able to apply Bohm's theories to breakthrough experiments in quantum mechanics, the unorthodox thinking encouraged students to explore new frontiers.

"It was a new age," Lazaridis explains. "We had this belief that all sorts of stuff was about to get transformed, from technology to the way we thought about the universe." Bohm's theories were so influential that when Lazaridis learned the scientist would be speaking in Ottawa in May 1983, he and a group of friends approached the pending visit like religious pilgrims. "We all wanted to go to Ottawa. We had no money. A couple of us said we can do this, it didn't need to be impossible," Lazaridis says.

The Waterloo students eventually made their way to Ottawa. Listening to the lecture, Lazaridis felt that he was in the presence of an "enlightened" man who "crackled" with confidence. He also remembers the small miracles that made his trip possible. A professor let the students drive a university van to the speech and friends secured rooms at an Ottawa fraternity. "The point was, we never gave up," he now says. "We just believed we had to get there and see David Bohm." Lazaridis would approach future challenges with the same sense of destiny.

At the University of Waterloo, Lazaridis distinguished himself as an entrepreneur. He landed a plum work placement at the Canadian branch of the Minneapolis supercomputer maker Control Data Corporation. He then earned his way out of a tedious night shift running computer diagnostics by designing a program that automated the process. Lazaridis was given a series of increasingly important assignments working with Control Data's "big iron" computers and was on track for a job in Minneapolis. The plans, however, were derailed by the company's financial woes. The big computer maker responded ineptly to the arrival of microcomputers and spent most of the 1980s and 1990s shedding assets. It is now called Ceridian.

The wrenching decline of a company staffed by so many smart and devoted engineers made a big impression on Lazaridis. Innovation could not thrive without corporate support and effective commercial strategies. Discouraged with the world of big business, he decided to be his own boss by starting a consulting company that designed computer solutions for local technology companies. For one of his first clients, he built a primitive memory card with custom software that eliminated the need for cumbersome floppy disks. He became so busy with his fledgling company that the university agreed to let him work for himself for his third-year co-op job placement. The $5,000 in profits he pocketed during the term allowed him to buy a new computer and take his father, Nick, on a fishing trip.

Lazaridis loved running his own business. By the fourth year he was consumed with an innovation that he and Doug Fregin had toyed with in Micsinszki's basement. By hooking up an early computer to a cathode-ray tube, the pair could transmit data to project information on a television screen. The device was a money saver for Micsinszki, who burned through expensive tubes broadcasting the recorded times and frequencies of his regular one-man ham radio talk show for fellow enthusiasts. At Waterloo, Lazaridis saw a grander application for the technology, and Fregin, who visited him frequently on breaks from his studies at the University of Windsor, shared his enthusiasm. During these get-togethers the old friends honed their high school innovation, creating a device with a custom-designed circuit board, computer memory, power supply, central processor, and a calculator-sized keyboard. Once wired into a cathode-ray tube, the system enabled users to type words that flashed onto television screens.

The system, Lazaridis decided, would be called Budgie, a fun, consumer-friendly name that he believed would endear people to an electronic system that was difficult to explain or understand. By spring of 1984 he was so convinced the device represented a breakthrough that he traveled home to Windsor to tell his parents and the Micsinszkis that he and Fregin would be dropping out of university weeks before graduation to launch a new business. Margaret Micsinszki said she and her husband were shocked by his decision, but they had learned to trust Lazaridis's determination. For Lazaridis, she says,

"There were no roadblocks. He would persist until the experiment succeeded or the project worked."

While Fregin and University of Waterloo co-op student Chris Shaw wrote software code and perfected hardware for the Budgie, Lazaridis pitched the innovation to local businesses as a kind of digital advertising banner that could effortlessly flash new messages. When a local hardware store and shopping mall agreed to test the Budgie, the trio attracted local media attention. A black-and-white photograph taken by a local newspaper of the young entrepreneurs, still very much Boy Electricians, remains a timeless portrait of innovators who misunderstood their market.

At the center of the photograph is a glass case with two televisions. One reads, "Advertise On Me - I Attract Customers," the other, "The Budgie System." Perched on top of the second TV set is a stuffed bird. To the left of the display, Shaw and Fregin join together, unsmiling, clad in plaid (Fregin) and a rumpled T-shirt (Shaw). To the right stands Lazaridis, at twenty-three sporting premature gray hairs, wearing an oxford shirt, V-neck sweater, and khaki plants. Clutching a vinyl briefcase and staring confidently into the camera, Lazaridis appears oblivious to a group of female shoppers gathered behind him. No one notices that the stand-in budgie is actually a toy parrot. Instead they are sifting through a large box of discounted goods placed in the hall by a nearby retailer.

In an unintended nod to the many lessons they had yet to learn about running a business, Lazaridis and Fregin formally registered their new company under the name Research In Motion Ltd. on March 7, 1984.

2 / / / ENCHANTED FOREST

Mike Lazaridis strode with purposeful confidence into an office tower on Eglinton Avenue in Toronto. He and Mike Barnstijn, a new Research In Motion partner, were hopeful that a meeting with a potential client would bring some badly needed luck. It was late 1989, five years after Lazaridis and Doug Fregin founded RIM. Their inaugural Budgie communicators never took flight because businesses didn't share the designers' excitement about the bulky digital advertising system. At the time RIM was surviving by designing electronic components in a berth above a Waterloo bagel store. It had a run making computerized digital display boards for General Motors Corp. and circuit boards for factory equipment. It even created automated bar code readers for film-editing machines that would later earn RIM Oscar and Emmy technical awards. The innovations were promising, but buyers were scarce. Cash was so low that Barnstijn was sometimes paid in RIM stock. If the pressure was getting to Lazaridis, he never let it show. He was not one to dwell on finances or grow nervous if products fell behind schedule. The schoolboy who fixed every mess at W. F. Herman high school, no matter how difficult, approached business setbacks as temporary problems. "There is always another life raft," was his mantra.

The raft of the day was Rogers Cantel Inc., a cellphone company controlled by Canada's cable pioneer, Ted Rogers. Having amassed a fortune feeding cable TV to Canadian homes in the 1970s and 1980s, Rogers had a habit of recruiting big thinkers who might deliver the next lucrative electronic breakthrough. One of Rogers' sages, an irreverent Brit who parlayed a chemistry degree into a mobile phone career, was seated in the middle of a warren of cubicles, smoothing a plush mustache, when Lazaridis and Barnstijn strolled in the door. David Neale was technically in charge of marketing at Rogers Enhanced Radio Group. More accurately, he was the Pied Piper to a team of employees known internally as the Enchanted Radio Group. The team tinkered with radio components and antennas and dreamed of data that could be carried over radio waves to mobile products. Could computers be refitted to fire messages and documents on radio signals to mobile couriers, salespeople, and other footloose professionals? Engineers and ham radio innovators experimented for years with text messages on radio waves. No one, however, had translated the breakthroughs into a viable business.

"No one believed we would amount to anything," says Neale. "Can you imagine a group of people who had been drawn together for the purpose of creating something, but weren't sure what it was? I was supposed to think up what that was."

Rogers enlisted RIM to assess recently purchased technology from Sweden's telecommunications giant Ericsson. When Neale and his team first opened the boxes of components, they were puzzled. Nobody could figure out what it was. And the big fat manual, more than a thousand pages, was in Swedish. What Rogers had purchased was a collection of wires and parts for a wireless data network called Mobitex. It was acquired to fix a persistent service issue: in an era before cellphones were ubiquitous, Rogers couldn't communicate with its service trucks. Customers wasted whole days waiting for servicemen, and Rogers lost money with idled trucks. If Rogers could figure out how to make a usable network with the Swedish equipment, it could manage its service fleet more effectively, improve customer satisfaction, and cut costs. Maybe Rogers could even sell Mobitex systems to other businesses.

Barnstijn, a Dutchman, knew enough Swedish to translate some of the Mobitex manual. What Rogers had acquired, he explained, was a network designed to deploy data over radio frequencies. It was the kind of technology bridge Lazaridis's teacher John Micsinszki had envisioned: a radio-based system that enabled communications on a network of computers and mobile devices. Lazaridis felt his pulse quicken. "I remembered what my teacher said, that the person who puts this all together is going to do something really big," he says.

For his part, Neale didn't have much faith that Mobitex would be commercially viable. All he saw was an electrical mess. "If you can figure out how this works, we'll hire you," he told his guests.

/ / /

Communication advances have marched at a sluggish pace for most of history. By the early 1800s progress was so limited that carrier pigeons and flag semaphores defined instant messaging. Things picked up speed in the mid-1800s with the advent of the telegraph. The rapid transmission of electrical messages over copper wires triggered such an explosion in communications that the breakthrough has been referred to as the Victorian Internet.[1] Just as the modern Internet boom inspired legions of start-ups seeking to leapfrog dot-com innovations, the dots and dashes of Morse code telegraph messages inspired competitors to race ahead with advances.

One of the most famous early pioneers was Guglielmo Marconi, an Italian inventor who devised a system for "telegraphy without wires." Dispensing with the wires and cables of the telegraph, Marconi devised a system that harnessed radio waves to transmit messages. Other scientists had previously experimented with transmitters to generate radio signals over short distances. But what these innovators lacked was Marconi's imagination and showmanship. He made headlines around the world in 1901 when his towering transmitter in Cornwall, England, successfully conveyed the world's first transatlantic radio message, three clicks, or Morse dots, for the letter *S*, to a receiving station Marconi was manning in Newfoundland.

Marconi's show business savvy allowed him to raise enough money to build a profitable global business for customers with deep pockets. Sales improved when it was revealed a Marconi operator went down with the *Titanic* after successfully sending an SOS to nearby ships. Naval and commercial ships, unreachable by telegraph wires, paid handsomely for Marconi's wireless equipment. But for the average company, his systems were too complex and expensive. Most consumers and businesses would have to wait nearly a century for more affordable wireless communication machines. In the meantime, innovation was driven by those willing to pay heavily for the convenience of portable communicators.

Ericsson designed what is believed to be the first car phone in the early 1900s for its wandering chief, Axel Boström. Boström was such a car enthusiast that his trips down Swedish country roads in rudimentary cars often left him stranded with a broken vehicle. The company assigned engineers to design a mobile phone so he could call for help. The solution was a car phone that could tap local landlines when Boström attached a metal-tipped pole to overhead telephone wires. The only problem with the system was the car had to remain stationary during calls.[2]

Detroit was home to the next major advance in mobile communication when the city's police force struggled to keep up with speeding getaway cars in the Roaring Twenties. To combat the crime wave, the police hired a local engineer to build a custom radio system that enabled dispatchers to send alerts about stolen cars or robberies from headquarters over a radio channel to receivers embedded in patrol cars. The radio messages sped up police response times, but the system had its limits. Radio messages could only travel one way from the station to cruisers, which meant police officers had to find a land phone if they needed to get more information or report back to headquarters. Despite the drawbacks, the innovation gave Detroit's finest an edge fighting bad guys. Other cities clamored for the crime-fighting device, a lucky break for a struggling Chicago radio manufacturer called Galvin Manufacturing Corporation.

Galvin was founded in 1928 to sell parts for home radios. Stiff competition forced the company to diversify into the emerging market for car radios. Its pioneering radios, called Motorolas, were created to tap into the restless American spirit. It was the Jazz Age, and cars and roads had replaced horses and trails. What better way to see and hear the country than a car radio. Soon, company founder Paul Galvin saw potential for another market—police cruisers. "There was a need and I could see it was a market that nobody owned," Galvin said.[3] He quickly dominated the market for mobile communicators by adding transmitters to specialized police radios, allowing two-way conversations between dispatchers and police.

Car and police radios marked the beginning of a decades-long race by Galvin to perfect wireless communications. Innovations with transistors meant it no longer cost a fortune to build the giant transmission towers of the Marconi era. Devices were getting smaller, signals more powerful. Galvin's next innovation turned the Illinois firm into a global player. More than forty thousand U.S. soldiers entered World War II with portable two-way radios that later became universally popular under the name "walkie-talkies."

Following the war, Galvin changed its name to Motorola and expanded into the professional classes with handheld pagers. Its first big paging success was the Pageboy, introduced in the mid-1970s. Backed by a network of powerful antennas that broadcast radio messages to pagers, Pageboys kept doctors, emergency workers, and other professionals connected when they left work. Like early Detroit police car radios, the fist-sized pagers were beeping one-way communicators, because network antennas lacked the signal power to send messages back into the system. Motorola changed the electronic conversation game again in 1983, unveiling the first commercial mobile phone, the shoe-sized DynaTAC. Nicknamed "The Brick," the device sold for $4,000 and came with a battery that lasted about an hour and took half a day to recharge.

Cellphones were a perfect solution for mobile professionals who didn't roam too far from headquarters, but charges rocketed if users called long distance. By the 1990s globalization was pushing so many employees to travel to distant locations that the costs and convenience of staying connected were becoming prohibitive. Wireless messages were a more affordable option, but devices and networks were primitive. Most big organizations had built custom networks and software programs to connect in-house desktop computers. But there was no standard communication language, no open, well-tended wireless roadway to shuttle mobile data to traveling employees or outside businesses, governments, and other organizations. It cost so much time and money to translate the Babel of network languages with custom software that many companies didn't bother. Early innovations by a surfing fanatic in Hawaii would prove instrumental in bridging the wireless data gap.

Norman Abramson left his job teaching engineering and physics at Harvard University in the late 1960s to accept a job at the University of Hawaii that put him within walking distance of the ocean. Abramson loved surfing, but he made his reputation riding airwaves. As head of a campus research project, Abramson created a wireless network based on radio signals that solved a local communications problem with University of Hawaii computers scattered among its campuses on four islands. Underwater telephone cables connecting the islands were expensive and not always reliable.

Abramson's solution was ALOHAnet, a network of software and equipment that radiated coded messages over radio signals. The advent of computers and digital communications made it possible to modulate radio waves, once shaped to convey the dashes and dots of Morse code, to relay digital bits known as 1s and 0s. This binary code was so efficiently processed that it was possible to relay data at faster speeds.

Ham radio enthusiasts had tinkered with radio-based digital data transmissions for years, but radio channels were scarce and the capacity for conveying large blocks of data over long distances was limited. The biggest problem with traditional analog radio channels was that they were so busy and noisy that data messages were at risk of being lost or so corrupted they were unreadable. ALOHAnet solved these problems by dividing data into coded packets. Each packet held a portion of the user's message and instructions about the destination and sequence in which the packet was to be arranged with other parts of the message when they arrived. If a channel was busy, packets were programmed to wait, like cars obeying a red light. As soon as a channel opened—*green light*—some packets continued their journey, a process that was repeated until all packets arrived. In the early 1970s, long before most people had heard of the Internet, Abramson and his colleagues were sending and receiving e-mails from various university campuses on their wireless network.[4] It would be years before the concept was commercialized.

Motorola and IBM joined forces in 1983 to create a two-way radio network for the computer maker's service technicians. The first commercial data network seemed an ideal partnership. IBM could keep tabs on roaming technicians; Motorola now had a blue chip customer to vouch for its breakthrough service and transmission equipment. IBM technicians were issued portable terminals. Initially, an IBM phone operator took customer orders, then routed computer messages in short, coded messages to the nearest technician. The device sped up IBM service response, but the experiment was costly and offered limited message capacity. The terminals sold for as much as $3,700 a pop, and there were access fees and messaging costs.[5] Few other businesses signed up for the service after they commercialized it in 1990. In 1994, IBM sold its 50 percent stake in the business back to Motorola.

Until the 1990s, wireless data networks were seen as a great engineering adventure that offered little commercial potential. It was an old story. Communication innovators often didn't know what they had. Alexander Graham Bell was so convinced his pioneering telephone would be such an unwanted intrusion that he initially promoted his invention in the 1880s at expositions and fairs as an entertainment system that conveyed music and theatrical performances over headphones to those who couldn't afford to buy tickets to the real thing.[6] Similarly, it would take years and hundreds of millions of dollars of investment in wireless data research and many wrong turns to convince the market that wireless data was a worthwhile service. In the meantime, there were enough profits to be made in the fledgling mobile phone business.

Within five years after Motorola launched its bulky brick phone in 1983, Finland's Nokia, Germany's Siemens, and Korea's Samsung joined the cellular phone race. Ericsson followed, but its engineering-driven culture struggled in a Madison Avenue world of slogans and product branding. Early Ericsson phones were lightweight marvels, but their dull brown and gray covers and plain female names, "Jane" and "Sandra," doomed what were then some of the more advanced cellphones on the market.

Like Motorola, Ericsson spotted a lasting opportunity in wireless plumbing. There was good money to be made selling expensive infrastructure that relayed and directed data traffic along radio channels. Ericsson had collaborated with Sweden's government-owned phone company Televerket in designing the Mobitex network, allowing ambulances and emergency response vehicles to send and receive data messages. Eyeing a bigger market outside its small home country, Ericsson launched a campaign to sell Mobitex globally. If customers bought the network, they would have to invest in Ericsson's expensive line of base stations, relay equipment, and portable terminals. The first set of Mobitex components sold in North America went to New Jersey–based RAM Mobile Data. The second was housed in the boxes Lazaridis examined in Rogers' offices.

/ / /

The basement ballroom of Toronto's King Edward Hotel was transformed into corporate Neverland. A dozen weeping fig trees had been stationed around the room, covered in small delicate lights to create just the look David Neale wanted: an enchanted forest for an enchanted radio team. On this late afternoon in May 1990, he had invited dozens of communications executives, journalists, and consultants to attend a presentation by Rogers on the new future in state-of-the-art wireless communications.

Guests were not disappointed. A short multiscreen slide presentation featured men in construction hats staring, eyes narrowed, at a glowing horizon, as 1s and 0s symbolizing binary code flew across a luminous rising moon. The wireless data revolution had arrived, a Rogers executive declared, and it was going to save businesses lots of money. Information would travel over radio waves to terminals in courier and service trucks, speeding the delivery of work orders, invoices, and payments. This was all possible because Rogers had

Mobitex. The Swedish network connected computers to mobile terminals that traveled wherever business went. Mobile data was no longer the stuff of science fiction. The future was here. To reinforce the point, tables were loaded with portable Mobitex terminals displaying test text messages dispatched from a distant location.

"What we were showing was very futuristic," Neale says. So futuristic no one visiting the enchanted forest realized the display was still a fantasy. None of the machines actually worked on Mobitex yet. The terminals were wired into a computer simulating radio transmissions. Lazaridis and his team at RIM had been making progress with the Mobitex network, but they were still months from designing software and components that would allow North American computers to communicate with the Swedish network. Neale couldn't afford to wait any longer. His enchanted radio team was in danger of being shut down if he couldn't convince his bosses and potential customers that there was a market for Mobitex's wireless network. "Everyone had a most pleasant time," recalls Neale. "We just didn't sell much." Five months later, Rogers began losing patience with the radio dream and transferred many of the group's staff to its rapidly expanding pager division. Neale left shortly after to join a telephone company, and RIM was left with contract scraps from Rogers and Ericsson.

/ / /

Rick Brock sped up as he exited Cambridge, Ontario, steering his car east onto Highway 401. Next to him sat Jim Balsillie. The men were going on a hunting weekend. Not the takeover variety, although there would be talk of that. Even though Brock's company, Sutherland-Schultz, was about to be swallowed whole by a Dutch acquirer, Stork MV, what he had lined up that fine fall day in 1991 was one of the most exclusive pastimes available to wealthy businessmen. They were going pheasant hunting on Nicholson Island, a secret escape in Lake Ontario, two hours east of Toronto. The island's clipped fields and tangled scrub were the property of a private hunting club. Only members, guests, staff, pointer dogs, and well-fed pheasants were allowed. Bing Crosby visited regularly in the 1960s and a who's who of Canadian, U.S., and European corporate chiefs made it their business to bag birds, fish, and deals in its fields and streams.

Balsillie and Brock had lots to discuss on the ride. It had been two years since the Harvard grad had joined Sutherland-Schultz and he was running much of the company. Balsillie's first assignment had been a corporate make-over. Sutherland-Schultz was spread too thin, with a mixed bag of technology, construction, and manufacturing contracts and assets. Some projects made money; a lot didn't. By his own admission Brock, an engineer, says his talent for solving technical problems did not come with "the ability to take it to market." Balsillie spent his first years identifying what assets and contracts to sell and renegotiate. When it came time to sell rights for a new gas compressor process, Balsillie found a buyer with deep pockets. A company owned by legendary Texas oilman T. Boone Pickens paid $2 million for the system. The young recruit was aggressive with suppliers and customers, pushing hard to renegotiate more favorable terms on signed contracts. His leverage? If terms weren't improved, Sutherland-Schultz would drag its feet with payments and orders.

"He was a unique great talent," says Brock. "He opened up the world of marketing opportunities to me—how to negotiate; how to do things."

Balsillie shaped Sutherland-Schultz into a more modern, focused business by capitalizing on innovations in construction and manufacturing sectors. He also relied on something else. At Trinity College he'd become intrigued by an ancient military manifesto. Sun Tzu wrote *The Art of War* around 500 BCE to document his successful military strategies in China during a time of marauding, warring rulers. In the 1980s, the slim treatise resonated with business leaders confronting an influx of foreign competition.

Balsillie revered *The Art of War* as a kind of spiritual guidebook for a small Ontario company facing ruthless global competitors. Forget about Peter Newman's *The Canadian Establishment*; the working-class kid from Peterborough was now following a different bible. "It is not a friendly world out there," says Balsillie. Sun Tzu, he says, taught him that "you can't panic. You have to stay focused. You go into a state. Emotionally you become formidable. You go into a warrior state."

Balsillie followed two Sun Tzu tactics religiously: appear strong no matter how weak your hand; and move to uneven terrain if an aggressor is overwhelming. For Balsillie, rugged ground meant keeping competitors, suppliers, and customers off balance. "Bung them up in wool and play obfuscation; promise them this and then do that," he says. "I am very good at that. I can send very uneven signals. Give them nothing to be certain with. Let them think they are getting what they want, but don't be overly provocative. I can do that forever."

Balsillie's warrior pose served him well in the short-term deals and negotiations. In the broader, more nuanced world of customer relations and employee management, however, he soon became a divisive figure. Many of Sutherland-Schultz's seven hundred employees bristled at Balsillie's impatience. Under Brock's leadership, no one had titles and employees pitched in to solve problems. In return Brock sent flowers to wives when husbands worked weekends; hired babysitters if a parent employee was needed after hours. When Balsillie arrived, he asked for the title executive vice president and made it his business to tell other managers how to do a better job. He was pushy and he didn't send flowers.

"I had trouble with him and other people. Jim made them feel like they worked for him," says Brock. "He'd piss people off and I would go patch it up."

Despite the flare-ups, Brock enjoyed Balsillie's company, treating him like a younger brother. Hence, the two-guy hunting trip. Sutherland-Schultz was about to be acquired and Brock wanted to talk to his young protégé. He was negotiating a side deal to buy a small Sutherland-Schultz division that specialized in simulation systems to test new factory equipment. The new company came with thirty-five employees, debt, and no budget. Brock was encouraging Balsillie to stay with Sutherland-Schultz and look after the new enterprise. Ride it out for a year, maybe two, earn some money, and, when Brock had a handle on the new company, they could acquire other businesses. Balsillie had no options. Unless you were interested in insurance, automotive, or small technology companies, there weren't many senior jobs for aspiring executives in southern Ontario. Moving was out, too. Balsillie had married his girlfriend, Heidi, and they were expecting their first child. Both had deep ties to the community.

As the two men talked, Brock's car phone rang. Set on speakerphone, it boomed with the voice of Dermot Coughlan, chairman of Derlan Industries and Brock's investment partner in Sutherland-Schultz. Coughlan had an update on the acquisition talks. The Dutch company had agreed to most major terms, but there were a few objections. Unaware that Brock was traveling with someone, Coughlan explained the issues.

"Stork doesn't want Balsillie. They are not going to hire him."

As the executive rattled off other items, Brock stole a glance at his passenger. Balsillie was staring vacantly at the phone. Blood drained from his face. He said nothing for a long time. "It just hit him in the car when they said they didn't want him. That was hard," says Brock. In retrospect, Brock says he should have seen the rejection coming. The Dutch executives negotiating the takeover ran their businesses like a bureaucracy, with layers of management, rules, and systems. In that world Balsillie, the restless corporate warrior, was an outlier. "They couldn't manage him. They knew it," says Brock.

Over the next few days Brock and Balsillie shot pheasant and swapped ideas. The best course, the pair agreed, was a small acquisition. Balsillie would get a healthy severance, enough to invest in a business. Brock suggested RIM, a Sutherland-Schultz supplier. Brock knew RIM was struggling because Lazaridis had recently approached him to invest. He was too busy to get involved, but he was impressed enough with Lazaridis's technical skills to recommend that Balsillie take a look.

Balsillie had met Lazaridis years earlier, shortly after joining Sutherland-Schultz. RIM designed circuit boards that Sutherland-Schultz sold with other equipment to manufacturers for controlling shop-floor production. Arriving in a jacket and tie, sporting his gold Harvard MBA class ring, Balsillie wondered if he had taken a wrong turn when he arrived in the space above the bagel store crammed with overflowing boxes of wires and equipment and unkempt staff hunched over computers. Lazaridis, wearing sweatpants, white socks, and sneakers, was resting his feet on his desk in front of a poster of a Porsche. Balsillie's first thought was "these guys are geeks"—a word Lazaridis hated, he would later learn. His second reaction, after listening to Lazaridis's confident projections of RIM's prosperous future in wireless innovations, was that he'd never met anyone who could be so mesmerizing about technology. "Mike had a gift," he says.

Balsillie had not come that day to talk shop. He had come in Sun Tzu mode to squeeze a lower price from a small supplier. His leverage, he warned Lazaridis, was that Sutherland-Schultz would end its business with RIM if it didn't capitulate. Balsillie came away from his first encounter with Lazaridis with two impressions. He was surprised the engineer acquiesced so quickly to what he calls his "tough guy" move. A bigger shock was Lazaridis's ambition, which Balsillie says was "audacious" for the ringleader of such a motley crew. RIM was going to be a leader in wireless communication. It was going to reinvent how people communicated. One day it would be a corporate giant, he told Balsillie.

When Balsillie later returned to visit Lazaridis in the spring of 1992, RIM's chief feared Basillie wanted to take over his company. Contrary to his earlier rosy forecasts about RIM's future, the company was perilously short of cash, in part because its biggest customers, including Sutherland-Schultz, were behind in their payments. Despite the setbacks, Lazaridis and Fregin were in no mood to sell. They had bailed the company out before; they'd do it again.

Rather than say yes or no to what they believed was a takeover overture from Balsillie, Lazaridis decided to stall, surprising his suitor. That was his game. "There was no way I'm going to negotiate with this guy because I know I'm not going to win," Lazaridis explains. As Balsillie persisted, however, Lazaridis came to view the would-be acquirer more favorably. He saw a driven, confident executive who understood banking, finance, deal making, and, best of all, how to sell a product. In other words, he had everything Lazaridis didn't. RIM's founder quickly realized: "I want this guy to work with me. . . . It was like meeting your future wife. You just know."

The courtship was a rocky one. Every time Balsillie pushed to close the deal, Lazaridis demurred. He was afraid of losing control of his eight-year-old company. In Balsillie's mind, however, control wasn't the end game. He was leaving Sutherland-Schultz, but his severance payment was not big enough to finance a takeover of RIM. Instead, he was angling for a partnership that would give him a stake in the company in exchange for cash that he would bring from his severance check and a mortgage on his home.

Lazaridis agreed in the spring of 1992 to have lunch with Balsillie at the Knotty Pine, a popular restaurant in nearby Cambridge. As Lazaridis recalls the lunch, Balsillie pushed again for a majority stake in RIM. Lazaridis said no, but offered instead to make his lunch guest a partner. In exchange for a $125,000 investment, he could buy a 33 percent stake in RIM, slightly less than the 40 percent share owned by Lazaridis but bigger than stakes owned by Fregin and Barnstijn. Balsillie rebuked his luncheon companion for leading him along. He threw his napkin on the table and bolted from the Knotty Pine.

Balsillie remembers the lunch, but not the outburst. If there was anger, he says, it may have been "posturing." Perhaps borrowing a page from *The Art of War,* his outburst threw his target off as he regrouped for a new strategy. Lazaridis did not know it at the time, but Balsillie had another plan. A generator factory owned by Westinghouse Electric in nearby Hamilton was up for sale, and Balsillie and Brock, who had more financial resources after the sale of Sutherland-Schultz, were quietly looking into a possible acquisition. Lazaridis didn't learn about the Westinghouse play until Balsillie showed up unannounced at his office. Weeks after he had stormed out of the Knotty Pine,

Balsillie was in another huff, Lazaridis recalls. This time, he explained, pacing frantically around the office, he was furious with Westinghouse and its advisers. Time had been wasted. The company had too many problems. There was no deal.

In mid rant, Balsillie stopped abruptly and turned to face Lazaridis. "What was that offer you made about a partnership?"

Lazaridis confirmed that the offer was still on the table. If Balsillie wanted to be his partner, there was one condition: Balsillie had to meet his fiancée, Ophelia, because, as he explained, "she is a great judge of character." Mike and Ophelia joined Jim and Heidi for dinner at their house in Waterloo. When they walked away from the Balsillie home after the meal, Ophelia offered a warning to her future husband.

"He's a shark."

"I know. He can be one on my team."

"As long as you remember he is a shark . . . it's a good idea."

3 / / / STAYING ALIVE

It was a challenge squeezing through RIM's offices on Columbia Street. Narrow rooms and hallways were crammed with desks and makeshift worktables, many of them just pressboard sheets perched on metal legs. Furniture had to be moved to allow for passing colleagues. The arrangement was so precarious that a table bearing heavy computer terminals and monitors once collapsed on startled workers.

Needing more space, RIM had abandoned its office above the bagel store in 1993, moving seventeen employees to a bland low-rise next to Lazaridis's Waterloo alma mater. A year later, the Columbia Street suite was overflowing. Balsillie and Lazaridis graduated from a shared office to separate rooms on opposite sides of a hallway. But the two penny-pinchers knew that they needed more space. When offices opened up next door, the co-CEOs had the adjoining wall torn down. The women's bathroom was converted into a storage room. A blue curtain divided the men's bathroom: on one side were showers and a toilet; on the other, four desks for a new software laboratory. One of the desks belonged to Matthias Wandel, a cheeky software programmer who joined in 1993 and quickly established himself as an inventive prankster. Shortly after being assigned a bathroom desk, he attached a cable to the nearby toilet's flusher. The other end was fastened beneath his desk. When his team eliminated a software bug, Wandel announced its demise by yanking the cord. The flushing noise prompted RIM engineers to throw up their hands and cheer.

The chaotic environment encouraged a subversive streak that soon became ingrained in RIM's engineering department. Engineers are by nature impudent, often staging stunts to show off their technical prowess. University of British Columbia engineers, for example, grabbed headlines in 2001 by hanging a Volkswagen Beetle from the Golden Gate Bridge. At RIM, acting out was a way of coping with financial uncertainty and deadline pressure. Lazaridis set aggressive product delivery timetables for the software and hardware contracts RIM performed for a range of customers. His team understood that the company's precarious health dictated urgency, and no one worked harder than Lazaridis, who sometimes slept underneath his desk while waiting for software to load. But the pace could be punishing.

RIM was still committed to helping get the Mobitex network off the ground and saw a big future for wireless data. "I think that, in another three years, wireless data [transmission] will be as successful as cellular phones, if not more," Lazaridis told his hometown *Kitchener-Waterloo Record* in 1992.[1] After developing programming tools for users to write applications for Mobitex, RIM wrote software for Mobitex users as well, including a wireless e-mail gateway service called RIMgate. But software didn't bring in much revenue; there weren't many wireless data customers, and they weren't willing to pay much for it. "You learn a lot of sobering things" trying to sell software, Balsillie told a trade publication in 1995.[2] Lazaridis and Balsillie believed RIM would have to start making its own hardware if it was to ever be more than a marginal player.

Neither Balsillie nor Lazaridis were big believers in praising or rewarding RIM's hardworking employees. The company was fighting for its survival, and the bosses wanted to keep staff sharp and hungry for success. Balsillie didn't want staff "getting sore arms" patting themselves on the back at a time the company's survival depended on overcoming so many obstacles. Its competitors were bigger, its customers predatory, and cash was in short supply. If RIM didn't quickly deliver what its customers wanted, the company would not endure. One RIM manager became so obsessed with deadlines he issued an edict requiring engineers to ask permission before leaving at night. Lazaridis reversed the decree, but his company's aggressive, need-it-yesterday approach fostered what would become a robust cynicism. "It got to the point that when schedules were made up I didn't bother to read them," says Wandel. "They were so made up, a fantasy."

Unrelenting pressure led to increased mischief. Wandel regularly invited colleagues into the parking lot to smash faulty prototypes with a sledgehammer. Another recreation was detonating large batteries. One engineer reconfigured a pipe gun, known as a potato cannon, to launch broken components into nearby fields. Others let off steam on local baseball diamonds. The RIM baseball team sported T-shirts with the initials DEM. Alluding to the company's uncertain fate, the letters were a play on the Latin phrase *Dextera Domini*—the right hand of God.

/ / /

The South Lawn of the White House was dotted with colorful tents that sagged under a heavy midday sun. It was July 22, 1993. Representatives from technology companies were gathered to show off the latest in mobile communications. President Bill Clinton led an entourage through the tents. Stopping at one, he examined a thick glass tablet and black electronic pen created by Eo Inc., a Silicon Valley start-up. Push the stylus across the surface of the EO Personal Communicator, Clinton was urged, your handwriting will automatically convert into a digital text message, poised to fly across radio waves to the person of your choice. Reflecting on dozens of American victims claimed by recent flooding in Illinois and nearby states, the president moved the stylus across the tablet: "Al, stop the rain in the Midwest. Thanks, Bill."

Minutes later, Clinton cited the message in a speech to a large gathering on the White House Lawn. Vice President Al Gore, an early wireless technology champion, was there. Joining them were Federal Communications Commission officials, media luminaries, and dozens of technology executives.

"I got to send the vice president that message over there and it's nice to know he'll be able to stop the rains in the Midwest within a few moments, remote control," Clinton said. The wireless note, he explained, was the beginning of a "new era of human communications." The Internet was taking off, updated federal technology laws were in motion, and a spectrum of radio channels was slated for auction to private companies wanting to build new wireless roadways for portable digital communications. These "information skyways," Clinton promised, were "a new avenue to send ideas and masses of information to remote locations in ways most of us never would have imagined. . . . Wireless hand-held computers and phones will deliver the world to our fingertips."

Clinton was right about the dawn of a new wireless data age. His timing, though, was off by several years. Mobile data ventures of all sizes were foundering because portable communicators were too expensive, slow, or complex. In the early 1990s, when less than 5 percent of North Americans owned a cell-phone, mobile messaging remained a sci-fi fantasy.

A year after Clinton scratched out his message on the EO Personal Communicator, the device was history. Buyers were turned off by its bulk and its price tag, fully loaded, of $4,000. Bigger players didn't fare much better. Apple Computer entered the wireless game in 1993 with a personal digital assistant called Newton MessagePad. For $699, consumers got a glass-covered notebook, with an electronic pen for writing documents, faxes, and messages. Unlike its namesake, the Newton was no genius. Indeed, its bumbling handwriting recognition feature soon invited widespread ridicule. *Doonesbury*'s creator, Gary Trudeau, featured the clumsy Newton in a 1993 comic strip that depicted him scrawling: "I am writing a test sentence" on the tablet. After several garbled electronic interpretations, the Newton yielded a last, desperate translation: "Egg freckles?" Apple abandoned Newton in 1998.

IBM launched a revolutionary phone at Disney World in Orlando in late 1993 called Simon. The phone offered mobile calling, an address book, calendar updates, faxes, and e-mails. Simon was a hit with technology buffs but flopped in the consumer marketplace. The machine was complicated and carriers lacked network capacity for the data-hogging phone. Simon passed away in 1995.[3]

One company that would draw millions of users to Clinton's promised super-highway was not invited to the 1993 White House event. Its DNA, however, was inside the EO Personal Communicator that shuttled the president's message. Embedded inside the doomed tablet were software programs guiding the message to a radio network. The software creator was Research In Motion.[4]

/ / /

Three years after Clinton's promise of a new communication era, the wireless data highway was going nowhere. The trade publication *Mobile Data Report* captured the frustrations of an impatient marketplace by lamenting the slow pace of innovation in 1995, which it called "the year of dullness."[5] Carriers and product makers charged too much for mobile devices that conveyed tiny amounts of data at mulishly slow speeds, the magazine complained. The only bright spot, it wrote, was a little Canadian company destined to "have a big impact" after unveiling a small, low-cost radio modem card that connected devices to the Mobitex network.

Research In Motion was reinventing itself in 1996. It had gained notice in the industry by making radio modems that connected laptops, delivery trucks, and other mobile data users to the Mobitex network. But Lazaridis and Balsillie had even greater ambitions: to make their own device. They started by making a point-of-sale terminal that stadium vendors could use to sell merchandise and food to fans in their seats in 1994; the machine was briefly used in the SkyDome where the Toronto Blue Jays played, but it didn't do well otherwise. What RIM needed was leverage in a field dominated by muscular companies demanding punishing terms, Balsillie believed. Ericsson and Rogers squeezed RIM by stalling payments of licensing fees.

Then, in 1996, the Skokie, Illinois–based modem maker U.S. Robotics dealt the company a devastating blow. Four months after ordering $16 million of wireless modems from RIM, U.S. Robotics reneged on the deal, potentially stranding RIM with insufficient cash to pay a multimillion-dollar loan borrowed to cover the cost of manufacturing the large modem order. "We were very vulnerable," says Balsillie, "a frog being cooked." If the company did not find new customers for the rejected modem cards it would not be able to repay its bank loan.

U.S. Robotics later asserted in legal proceedings that the modems were defective. Balsillie had a different take: he saw another wolf trying to wound RIM by squeezing its cash flow. The Skokie company was led by a former hippie named Casey Cowell who started building modems in his bathroom in 1976 in his early 20s.[6] From there he muscled past established players to build U.S. Robotics into a $2 billion industry leader, snapping up other modem makers along the way. One of his targets was RIM. "For their size they were very independent and aggressive. Those were qualities we liked to have," Cowell says.

From Balsillie's perspective, if U.S. Robotics couldn't buy RIM, it would make the company's life difficult. U.S. Robotics agreed in December 1996 to end the dispute and resume purchasing modems, this time at a higher price. That arrangement lasted less than a year. In August 1997, U.S. Robotics again refused to buy the modems. The ensuing legal conflict dragged on until an arbitrator ordered U.S. Robotics to pay $2 million in July 1998.[7]

Balsillie learned his lesson after U.S. Robotics' first cancellation. To survive, the pint-sized company needed new customers. Balsillie's prayers were answered by two of his most industrious salesmen: Don McMurtry, a RIM veteran of four years, and Justin Fabian, two years out of university. When Balsillie asked the pair for leads, McMurtry reached for a stack of faxes on his desk, all inquiries from buyers. The sales team had previously paid little attention to the requests. RIM barely had enough capacity to make modems for U.S. Robotics. When he went over the faxes again, McMurtry realized a lot of Korean technology companies were inquiring about the modems.

Months later, in January 1997, Canadian prime minister Jean Chrétien and a team of provincial premiers and corporate chiefs flew to Korea on a trade mission. Included on the trip were three young executives who were pretty well unknown to the rest of the Canadian delegation. Balsillie, McMurtry, and Fabian worked fast in Korea: they signed deals negotiated earlier to sell more than ten thousand modem cards, enough to keep RIM alive. For the RIM trio the trip was a victory lap. "We dumped a lot of radio modems," McMurtry says. After the bruising encounter with U.S. Robotics, RIM's co-CEOs would remain wary of U.S. tech behemoths. "It was really the awakening for Mike and Jim as to how savage the computer industry is," McMurtry says.

The U.S. Robotics experience had a profound impact on Balsillie. RIM could no longer operate as an obliging laboratory of ideas, a place where innovator-in-chief Lazaridis shared thoughts about wireless data innovations. In a jungle of technology predators, the small company had to be as ruthless as the giants. For Balsillie, every potential customer, supplier, and business partner was a potential opponent. "It was a massively predatory and high-stakes gambit all day, every day," he remembers. "If you're sentimental and emotional, you'll get eaten up. You're dead."

The dark view was a stark contrast with Lazaridis's sunny faith that RIM was destined to succeed through innovation. "Jim believed everyone was out to kill us and he couldn't trust anyone," Lazaridis says. "I had a different point of view. I liked long-term relationships. I believed our capabilities allowed us to succeed."

Though philosophically opposed about many things, the partners were united in a belief that RIM needed a more ambitious strategy to prosper. Balsillie was convinced they had to borrow from the playbook of the ravenous technology trailblazer, Microsoft. Based in Redmond, Washington, Microsoft had transformed itself into a global titan by positioning its core product, the MS-DOS operating system, as an invasive force inside the nation's computers, grabbing an ever-bigger share of desktop applications. By the mid-1990s, 86 percent of U.S. computers operated with Microsoft systems delivering everything from Internet searches to games.[8]

"Everyone wanted to do a Microsoft, get a product like DOS, then wedge the business open, dominate the economics, and kill anyone trying to make a product," Balsillie says. To chase this dream, RIM would develop a signature wireless product. That product, Lazaridis was convinced, was a mobile message device. Not the expensive and awkward Newtons and Simons that belly-flopped, but a small, simple, inexpensive device that did one thing well: send and receive digital messages instantly.

In 1996 three major companies were leading the quest for the perfect palm-sized communicator. Referring to a scene in one of his favorite films, the 1981 blockbuster *Raiders of the Lost Ark,* Lazaridis was convinced his competitors, like German soldiers searching in the desert for the Ark of the Covenant, "were digging in the wrong place."

The competitor digging with the largest shovel was Motorola, then the dominant global maker of cellphones and pagers. The Chicago firm opened a new market with Tango, a pager that not only received messages but enabled responses. Unlike the elegant dance that inspired its name, the device was clumsy. Tango expertly received short text messages over Motorola's Re-FLEX paging network, but it stumbled with replies because it didn't have sufficient transmission power. Message replies were limited to a series of canned responses, such as "running late" or "will call later."

Another contender was Nokia's 9000 Communicator, a book-sized tool that looked like a cellphone strapped onto a mini keyboard. A precursor to the smartphone, the 9000 combined computing, cellular, and Internet applications such as browsing and e-mail. The Finnish phone was so glamorous it was used by Val Kilmer's Simon Templar character in the 1997 remake of *The Saint.* Few consumers, however, could afford the $800 price tag, and wireless cellular network carriers more accustomed to handling voice traffic charged a fortune to relay such data-heavy communications.

One company had more success creating a portable office aide: RIM nemesis U.S. Robotics. Its Palm Pilot 1000, launched in 1996, the year after U.S. Robotics bought California startup Palm computing, was a sleek device storing calendar, contact, and other information that could be synchronized with users' computers. Promoted as a personal digital assistant, the Palm was an instant hit with professionals. You didn't need an engineering degree to operate the machine. And unlike Newton's faulty handwriting, the Palm came with a digital keyboard that was easily operated with a stylus. No more "egg freckles." Missing from the Palm Pilot, however, was a wireless connection. Fans would have to wait until 1999 for a new Palm Pilot to be linked wirelessly to the Internet and e-mail.

RIM was quietly putting the finishing touches on its own handheld communicator in the spring of 1996. Its conquer-the-world strategy was audacious for a company with fewer than one hundred employees, but RIM's low profile had its advantages: bigger global companies didn't take the small Waterloo company seriously. "We seem to be doing quite well without anyone knowing," Lazaridis told the *Globe and Mail* in one of his first mainstream media interviews. Working in the shadows, Lazaridis's team had accumulated eight years of experience helping Sweden's Ericsson, Toronto's Rogers, and New Jersey's RAM Mobile Data, the small wireless data arm of BellSouth, transform Mobitex into a working radio network with better coverage across the continent than its main rival, ARDIS, the data network that was created by Motorola for IBM and sold to American Mobile Satellite in early 1998.

By the mid-1990s, Rogers and RAM Mobile had little to show for hundreds of millions of dollars spent expanding the networks. Radio-transmitted data was an expensive and nonessential service. Mobitex and ARDIS had fewer than fifty thousand customers.[9] Media and industry players questioned the future of radio networks. AT&T was developing a faster network technology that was due to be launched imminently. If Mobitex didn't attract more traffic, Rogers and RAM Mobile would surely abandon the costly wireless exchange. Such a move would be fatal for RIM. Lazaridis had devoted years to Mobitex by designing many of the on-ramps to the rickety information highway. It was RIM that created a software-based system of universal digital rules that allowed different types of computers to exchange data. And it was RIM's portable radio modems that drew laptop and mobile device users to the Mobitex roadways.

When RIM's radio modem went into production in 1995, Lazaridis believed it was a watershed moment. RIM had hired a team of radio engineers from McMaster University in nearby Hamilton who designed a portable radio card that was small and powerful enough to be housed in a handheld device. The radios worked better than those made by Ericsson, costing less and draining less battery power than the competition. For Lazaridis, who had been sending electronic mail since university, the most logical device would be one that sent and received e-mail. His counterparts at RAM Mobile Data disagreed. Motorola was generating a lot of attention with its two-way Tango pager, which sent short paging messages, not lengthy e-mails. The media was heaping praise on the gadget. Paging was a booming market with nearly 40 million subscribers. Some experts believed the two-way paging market could attract nearly 80 million subscribers by 2005.[10] If RAM Mobile and RIM wanted in, they'd have to move fast. In the summer of 1995, Lazaridis set a deadline for his engineers. RIM would have a working prototype by Christmas for a two-way pager that would be called Inter@ctive 900. Production would begin in 1996.

To the engineers, the decree was yet another impossible demand. RIM employees respected Lazaridis for his drive and design ideas, but when it came to deadlines, he was starry-eyed. Did he really think they were going to beat Motorola and its sprawling army of engineers with a new two-way pager in a yearlong sprint?

"Mike would make these bold calls and I thought he was nuts," says RIM's radio software prodigy Matthias Wandel. To Lazaridis, the tight deadlines were a matter of survival. Without a new product, the company would not last.

/ / /

RIM was months behind its promised December delivery of a pager prototype to RAM Mobile Data, the New Jersey–based wireless data carrier that was desperate for wireless messaging devices it could sell to customers to boost data traffic on Mobitex's empty roadways. The Inter@ctive 900 project had suffered so many setbacks that by early 1996 RIM engineers were questioning Lazaridis's unwavering optimism about the handheld device, a thick, fist-sized machine with a keyboard and a screen on a pop-up clamshell cover that Lazaridis's wife Ophelia nicknamed "Barbie PC." Lazaridis drew some of his confidence from an unlikely alliance with one of the United States' most powerful technology companies: the semiconductor maker, Intel Corp. Graham Tubbs, an Intel business development executive, visited Lazaridis in early 1995 as part of a search for new Canadian customers. Tubbs was initially doubtful that wireless devices or pagers would be a big enough market for Intel chips, but he changed his mind upon hearing Lazaridis's description of the Inter@ctive 900. If RIM got it right, the potential for a two-way messaging device was enormous. The problem with such a small unit, Lazaridis explained to his American guest, was that conventional chips drew so much power that the Inter@ctive's battery drained too quickly. No one wanted a portable communicator that worked only for a few hours. Tubbs saw RIM's problem as Intel's opportunity. By making a bet on RIM, Intel could help Lazaridis solve his problem and open a new market in mobile communicators for Intel.

Tubbs and Terry Gillett, Intel's division manager for microcontrollers, drew up a proposal to redesign an existing Intel microprocessor—a silicon chip housing the central processing unit—for a two-way pager. Development costs would run to $2.5 million, they advised Intel. Sorry, you're only getting $100,000, they were told. The minuscule budget should have killed the microprocessor project. But Tubbs and Gillett realized that by reconfiguring another existing chip they could fashion a power-efficient microprocessor for RIM for less than $100,000.[11]

By the time the Intel microprocessor arrived in the spring of 1996, RIM had missed the December 1995 deadline to deliver a pager prototype to RAM Mobile Data. The chip was one of many components RIM's engineers struggled to integrate into the Inter@ctive 900. The pager's internal antenna interfered with the radio signal. The transmitter conked out. RIM had outsourced design and manufacturing to Canadian firms that did such a bad job the device's plastic case parts had to be glued together, while the hinge that attached the screen lid to the body of the device easily wore out. RAM Mobile, growing impatient for a competing pager to Motorola's Tango, requested a demonstration at its head office in Woodbridge, New Jersey, on April 19, 1996.

That morning, RIM's office was a high-tech war zone. Parts and wires were scattered everywhere, engineers were slumped asleep in chairs. Lazaridis and a few RIM soldiers stood over a gray plastic object shaped like a hamburger. The device consisted of two puck-shaped plastic components connected by a hinge. The top held a small screen displaying four lines of text; the bottom, a tiny keyboard. It was a fully interactive two-way device. Unlike pagers, which operate with radio receivers capable of capturing messages, RIM's device came with a transceiver that could receive and reply to electronic notes. When it worked, that is.

Cupped in Lazaridis's hand was the only working prototype of the Inter@ctive 900, a device that would become known internally as "the Bullfrog." Most of the bugs had been eliminated, but the transmitter was so finicky it wasn't sending messages. Wandel was pulled out of bed at dawn to change the configuration. "If we don't get this done," Lazaridis warned, "we might as well shut down the company."

Wandel was able to tweak the transmitter, but it was only capable of sending radio signals short distances. That would have to do. Lazaridis slapped the clamshell shut, grabbed his briefcase, and headed out the door for the airport. In Woodbridge, Lazaridis took the stage at a presentation center in front of dozens of RAM Mobile engineers and managers so his demo could be broadcast on a large screen. Holding the Bullfrog aloft, he tapped out a short message that was relayed to a nearby computer.

"It worked. We got through it. Everyone clapped and cheered," Lazaridis recalls. After that day, the prototype never worked again.

/ / /

Jim Hobbs, vice president of BellSouth's mobile data group, knew he had to call Lazaridis. Hobbs had lots of time for RIM's innovator and loved being astonished by the gadgets Lazaridis pulled from his pockets. Lazaridis always seemed to know what was around the corner. On this day in May 1997, however, it was Hobbs' duty to surprise Lazaridis. And it wasn't with good news. BellSouth was running out of patience with RAM Mobile's expensive Mobitex network. The Bullfrog hadn't made much of a splash. Customers loved the immediacy of its two-way paging, but the device was clumsy to hold and jutted out of users' hip holsters. Bump into a doorframe and it sheared off the belt, damaging the device. RAM Mobile's sales staff nicknamed the ungainly pager "Fat Boy."

When he reached Lazaridis on the phone, Hobbs was uncharacteristically terse: "If things don't pick up, something bad is going to happen." BellSouth hadn't set a date, but budget season was coming, and it looked like the carrier might mothball its mobile data experiment unless RAM Mobile could find some new devices to generate traffic.

"Mike, I'm telling you this for your own good. We've got to make something here and we've got to do it quick," Hobbs warned.

Lazaridis gently put the phone back in the cradle and walked out of his office to Balsillie's corner room across the hall. "I think we're dead," he said. "They're going to pull the plug on Mobitex. We have two weeks."

Balsillie got the "dead" part. Products designed for Mobitex generated the bulk of RIM's sales: software, modems, and the Bullfrog. RIM was so committed to the network that a new project was underway to make a more sophisticated two-way pager. Balsillie was cautious about developing another device after Bullfrog's poor debut. Costs were rising faster than sales; it would be reckless to make another big bet. Hobbs' call changed the stakes. This was no time for caution. RIM had to convince BellSouth that RIM had a game-changing product.

The call from Hobbs was more than a tip from a buyer to its small supplier. The BellSouth executive understood that its wireless data venture in

New Jersey needed RIM's wireless devices as much as the Waterloo business needed the carrier. Their marriage of convenience was often rocky; Hobbs and Lazaridis engaged in back-room diplomacy to keep the union alive. A major difficulty was the relationship between RAM Mobile's CEO, Bill Lenahan, and Balsillie. Since joining the New Jersey carrier in 1995, Lenahan had been put off by Balsillie's abrasiveness toward BellSouth. Lenahan pressed for low prices on RIM's modem cards and Bullfrogs to attract customers and keep BellSouth off his back. Balsillie pushed back like a tier-one manufacturer. Lenahan wasn't used to such behavior from small suppliers.

"Jim is not an easy guy to work with on this stuff. He wants to be the smartest one in the room all the time. . . . I think he has a certain amount of arrogance about him," Lenahan explains today.

Balsillie saw RAM Mobile and BellSouth as two more in a series of out-sized customers who were out to squeeze the little guy. If he didn't play "hyperaggressive," Balsillie says, RIM was roadkill. Lenahan concedes he was preoccupied with managing his demanding parent, BellSouth, "the big guy in the room." The Atlanta carrier wanted to see sales gains from RAM Mobile every quarter. The more pressure he got, the more he muscled RIM and other suppliers for lower prices and new products. "RIM had to keep showing us what they could do for us to keep moving forward," Lenahan says.

A long-term player, Lazaridis saw no point in playing tough after the call from Hobbs. The burden was on him to convince the Atlanta carrier's senior executives of the vibrant future for wireless messaging. The solution was a new two-way pager that RIM had under development. Showing them a prototype wasn't enough; he had to convince buttoned-down BellSouth executives that innovations in wireless devices were on the verge of changing how the world communicated.

The sun was setting when Lazaridis finally parked his car in front of his house, hours after Hobbs' call. At the front door he was greeted with a screaming child. After a difficult day with their cranky son, Ophelia was passing the torch. Lazaridis's plans to craft a presentation for BellSouth had to be put on hold. He sat down to play with his two-year-old. Hours later, the youngster drifted asleep. Most working fathers would have been ready for scotch and sleep by now, but Lazaridis felt strangely energized. Time with his son had cleared his head and he was ready to write. Popping an album by rock guitarist Joe Satriani on his stereo, he began strumming his keyboard. Three hours later, he had written a roadmap for the future of mobile messages entitled: "Success Lies in Paradox."[12]

Early wireless data innovators failed because they crammed multiple office tools into book-sized devices. The products were battery and bandwidth hogs and a headache to operate. Tapping out messages with a stylus was unreliable and time-consuming. Keyboards were small and difficult to manipulate. What these device designers misunderstood was that most professionals already had office computers, faxes, cellphones, pagers, and personal digital assistants. They didn't want more technology. They wanted convenience. In 1997, that meant keeping up with a torrent of modern office messages. The introduction of voice-mail in the late 1980s made remote access to phone messages possible. What about e-mails and paging messages? If bosses were sending urgent electronic notes, surely the answer was not standing sentry at an office computer or scrambling for a phone if your one-way pager beeped an alert.

The paradox of success, Lazaridis wrote, was that handheld devices did not need more functions; they needed fewer. "We must maximize adoption by minimizing complexity" of a powerful, reliable, and simple device that filled the mobile text message gap. A reinvented two-way pager half the size of the Bullfrog with a new, doubly powerful Intel microprocessor was the answer. The new pager was formally named Inter@ctive 950, but it was known internally as Leapfrog. A single AA battery lasted nearly a month, and its larger screen was easily navigated with a trackwheel, a concept Lazaridis borrowed from a VCR remote control. The two-way pager also came with limited e-mail capacity. As for the keyboard, the answer was not ten fingers, but two thumbs. Leapfrog was small enough to be cradled in two hands, freeing thumbs to work an artfully curved keyboard with concave keys that minimized typos. Even the clumsiest typist would be comfortable with the device because the small screen above the keyboard allowed users to monitor accuracy. "We must revel in its limitations," he wrote.

The best thing about Leapfrog was that there was no need to reinvent the network. Mobitex already reached 50 percent of U.S. cities. If BellSouth was willing to extend the network's reach, Leapfrogs could toss and catch messages across a national Mobitex network. Not just simple text pages but also e-mails. Leapfrog and Mobitex had the potential to transcend the jungle of incompatible corporate and government computing systems by building wireless bridges to convey mobile e-mails. No one else had solved the mobile e-mail riddle.

"Let's make e-mail our transport and payload and beat them all to the punch!" Lazaridis wrote.

4 / / / LEAP

As he rode the elevator to the twentieth floor, Lazaridis realized something was missing. He drove his hands into his pockets, rifled through his briefcase. *They weren't there!* It was late spring, 1997, and in seconds he and Balsillie would step off the elevator in BellSouth's Atlanta headquarters on Peachtree Street to present the results of the "Success Lies in Paradox" manifesto. But where were the two industrial foam prototypes prepared for the session? "I left them in the taxi," Lazaridis told Balsillie and BellSouth's Hobbs as they approached their fate in the clouds.

Delaying the meeting was impossible, Hobbs explained, because they were pitching to RAM Mobile's owners and top executives. Hobbs gave his secretary Lazaridis's taxi receipt to track down the driver. Waiting for the RIM duo in a conference room was Michael Kulukundis, the Greek shipping magnate and founder of RAM Mobile; Earle Mauldin, CEO of RAM Mobile's other investor, BellSouth Enterprises; Mike Harrell, president of BellSouth Mobile Data; along with Ron Dykes, CFO of BellSouth, and Bill Lenahan, RAM Mobile Data's boss. Hobbs and Lenahan were so excited after reading Lazaridis's manifesto that they had invited Kulukundis and Mauldin in order to win backing for an expanded network.

Lazaridis began by talking about the coming boom in wireless data messages and unique market window for Mobitex and RIM's Leapfrog. After several minutes, Lazaridis stopped himself. "I'm embarrassed," he told the room. He did not have the prototypes—they'd been left in the cab. "It was a big letdown," Lenahan recalls. This is not what he'd invited his bosses to witness. As the meeting wound down, the doors to the room flew open and a BellSouth employee walked in with foam blocks the size of soap bars. The missing Leapfrogs! The dramatic entrance, Hobbs says, transformed a run-of-the-mill conference into a "come-to-Jesus meeting."

The Leapfrog was a big step up from its predecessor. Lazaridis had been so dissatisfied with the work of the Montreal industrial design firm that built the Bullfrog on contract that he determined all future products would be designed in-house. He charged a twenty-four-year-old mechanical engineer hired right out of University of Waterloo named Jason Griffin with building and leading a design team. It was an expensive investment that included customized workstations with cutting-edge 3-D design software costing tens of thousands of dollars, but the decision paid off as Griffin and his team got to work.

Lazaridis felt the Leapfrog had to be as small as a pager so it didn't sit awkwardly in a belt holster like the Bullfrog. With little space to work in, Griffin had to be as sparing as possible in the keyboard design. "We didn't want the keys to be too tiny, so we had to get rid of every key that wasn't needed," says Griffin. There would be just one shift key, not two like a normal keyboard. Punctuation marks were doubled onto letter keys in a standard QWERTY configuration so those keys could be stripped out as well. The trackwheel to the right of the screen handled the job that four direction and eight function keys had done on the Bullfrog.

After experimenting with key shapes and layouts, Griffin and Lazaridis settled on a keyboard customized for the thumbs that used it. Keys on the right half were oval and tilted right, toward the right thumb, mirrored by the keys pointing the other way on the left side. Inside the device, Griffin pushed to have the keys sit on a piece of metal known as a dome, rather than plastic, the industry standard; that way, users would feel a crisp "click" every time they pressed a key, just as they did on a regular keyboard, rather than a "mushy rubbery feel, like a TV remote control," says Griffin. It was more expensive and RIM's manufacturing team pushed back, "but Mike said, 'No, the interaction with the device is important here,'" Griffin said.

As the blocks were passed around the BellSouth boardroom, executives cupped the devices, marveling at slips of paper substituting as text on a small screen resting above small keyboard buttons. Click the plastic trackwheel to the side, Lazaridis explained, and users could scroll through any number of messages. This was just what the worker-on-the-go wanted. "I was very excited," Lenahan says. So were his bosses. BellSouth's technical group blessed the device a few weeks later, committing to a $50 million order of Leapfrogs, then the company's largest contract. BellSouth was so convinced that two-way paging was the mother lode that in 1997 it acquired full control of RAM Mobile, renaming it BellSouth Wireless Data. In addition it approved a multimillion-dollar budget to expand Mobitex by doubling its relay network of 1,200 base stations in order to reach 90 percent of the U.S. population.

"We bet the ranch," says Hobbs.

/ / /

As Lazaridis pushed RIM's technology forward, Balsillie struggled to pay the bills. The two kept in close contact, spending hours on the phone on evenings and weekends, and fully trusted the other to handle his area of expertise. "He was a shark in the sense that he is perfectly evolved for that line of work—finance, business contracts," says Lazaridis. "You can say I'm a shark when it comes to technology and business opportunities, but I don't have time for banks and finance and contracts and running a company."

When Balsillie checked RIM's bank accounts a day after he joined the company in 1992, he was stunned to learn his entire $125,000 investment had immediately evaporated to pay overdue bills. Early on, the Harvard Business School grad kept the company afloat with low-cost loans from RIM's largest customer, Ericsson, and an Ontario government venture agency. In 1994, he convinced the founder of a prominent Canadian technology company to invest $2 million. Val O'Donovan became a local business hero when he moved his satellite equipment company and dozens of employees from Montreal to Cambridge, Ontario, in 1979. Balsillie courted O'Donovan as a mentor, invited him onto RIM's board, and sold him a 30 percent stake in the company.

RIM was growing steadily—revenue doubled to C$4.2 million in its 1995 fiscal year from two years earlier, and doubled again to C$8.4 million the following year. The company hired dozens of employees and took over more space in its rented building, but its small size left RIM vulnerable to any glitches. By spring 1996, RIM was in a precarious spot, with U.S. Robotics balking at paying RIM and the Bank of Montreal threatening to call a loan. Balsillie teamed up with his young CFO, Dennis Kavelman—his wife's cousin—to see what opportunities Canadian stock markets offered.

In the early 1990s, big technology players were rare in Canada. Natural resource companies dominated domestic stock exchanges, and there was nothing comparable to New York's NASDAQ market, which catered to technology start-ups. Few promoters or financial analysts went to bat for small Canadian tech stocks.

When Balsillie and Kavelman made their pitch to Bay Street, Canada's equivalent of Wall Street, the big Canadian investment banks treated them like small fry. The typical fee charged by Bay Street banks was about 7 percent of any money raised through a securities offering. In exchange for an exclusive eighteen-month investment banking relationship, Bay Street firms offered only "best efforts" to help the Waterloo company raise capital. "One of the big bank dealers told him, 'Come back when you need $50 million,'" says Daniel Hachey, then an investment banker with independent brokerage Midland Walwyn who got to know Balsillie. "He felt he was getting the message: 'You're not big enough or good enough for us right now; come see us when you're a more serious player.'"

One underwriter was different: Griffiths McBurney & Partners, an upstart investment banker that specialized in junior mining and tech companies. Balsillie visited GMP hoping the firm could help RIM sell C$15 million of securities. But after one day of visiting GMP clients in Toronto in May 1996, investors pledged to invest C$90 million in RIM. One, Frank Mersch, a well-known local fund manager, was so taken by the RIM story he offered C$50 million on the spot for an entire RIM securities offering. Balsillie drove home that night feeling much better about RIM's financial prospects. Now, he and Lazaridis had to find an excuse for raising more money than they'd anticipated. They upped their needs to C$30 million when Lazaridis said it would be nice to build a factory. RIM then raised C$32 million by selling "special warrants," a popular financing mechanism for small Canadian companies not quite ready to go public; it gave investors the right to convert their investment units into shares when the company did list. RIM paid off its loan and was out of financial trouble.

In October 1997, Balsillie parlayed BellSouth's commitment to buy the Bullfrog into a C$115 million initial public offering at C$7.25 a share on the Toronto Stock Exchange; it was the largest Canadian technology IPO of its time. The warrants investors more than doubled their money, and suddenly the struggling entrepreneurs from Waterloo were wealthy, at least on paper: Lazaridis's 9.8 million shares were worth C$71 million, while Balsillie's 8.1

million shares were worth C$59 million. They celebrated by taking the IPO check back to RIM headquarters for employees to pass around.

/ / /

RIM's engineers were at it again. In early 1998 voice-mails circulated around the office. Each delivered messages in a robotic baritone reminiscent of Freddy Krueger, the gruesome killer of *A Nightmare on Elm Street*.

"Why won't you die?"

"Welcome to my nightmare."

"Come to Freddy."

The engineers exchanged these joke messages as Leapfrog neared the final stages of development. The spark was BellSouth Wireless Data's push to add gimmicks to the two-way pager. The latest was a service that enabled senders to convert text messages to spoken messages sent to recipients' voice-mail. Senders could select from four preprogrammed digital voices. One was a dead ringer for Freddy. The contrivance was an affront to RIM engineers who worked tirelessly to create a reliable, efficient communicator. BellSouth's Freddy Krueger murmurings were like hanging fuzzy dice on the Hubble telescope.

"This kind of stuff really bothered Mike," Balsillie says. "It was debasing his product."

This was not the future of wireless communications Lazaridis had promoted in Atlanta a year earlier. He and his engineering team believed in a new era of instant, efficient, and mobile e-mails. BellSouth executives loved Leapfrog, but they weren't ready to embrace RIM's e-mail vision. The core market for the new device was two-way paging, they insisted. More than 40 million North Americans were now using one-way pagers in a market dominated by Motorola. Leapfrog was going to crack the market open for Bell-South because of the device's groundbreaking capacity to send and receive paging messages.

To Lenahan, mobile e-mail "was the next generation" and his struggling network had no time to wait. "You have to sell what you have today, not what's coming. Paging happened to be what we were selling."

Lenahan's concerns were understandable, but he misunderstood how quickly businesses would flock to a service that brought order to the chaos of digital chatter. By the mid-1990s e-mail had moved out of university labs and into everyday life. Hotmail, the Internet-based e-mail service, launched in 1996, attracting millions of users and the attention of Microsoft, which acquired the start-up in 1997. E-mail even went Hollywood in 1998, turning up as a digital matchmaker in the Tom Hanks–Meg Ryan romance, *You've Got Mail*. In business, electronic mail was now the medium of choice. At the time, mainstream e-mail programs such as Microsoft Outlook or Lotus Notes were moored to company desktops or laptops that communicated with each other through a central server. Data could only be sent wirelessly through special modems and a subscription to a network such as Mobitex, but the process was expensive and cumbersome.

With the Leapfrog still in development, RIM engineers first experimented with using the Bullfrog themselves in 1997. RIM engineer Perry Jarmuszewski regarded the Bullfrog as a plaything until he got lost on a trip to San Francisco. With no map and no cellphone he e-mailed a friend back in Waterloo to ask him how to find the famous curved switchback section of Lombard Street. Within minutes an e-mail returned with directions. "That's when the lightbulb went off," Jarmuszewski says. "I didn't have to call anyone and I got my answer instantly. [I realized] this thing is going to revolutionize communications."

RIM employees discovered that in addition to sending and receiving paging messages, it could channel e-mails. By making a small change on each employee's desktop in-box, they were able to forward work e-mail to a separate Bullfrog pager address. The discovery was liberating for RIM employees suddenly able to read business correspondence from car and home on the clamshell mobile device. "Once you got this thing in your hand it evolved e-mail pretty quickly into instant messaging," says David Castell, who received a Bullfrog when he was hired as product planning manager by RIM in 1997.

It didn't take long for RIM employees to see how invaluable and distracting mobile e-mail could be. In meetings they would often only see the top of Balsillie's forehead. RIM's hypercompetitive co-CEO had become one of the world's first mobile e-mail addicts, conducting meetings while scanning his Bullfrog for the latest from sales staff, customers, and investors.

The Bullfrog was far from perfect. The biggest headache was responding to e-mails. Messages arriving on Bullfrogs were conveyed to the device by the user's desktop e-mail program. Hit reply and the message returned only to the user's desktop in-box, instead of the original sender. When the Mobitex network crashed, a frequent occurrence, new e-mails set off a frenzy of unwanted responses. BellSouth automatically returned error messages to send-ers during an outage. This meant that any new message forwarded by a user's desktop to a Bullfrog was greeted with an error alert that was automatically forwarded right back to the device. This self-perpetuating loop of error alerts continued until the network recovered. Some RIM employees returned from holidays to find hundreds of error messages in their in-boxes.

When it became clear that BellSouth had no interest in promoting Leap-frog's e-mail capacity, Lazaridis decided RIM would press ahead with a plan to refashion Leapfrog as an e-mail device. One day in early summer 1997, Lazaridis summoned software engineer Gary Mousseau into his office. Lazaridis started scribbling excitedly on his whiteboard as he talked. "Gary, we're going to solve this two-mailbox problem," he said. "We're going to do something big. We'll build a product that works with Outlook and Exchange," Microsoft's recently launched corporate e-mail system.

Lazaridis explained that he wanted to bring proper "push" e-mail to the Leapfrog—e-mail that arrived automatically on the device without requiring users to log in and download their messages. Users shouldn't have to forward their work e-mails to the handheld devices—they should be able to send and receive e-mails wirelessly as if the Leapfrog was a portable, synchronized ex-tension of their desktop computers. Surely the company had the know-how and technology to do this.

There were two major issues, security and bandwidth. An e-mail had to be encrypted at the point of transmission and only decrypted when it reached its destination. And whatever RIM designed had to respect the limited capac-ity of the Mobitex technology: a message would have to be limited to a kilo-byte or two of data. Anything longer would have to be truncated or sent in stages. Mousseau furiously scribbled notes in his lab book as the two batted ideas back and forth. He couldn't wait to get started. He already had a name for the project: Outreach. Over the coming months, Mousseau and a handful of other RIM engineers mapped out the basic concept. Mousseau developed a software program, known as the "redirector," to be installed on a user's desk-top computer that would copy every e-mail, compress the information, and repackage the contents into a new message sent to the mobile device.

Ideally, the package would be sent electronically through the Mobitex wireless data network, then transmitted and decrypted to the user's mobile device, but that wasn't practical because it meant that every user would have to wait months to get the phone company to install a Mobitex modem.

Lazaridis had another idea: Instead of sending messages directly into the Mobitex network, it would fire user e-mails over the Internet to a transfer point at RIM. Since RIM already had its own connections into Mobitex, the messages would pass through this transfer point, a server which RIM called "Relay," then funnel into RIM's connection to Mobitex and on to the wireless device. The Relay would act as a clearinghouse for all messages sent to and from the wireless devices.

The system would also have to work in reverse: if a user tapped out a message on his or her handheld device, the machine would need to compress and encrypt the package and transmit it wirelessly to the nearest Mobitex tower. From there it would be sent through wires into RIM, then relayed to its destination. Every e-mail sent by the device would also find its way back to the user's desktop computer, where the redirector would decode and unbundle it and place a copy in the sent box as if it had been typed out there to begin with.

For Lazaridis, it was important that the user had no sense of the complexity involved: the device should simply send and receive e-mails in sync with the desktop, like magic. As for his engineers, they would spend well over a year building the software and relay system to make wireless e-mail a reality.

By fall 1997 Mousseau was overwhelmed. He was working long hours and rarely able to see his four children. He was getting lost in the possibilities of what the device could do. Around the office, his colleagues began to call him "the Blur." Late one night, RIM cofounder Doug Fregin peered into Mousseau's office to see the software engineer seemingly frozen in his chair, his hands on his keyboard. Mousseau's eyes were open but he was asleep.

Lazaridis could see Mousseau was struggling. He reined in the developer's ambition to add such features as synchronized calendar and contact information—like the hot product of the moment, the Palm Pilot personal digital assistant—and Internet browsing. "We're going to focus on mail only," Lazaridis told him. He also promised to get Mousseau some help. One engineering co-op student recruited from University of Waterloo subsequently got pulled so deeply into the project that he failed several courses. (As a consolation, he was eventually hired on at RIM.)

Despite the brutal hours, Mousseau and the team were able to deliver what Lazaridis had requested: a working system to route work e-mails to and from its wireless devices.

Now, RIM just needed a wireless network to put the system into operation. Since BellSouth wasn't willing to offer wireless e-mail, Balsillie and

Lazaridis crafted an alternative idea in late 1997: buying airtime on the Mobitex network from the disinterested carrier and running a service themselves. "What if I go in now and offer to buy $5 million worth of airtime, cash, now, and then I could sell it over a period of time?" Lazaridis asked Balsillie. "If we did that, then we could sell the devices for $500, but sell the airtime for $50 per month"—at a time when BellSouth was charging about three times as much each month for two-way paging service. "That would be much more appealing to the customer. We can sell it ourselves."

It was an audacious move by a small device maker, to even think a big carrier would allow a puny upstart to start its own wireless data service and set its own terms. BellSouth's Lenahan thought the idea was preposterous. Wireless carriers did not resell airtime; it weakened their hold on the market. What was RIM thinking? It was a small company with no back office staff to handle billing, sales, or customer service. "I thought RIM was getting itself into something they were not going to be any good at," says Lenahan.

What Balsillie and Lazaridis understood was BellSouth Wireless Data's vulnerability. Always on the lookout for potential opponents' frailties, the RIM co-chiefs had learned that the Mobitex operator was facing a $10 million budget shortfall. It was still a weak ward of a large telecom company, and it needed to show any kind of return for the big investment its owner had made. The RIM bosses offered to pay $5 million up front out of the cash from its stock offering for two years of unlimited airtime on Mobitex. Although Lenahan was uncomfortable giving up airtime to a supplier, the lure of up-front cash was irresistible. He agreed that RIM's cash offer was a better bet than RIM's long-shot chance of generating profits selling airtime for an e-mail device. "I felt like it was our best option at the time," he says.

RIM forged a similar deal in the smaller Canadian market with Rogers for $1 million. By 1998, the enchanted forest's marketing guru, David Neale, had returned to Rogers and, like Lenahan, was keen to accept an offer that yielded "up-front revenues on an otherwise empty network."

The novel agreements gave RIM full control to sell, promote, and manage e-mail traffic using the same device that was expected to deliver two-way paging to the masses. The two carriers would regret underestimating the potential of RIM's wireless e-mail plan.

/ / /

Handheld wireless e-mail was a breakthrough product nobody knew they wanted. When Balsillie and his new product manager, David Castell, began testing consumer appetite for a mobile e-mail service on the Leapfrog device, they assumed traveling salespeople and other busy professionals would line up for a product that constantly relayed urgent e-mail updates. Instead, focus group research revealed there was no burning desire by participants to quickly read or reply to electronic messages. If they needed to reach colleagues urgently, a phone call would do. At a focus group in Sunnyvale, California, one participant grew antagonistic when showed a device announcing e-mails with a buzzing noise. "If this thing buzzes every time I get an e-mail, you'd better ship it with a hammer," he warned.

A more helpful insight came from a participant who spent much of his professional life on the road. He approached with dread his evening hotel ritual of downloading the day's flood of e-mails on his laptop. It was a chore that inevitably involved hours of reading and replying. "If I just had a tool to help me with my volume of e-mail on the road, I'd pay anything," he said. Convenience, not urgency, was a more potent marketing pitch. This was a device that could free customers to catch up on office communications on their terms. Idle time between meetings or lost time in taxis and airport lounges could be productively spent processing e-mails. Employers would be able to reach staff any time of the day and employees would not have to be tethered to computers. Bosses would never know e-mails were coming from baseball games, the golf course, or family homes.

The next step was positioning the service in the crowded technology market. Lazaridis was so captivated by the concept he argued RIM should sell the Leapfrog as a new product category: e-mail pagers. Castell and RIM's marketing vice president, Dave Werezak, disagreed. Too many other innovative communicators, such as IBM's Simon or the EO Personal Communicator, had failed in part because they tried to define new categories and consumers didn't appreciate or understand what the products offered. RIM managers were influenced by management guru Geoffrey Moore, who argued in his influential book *Inside the Tornado* that innovative technologies had a better chance of success if sold within a proven product category.[1] The most popular handheld device going in 1998 was the Palm Pilot, sold as a personal digital assistant, or PDA. Palm Pilot was a huge hit because it allowed busy professionals to easily store and update calendar and contact information on a pocket-sized device. If the e-mail-enabled Leapfrog came with calendar and contact applications, Castell urged Lazaridis, then RIM could position its product as the most comprehensive PDA on the market. Lazaridis, who used a Palm, worried RIM would be seen as a weakling against the Silicon Valley darling. Castell's pitch, however, was compelling: "If you want addresses and calendar, go for Palm. If e-mail is important, we're the PDA to choose." Lazaridis was swayed. His busy engineers were handed another impossibly short deadline to add calendar and contact applications to the device.

Lazaridis believed RIM's new device was such a convenience that it would become the preferred mode for exchanging e-mails. For that to happen, the user interface on the Leapfrog—what the customer saw and experienced when using the device—had to be intuitive and easy to operate. "Remove think points," was one of his favorite phrases. "I liked teaching people to put themselves in the minds of the users," Lazaridis says. "I wanted to get to the point where users prefer to use [the device] to send messages than actually power their computers."

E-mails often arrived with a thicket of coding and header information. Because the Leapfrog screen was so small, all unnecessary information was pared from the display. All that users would see when an e-mail arrived was who sent it, when it arrived, the subject line, and the first two lines of text. Lazaridis didn't want a help menu—the device should never be that complicated. He believed that using the Leapfrog for e-mail should be so instinctive that users would never have to interrupt their train of thought to hunt for a command. "We found 90 percent of the time you did the same thing," says Lazaridis. "So at any one point, there's a high probability you'll do the same thing. For each one, we tried to anticipate what the user would do next. If we got it right, everything became a double click [of the trackwheel]: one click to pull up the command, one click to execute."

To Lazaridis, it was important that users only ever had one menu to choose from, rather than a multitude of options like most software programs. If you were typing a message and clicked the trackwheel, the menu would only bring up items that were relevant to crafting and sending an e-mail. It would also automatically highlight the Send function. The team developed other shortcuts, giving full functionality to thumb-typers without adding extra buttons. If a user typed two spaces, a period would appear at the end of the previous word and the next word would be automatically capitalized. If a user held down a letter key the machine would capitalize it, eliminating the need for the shift key.

Ideas began to spill forth from across the company and got coded into the platform: if a user typed B while reading an e-mail, the e-mail would scroll to the bottom; T brought the user to the top, and U to the next unread message. To send a new e-mail, a user had to type only the first few letters of the recipient's name in the To: box and all potential matches would show up until enough letters had been typed to eliminate all others. Clicking on a person's name in a calendar item would bring up a new e-mail, with that person's name already in the To: slot.

Perhaps the neatest trick was making wireless e-mail appear faster and more instantaneous than it actually was. On other devices users had to log in, pull down messages, and wait for their device to process them. With RIM's e-mail device messages arrived automatically, but the device still had to process them. That took time. Users didn't need to know that. Lazaridis instructed his developers to hide the back-end process: users should be buzzed not when the e-mail arrived, but after it had been decrypted, decompressed, and dumped into their in-box, ready to read.

/ / /

The thirty-minute ferry ride from San Francisco to Sausalito is one of the world's more beautiful commutes. Passengers float by the Golden Gate Bridge and tree-topped Berkeley Hills as they make their way to the pastel-colored shops and restaurants of Sausalito. In the spring of 1998 a few dozen professional commuters arriving in Sausalito for some downtime were greeted with unwelcome work questions.

Stationed at the wharf was a trio of employees from Lexicon Branding, a local company renowned for its gift of selecting memorable brand names, particularly for nerdy high-tech products. Intel's Pentium chip and Apple's PowerBook laptop brand names were born in Lexicon's Sausalito headquarters. On this day, Lexicon's staff was assigned to test commuter attitudes about mobile devices. When the questions turned to e-mails, the results surprised them. E-mail wasn't a convenience; it was a stress point. Mentioning the word inspired dread about work piling up in in-boxes.

This was a new insight for Lexicon's client, RIM, which was searching for a name for the mobile e-mail device it was to launch in 1999. Lazaridis's engineers loved PocketLink, the name RIM was using internally. Other choices included EasyMail and MegaMail.[2] It was clear now to marketing vice president Dave Werezak, who had hired Lexicon, that these names didn't work; "mega" and "mail" were anxiety triggers. What RIM needed was a name that lowered workers' blood pressure. Back in Lexicon's office, staff brainstormed, writing soothing and positive words such as "summer vacation," "melons," and "strawberry" on paper taped to a wall. Lexicon founder David Placek didn't like strawberry; it unfurled too slowly when he said it. That would not work for a device speeding up communications. Next to the name of the red fruit, one of his employees had scrawled "blackberry."

Placek liked "blackberry" for a number of reasons. Lexicon had recently commissioned a "sound symbolism" study by a linguistics professor to gauge people's reactions to sounds and letters. The professor concluded that the letter *b*, repeated twice in "blackberry," was a positive sound evoking speed and efficiency. It was also an unexpected name for a technology product, one that would stand out, with both *B*s capitalized. Another connection was the device's miniature elliptical keys; they resembled the tiny black fruit sacs of the blackberry. "That was important; it made it logical," says Placek.

When Placek traveled to Waterloo in June, he carried a stack of forty cards, each inscribed with a potential brand name for RIM's new product. As Placek presented each offering to a group of company executives, Lazaridis grew uncomfortable. Options such as "Byline," "Outrigger," and "Blade" didn't impress him. The engineer who years earlier named his clunky digital advertising unit "Budgie" wanted something friendlier. When the fortieth and final name was presented, Lazaridis perked up:

"BlackBerry."

"This is it, this is the name," Lazaridis exclaimed. "I loved it at first sight," he would later say. Balsillie liked the name but was a bit slower to come around. Many of their RIM colleagues, however, didn't like the name at all. The company's pragmatic engineers thought PocketLink perfectly explained the engineering advances of a pocket-sized product connecting people to wireless e-mails. Focus groups agreed. "They all hated BlackBerry," says Castell. "'What, was it invented by Mr. BlackBerry? Why would you name it that?'" he says, imitating one of the participants. "They were like, 'We all liked Pocket-Link better.'"

RIM's sales staff had another preference: Blade. RIM's mobile e-mail device was the perfect tool for road warriors like them. A blade could cut through a thicket of e-mails. Lazaridis disagreed. Blade sounded cold and menacing.

After several days of debate, Lazaridis phoned Placek for help with the naming impasse.

"Mike, compose an e-mail to the people pushing for Blade," Placek told his client. "Type out the following in the e-mail: www.blade.com. Hit send and do not, I repeat do not, look at the Web site," Placek urged. Moments later Lazaridis heard a chorus of objections from a nearby office. "Ewwwwww," was the cry from some of RIM's salesmen. The Web link had taken them to an explicit porn site.

There would be no further challenges to the BlackBerry name.

/ / /

The summer of 1998 was an anxious time for RIM. The company was late getting the two-way pager to market, and after it finally shipped tens of thousands of Leapfrogs to BellSouth warehouses, the company uncovered a serious flaw. A software bug caused devices to drain so much power from the batteries that they leaked white electrolytic fluid. To avoid alarming BellSouth, RIM told the carrier it was dispatching employees to upload a new software program. RIM's sales vice president Don McMurtry and newly hired product manager Patrick Spence took a team of interns on a tour of sweltering warehouses, some located in derelict inner-city neighborhoods. The stealth rescue team spent weeks of thirteen-hour days unwrapping boxes, replacing thousands of batteries, and uploading software fixes that would stop the battery drain. "It was the kind of work you didn't really sign up for, but we had to get the job done," says Spence.

Balsillie made his boldest move when BellSouthWireless Data placed its initial $50 million order for Leapfrogs. The deal came after weeks of acrimonious negotiations. Under pressure from his BellSouth masters to stoke profits, Lenahan leaned on Balsillie to sharply discount the Leapfrog. The carrier had poured hundreds of millions of dollars into an expanded Mobitex network on the bet that the Leapfrog would stimulate wireless data traffic. Competitors were selling pagers at the time for about $400 each and charging monthly network fees. Lenahan wanted to lure customers to Mobitex by driving the Leapfrog's price tag below $250 a unit. Balsillie and Lazaridis thought the demand was ludicrous. RIM would barely earn a profit. Lenahan says contract talks were "testy" because Balsillie would agree one day to terms in the sales contract and call back the next demanding a sweeter deal for RIM. Several phone calls "ended with somebody hanging up" abruptly, Lenahan says.

After weeks of haggling, the companies had a deal. BellSouth announced in August 1998 a plan to sell RIM's Leapfrog for an introductory price as low as $249 until the end of December. The cost rose to $359 in 1999. Balsillie signed off on the terms, but he wasn't happy. Once again a big company was trying to push RIM around. On top of that, BellSouth insisted on an exclusive right to sell the device. At $249 each, Balsillie believed BellSouth was asking for too much.

Weeks after the carrier announced its deal with RIM, Lenahan learned at a wireless industry conference in Orlando that the exclusivity deal he believed he had with RIM wasn't quite so exclusive. On September 23, BellSouth's archrival, American Mobile Satellite, issued a press release announcing a "close relationship" with RIM to sell the Leapfrog two-way pager on its ARDIS network. The release quoted Balsillie praising American Mobile as an "important partner" that was "instrumental" in the success of the new pager.

"Lenahan was spitting feathers," says Rogers' marketing head, David Neale, who had breakfast with the BellSouth executive minutes after the deal with ARDIS was announced. Neale and a handful of executives from parent company Rogers Communications spent the rest of the meal listening to Lenahan rage about the betrayal. "I hated to lose a deal to ARDIS," Lenahan says. "I felt that because of the relationship we had with RIM and Balsillie himself, we should have gotten more respect."

As far as Lenahan was concerned, Balsillie had verbally agreed to sell Leapfrog solely to BellSouth. Balsillie concedes he never dissuaded the carrier's top officials from thinking they had an exclusive but argues BellSouth's terms were so punishing that RIM had to protect itself with another carrier partner. Lenahan says his initial response was to cancel the contract. After some "hard conversations" with Balsillie and a few exchanges between the companies' lawyers, BellSouth stuck with the deal. The carrier's relationship with RIM, however, would never be the same. Lenahan would be wary about future deals with RIM. "They were on notice. If this kind of thing happened again, there wouldn't be a second order," Lenahan says.

Balsillie recalls the ARDIS deal as the moment RIM put formidable U.S. carriers on notice that the Waterloo bantamweight could play just as rough as the big guys. Steering RIM, he says, meant being "massively scared shitless and fucking terrified" that carriers or competitors would one day toss the company over a cliff. After "trying to bob and weave" around bigger hitters for years, he saw a unique chance to grab the advantage when ARDIS came calling. He correctly gambled that BellSouth was in a corner because it had already signed its contract to buy the Leapfrog, a pager its network badly needed.

Recalling the controversial transaction, Balsillie throws his hands in the air and breaks into a broad grin: "I played the leverage," he laughs. "Welcome to business."

Balsillie's cutthroat tactics were designed for competitors and pushy customers that he believed threatened RIM. Company employees knew better than to cross him. He had a short fuse and could be unforgiving when staff didn't follow orders or weren't prepared. Some RIM employees believed the best strategy was to steer clear of the prickly boss.

Not everyone—or everything—listened to the advice. Late one evening in RIM's offices on Phillip Street, RIM's radio software prodigy, Matthias Wandel, had a close call when demonstrating his latest gadget to some colleagues. He had created a small car out of knobs and plastic scraps that was designed to run on software code embedded in a tiny radio. The vehicle was programmed to respond to basic signals. When its front bumper hit an obstacle, the car backed up, turned, and continued its journey.

After a few crashes into desks and walls, the car started rumbling down a narrow hallway. It traveled without interruption until it neared the end, where two offices sat on either side of the hall. When the car lurched toward one of the open doors, Wandel and the engineers went quiet. It was Balsillie's office. Before the car reached the threshold, however, it veered unexpectedly toward the other room, Lazaridis's office. Watching the car disappear into the office, the engineers started laughing.

"Even this thing is afraid to go into Jim's office," one said.

5 / / / SPREADING THE GOSPEL

Justin Fabian drew a BlackBerry out of his holster, holding it aloft.

"Just give them a taste," he said, snapping the device back into its black sheath.

A moment later, he again slapped leather.

"Cradle it in your hands like it's a valuable object," he said. "Get them interested."

Back into the belt holster it went.

"But you don't want to satisfy their curiosity just yet."

Just twenty-two and fresh out of college, Phil McRoberts hung on Fabian's every word. It was August 1998, and Fabian, RIM's vice president of sales, was showing the newly hired sales rep how to pitch technology. The trick, Fabian said, was to reveal the fun and tactile pleasure of using a BlackBerry. Fabian and Balsillie knew this to be true from watching tapes of focus groups several months earlier: When moderators described e-mail, viewers grew heavy-lidded. But once focus group participants actually handled the device, everything changed. "It takes BlackBerry a few days to grow on you," Balsillie said.

The key was to get buyers to take it for a trial run. Once they knew what a BlackBerry felt like, RIM had them. They wouldn't let go. It was important at first to offer prospective buyers no more than a feel, though—"a taste," as Fabian put it. It was part sales tactic and part defensive move: with giants like Microsoft and Motorola crowding into the wireless data business, the less said about the elaborate invisible system that made BlackBerrys work, the better, Balsillie warned.

BlackBerry's guerrilla sales tactics called for a new breed of salespeople. Balsillie told sales VPs Fabian and Don McMurtry to spike résumés from cellular and computer industry veterans. No jaded old-timers: Balsillie wanted young recruits, brave pioneers—"wireless e-mail evangelists."[1] The ideal candidates were middle-class Canadians from small towns who had been class valedictorians: young men and women who were energetic, competitive, confident, and game for adventure—hungry outliers much like Balsillie.

RIM found most evangelists, like McRoberts, from the co-op business program at nearby Wilfrid Laurier University. Prospects had to show they could think on their feet. McMurtry tested interviewees by tossing a pen at them. "Sell it back to me," he said, a trick also used by the notorious Wolf of Wall Street, stockbroker Jordan Belfort. Evangelist Eric Klimstra won over McMurtry by convincing him to buy advertising on the pen. Once RIM's sales team was in place, Balsillie earmarked $5 million for a launch campaign—peanuts compared to a huge product rollout from the likes of Microsoft. There would be no glossy advertisements, launch parties, or celebrity spokespeople like supermodel Claudia Schiffer (a Palm pitchwoman). Instead, RIM offered thousands of free tastes. Within a few months, as BlackBerry gained initial market acceptance, Balsillie changed the plan to what he called the "puppy dog pitch"; prospective customers would be allowed to take the device for a free one-month trial, as in "take this puppy home; if you don't like it, bring it back." The idea was that few would do so after falling for a new object of affection.

/ / /

McMurtry was still in the office on the night of September 9, 1998, when the phone rang. It was Fabian, in Boston. "Get the team down here immediately," Fabian said, "It's a sell-a-thon!" Fabian and Klimstra had landed in the middle of a marketing brawl between two of the world's leading software makers. Microsoft was staging a national sales show in the backyard of Cambridge, Massachusetts–based Lotus, maker of popular e-mail and spreadsheet programs. Microsoft's corporate e-mail offering, Exchange, was about to surpass Lotus's market lead, and the Cambridge company was not taking the challenge quietly. Shuttles plastered with yellow Lotus ads offered free rides to conference goers arriving at Logan International Airport. Outside the conference's exhibition hall, Lotus employees handed out branded T-shirts and buttons and invitations to a Lotus-sponsored "Boston 'E' Party." If attendees wore Lotus shirts inside, they could win Red Sox tickets.[2]

While Microsoft and Lotus duked it out, Fabian proceeded with RIM's guerrilla marketing campaign. He had chosen this venue to reveal the first advance peek at BlackBerry, which would be launched four months later. More than four thousand information technology executives and experts attended the three-day show at Boston's Fleet Center, ordinarily the home of the Bruins and the Celtics. Fabian and Klimstra walked the floor in search of anyone using mobile communicators. The most popular was Motorola's two-way pager, the PageWriter 2000. It was easy for RIM's evangelists to impress Motorola users. PageWriter customers racked up massive monthly data bills, and the device's capacity for exchanging messages didn't compare to BlackBerry. "Hey, do you get e-mail on that?" Klimstra would ask. "How would you like e-mail on your hip for way cheaper and in a smaller package?" By the end of the first day, Klimstra's pockets bulged with business cards. "It was like shooting fish in a barrel," he said. The next day, McMurtry and a few more evangelists were on the first plane to Boston.

Conference goers hadn't seen anything like the BlackBerry. At a time when primitive two-way paging was considered the new new thing and Internet browsing was still a novelty, a device offering instant access to office e-mails was startling. Initially, the miniature keyboard baffled conference attendees. Some scrunched fingers to try to type on the tiny keyboard as they would on their personal computers. Others poked at the tiny keys with a pencil. Klimstra quickly corrected them, demonstrating how thumb-typing worked: you had to cradle the device in your hands, with thumbs hovering above the keyboard to type. "Trust me, you get used to this quickly," he said. He encouraged people to *feel* the product to see how sturdy it was, and dashed off messages to everyone he met, instructing attendees to remember when he sent the e-mail and to check the arrival times when they logged into computers; that way they would understood how quickly BlackBerry worked.

In coming months, RIM evangelists fanned across the United States spreading the BlackBerry gospel. In airports, they approached anyone with a laptop or handheld device.[3] McMurtry demonstrated how his product was more rugged than Motorola pagers by dropping BlackBerrys on tables and concrete floors. McRoberts went further: in presentations, he began flinging the device against walls. "It just became my thing," he says—an icebreaker to impress skeptical executives twice his age. To their amazement, it never broke, though McRoberts sometimes had to chase down dislodged batteries. Once he sidearmed the device so hard in a roomful of IT executives it took out a chunk of boardroom paneling. To McRoberts' relief, everyone laughed.

/   /   /

RIM's CFO, Dennis Kavelman, approached Balsillie in the late summer of 1998 with an idea. Months after hitting the Toronto Stock Exchange with an initial public offering, RIM's stock was going nowhere in Canadian capital markets, trading well below its IPO price of C$7.25 a share in 1997. Local investors don't get RIM. Maybe it's time to court international investors, Kavelman concluded. RIM was still in its messy legal battle with U.S. Robotics and some local financial analysts were publishing negative reports about the Waterloo company's prospects. Balsillie grew so frustrated with hometown naysayers he rebuked one analyst at a public meeting for asking a "dumb" question about RIM's chances of survival.

RIM's largest shareholder delivered more bad news in September 1998, selling 3 million shares, one-third of its holding in RIM's stock. Five years earlier, Waterloo satellite equipment maker COM DEV International had bought the stake in RIM. COM DEV founder Val O'Donovan was a mentor to Balsillie and a strong presence on RIM's board. The companies were so close that when RIM officials took guests on a tour of its facilities, visitors were also shown COM DEV's nearby operations. By 1996, however, the partnership was fraying and COM DEV spun its RIM shares off into a separate company controlled by O'Donovan, which then sold down its RIM stake on September 3, 1998. RIM was days away from announcing quarterly results. The optics were terrible, leading some investors to fear the worst, since an insider was selling during the company's sensitive pre-earnings "quiet period," a contravention of RIM's trading policies for officers of the company. O'Donovan resigned from RIM's board at Balsillie's insistence.[4]

To Balsillie, the setbacks were wearying evidence of Canadian hostility to hometown success. Fellow Peterborough resident and celebrated author Robertson Davies called it Canada's "tall poppy syndrome": the inclination to cut down those standing above the crowd.[5] The solution, RIM's executives decided, was to go where poppies can never grow too high. For months, Balsillie and Kavelman had discussed cross-listing RIM on New York's NASDAQ exchange and had even brought in a U.S. tech brokerage, NationsBanc Montgomery Securities, as part of the underwriting syndicate for the IPO a year earlier to warm up American investors. Kavelman tested the waters when he traveled to Manhattan in September 1998 to speak to an investor conference hosted by the boutique Connecticut banker Soundview Technology Group. Officially he was there to promote RIM's two-way pager, the Leapfrog, but some in the audience were less than enthusiastic. "I don't want yet another e-mail address," Michael Gartenberg, Gartner's influential research director, complained. "When will someone finally give us the ability to access corporate e-mail on the go?" Kavelman saw his opening, pulling Gartenberg aside to demonstrate his BlackBerry, still months away from a public launch. "It was love at first click," Gartenberg recalled years later.[6] "The first time I saw a BlackBerry, I knew it was going to change the game."

By the time Kavelman left the conference, he and his BlackBerry had been swarmed by other Wall Street professionals curious to see what he had shown the Gartner executive. Kavelman called Balsillie from the airport. The time was right to move on a NASDAQ listing, he told Balsillie. There was something else. "Jim, we need to get someone from sales down to New York right away," Kavelman said. "I have tons of business cards already. People want BlackBerry."

/ / /

It was the fall of 1998 and Eric Klimstra felt his stomach flutter as his boss, Jim Balsillie, with one hand on the steering wheel and an ear fastened to his cellphone, sped from Waterloo to Toronto. Engrossed in negotiations with a BellSouth official, RIM's chief ignored his young passenger during the eighty-minute drive. With nothing to do, the recently hired computer science grad reviewed his instructions from Balsillie for their forthcoming meeting with Intel, creator of the powerful semiconductor chip embedded in BlackBerry. Intel was getting its first look at the near-finished device; if the Silicon Valley giant was interested and ordered a batch of devices for its senior executives, other U.S. businesses would take the small-town Ontario company more seriously.

To Balsillie, meetings were corporate theater. You had to memorize your part before the curtain rose. Usually, Balsillie was the leading man, but he was willing to take on any role his team required for customer meetings. He could play the flinty, ice-veined negotiator or maintain a quiet presence, depending on what was needed. Tyler Nelson, who led several key business development initiatives after being hired by Balsillie in mid-1998, says: "Jim would say, 'If you bring me into a meeting, use me for effect. What do you want me to do?'—but you had to make sure he was 100 percent [onside]. If not, a meeting could go sideways fast."

Once Balsillie approved a meeting agenda, everyone on his team was instructed to stick to the script. "I hate being thrown off by others in a meeting," Balsillie says. "I get edgy when people are not prepared." Even though Intel was a RIM partner, Balsillie was wary. You could never be certain of any customer, supplier, or competitor. Meetings were a potential minefield. "You learn quickly that this is serious business," Balsillie says, "and you don't make an independent move unless you know all aspects of the plan and exactly what you're doing, because the penalty for a misstep is severe."

Overprepared and inexperienced, Klimstra knew his role: to answer technical questions. Otherwise, Balsillie had told him, say nothing. While Klimstra viewed Intel as a friendly ally, RIM's chief saw the semiconductor giant as a dangerous, tricky heavyweight whose every employee lived by former CEO Andy Grove's mantra, "Only the paranoid survive."

The meeting started well enough. Balsillie explained how BlackBerry could be synchronized with a user's desktop computer calendar and contacts. You just have to put the device in this cradle, he said, pointing to a prototype. Normally, the cradle would have had a cable connecting it to the computer, but the cord was missing from the demonstration. One Intel executive, Sean Maloney, VP of worldwide sales, was confused. "What are you saying, how does it do that?" Maloney asked.

Klimstra saw why the Intel executive was puzzled. *He doesn't realize there's supposed to be a cable connecting the cradle to the computer,* he thought. Balsillie appeared stumped too, saying nothing. To Klimstra, the lengthy silence that followed was agonizing. *This must be my cue,* he thought. Clearing his throat, Klimstra piped up: "That cradle is just a mock-up." Maloney nodded as Klimstra explained it would normally have a cable attached. Balsillie turned to Klimstra. "Eric," he said, growing cold with fury. "Don't you ever, ever, ever, *ever*"—Klimstra's stomach twisted with each "ever"—"interrupt me in a meeting again."

After an awkward silence, Balsillie continued the presentation.

As they filed out after the meeting, Maloney's eyes met Klimstra's. The young evangelist could read the look: "*Kid, I'm sorry if I got you fired.*"

Outside, Balsillie was unapologetic. "Never interrupt me when I'm in the zone," he said. "I was very specific in directing them in a certain way and I didn't want to go down any other path." It wasn't that Klimstra had said anything wrong. What bothered Balsillie was that he had said anything at all. "He could have been about to take us over a cliff" by inadvertently blurting out a corporate secret as he explained how the system worked, Balsillie says of his strict stick-to-the-script rule.

In the end, the meeting was a success. Intel ultimately ordered two thousand devices. And Klimstra, though chastened, was not fired or subjected to any further consequences. He sat silently, watching Highway 401, Canada's busiest roadway, unfurl as Balsillie spent the ride back on another call. Balsillie does not recall the details of the interaction, but Klimstra, who stayed with RIM another eight years, never forgot. To him it is an enduring tale of his boss's tactical prowess, and it only cemented his loyalty to Balsillie. "Honestly, I would follow [Balsillie] into a fire," Klimstra says.

/ / /

Patrick Spence was returning to Manhattan in style—new suit, shiny shoes, and polished patter. Weeks earlier, he had been cleaning up battery-leaking Leapfrogs in steamy New York warehouses. Now, after Kavelman's enthusiastic reception in New York, he was returning as RIM's Wall Street evangelist. The tall, former varsity volleyball player was armed with a cheat sheet of local bank and brokerage executives furnished by a local Microsoft reseller. He quickly learned that the Winter Garden Atrium of the World Financial Center was the place to approach dealmakers and analysts to offer demonstrations. Some prospects invited Spence up to their offices. One senior banker practiced putting golf balls as Spence installed BlackBerry software on his desktop computer. The banker laid down his putter and looked on in amazement when Spence showed him that a test e-mail sent from the banker's computer to himself arrived faster on the BlackBerry than it did to his own desktop in-box. The banker ordered two BlackBerrys that afternoon—one each for himself and his assistant.

BlackBerry's first users weren't typical early adopters—gearheads who routinely rushed out to experiment with any new technology. The first converts were senior legal and banking advisers who needed to be first with information. Once Fortune 1000 CEOs saw their bankers and lawyers cradling BlackBerrys at meetings, they wanted their own. The constancy of Black-Berry e-mails gave new urgency to business communications. Bosses with BlackBerrys chastised lieutenants for slow responses to e-mails that many still took a day or two to read. They made sure that changed. Senior BlackBerry-using executives in turn ordered BlackBerrys for *their* direct reports so they could stay in touch constantly. The BlackBerry virus was starting to spread.

Although corporate bosses were starting to embrace BlackBerry, Lazaridis and Balsillie knew they faced a challenge selling bulk orders to big businesses. Technology purchases were the domain of chief information officers (CIOs). These executives were conservative and frowned on technology that exposed internal communications. "The problem with going through IT is they had to approve everything. It would take a year," says Lazaridis. "You had to test everything, approve it, and most of these [CIOs] didn't want it anyway. It was just another thing to deal with. But once a CEO tried it, that was it."

The solution, Lazaridis and Balsillie decided, was an unorthodox plan to infiltrate Fortune 1000 companies. RIM made it easy for influential managers and executives to link the addictive BlackBerry system into their corporate e-mail without involving the IT department. Their secret weapon was the software designed by RIM engineer Gary Mousseau. The program was included free with every BlackBerry purchase and took only fifteen minutes to install on any computer. Once it was running, it connected the BlackBerry to a user's e-mail and the device was operational. RIM even priced the devices so they fell within executives' discretionary spending budgets. The idea was to get a critical mass of top executives in a company to use BlackBerrys before their CIO realized a new technology had infiltrated the business. This would be all the leverage RIM needed, Balsillie and Lazaridis believed, to convince CIOs to acquire sophisticated RIM servers to centrally manage large volumes of BlackBerry devices from within their IT departments. The CIO end run was a unique strategy, making BlackBerry the first IT product ever sold from the top down, pushed by senior management onto their IT organizations.

One of BlackBerry's big early converts was financial services giant Merrill Lynch. John McKinley, chief technology officer for the brokerage and banking Goliath, was standing near Kavelman at the Soundview conference as he demonstrated the BlackBerry to others. "This was really eye-opening," McKinley says. Unlike other mobile devices, "it wasn't trying to solve all problems, but taking one use case—e-mail—and trying to deliver it in a new paradigm. It struck me these guys were onto something new and distinctive." He wanted to bring BlackBerry to Merrill as soon as possible.

RIM couldn't have asked for a more influential customer. When Black-Berrys first arrived at Merrill in early 1999, the company had forty-five thousand employees across the country. Merrill employees soon became addicted. "It quickly became a Web of people that had one saying, 'Hey, you have to get this guy one and this guy one,'" says Spence. "I was seeding it with reckless abandon into Merrill because it was the best marketing and sales investment we could make."

/ / /

Spence was back in Waterloo in late January 1999 when RIM received one of its first BlackBerry online orders. The buyer was Michael Dell, founder of computer maker Dell Inc. Spence couldn't believe it. RIM had only launched BlackBerry days earlier, and its Web site ordering system was still a work in progress. How could a Waterloo company be on the radar of one of America's most successful entrepreneurs? It had to be a hoax, Spence figured. But when he e-mailed Dell to offer his assistance, he got an immediate reply from the billionaire. Spence was soon on his way to Round Rock, Texas, where he worked with Dell's IT department to deploy devices for about one hundred executives and IT specialists in the following weeks.

Soon the rave reviews rolled in. *BusinessWeek* called BlackBerry "close to perfect pocket E-mail." *PC World* dubbed RIM's latest the best wireless communications device of the year. *Fortune* named BlackBerry one of seven "cult brands," alongside Ben & Jerry's and Nike.[7] Celebrities from Pamela Anderson to Howard Stern would not part with the device.[8] Microsoft's Bill Gates and General Electric's Jack Welch were early champions. Every time GE's world-trotting boss stepped away from a golf game or social event to scan his BlackBerry, he signaled to influential friends and associates that effective leadership includes instant e-mail access.

Stories abounded about how BlackBerry transformed corporate life. One of Welch's top lieutenants, GE Capital CEO Michael Neal, slept with a BlackBerry under his pillow, Don McMurtry says. Spence began noticing a change with the lunch crowd in lower Manhattan. People were ignoring their tablemates and peering down at their BlackBerrys instead. Traders nicknamed the device "CrackBerry." If you were bent over the cradled device, oblivious to your surroundings, you were doing the "BlackBerry Prayer." Before long, the ranks of RIM's evangelists had grown to include thousands of its customers.

Spence and fellow evangelists were greeted like conquering heroes when they returned with weekly tales from the trenches. Colleagues who had worked long, frustrating hours to perfect the BlackBerry were astonished by its fame south of the border. "You knew and could feel you were part of something special," he says.

/   /   /

The dot-com bubble was the era of the rock-star tech analyst. With one call, Morgan Stanley's Mary Meeker and Merrill's Steve Milunovich could make or break a young high-tech firm's prospects. Milunovich shared his views on RIM for the first time in May 18, 1999. His report raved about BlackBerry's ease of use, durability, and market potential. Impressed, the analyst put a $13 price target on the stock, 20 percent higher than its last price.

Milunovich's call jolted RIM stock awake. Three months earlier, RIM had debuted on the U.S. public markets, opening at just under $13 in early February on the NASDAQ. It then began to sink, losing more than a third of its value in the following weeks. The stock wasn't going anywhere—until Milunovich's report came out.

On the day of the Merrill report, 24 million RIM shares traded hands on NASDAQ—more than the combined volume of the previous ten days on the exchange—pushing the stock above Milunovich's optimistic $13 target. Other analysts followed with glowing reports. Two months later, the stock was trading at $26. By mid-November it had doubled again. In March 2000, the stock hit a new high-water mark, closing at more than $156 per share on Nasdaq (and C$227 on the Toronto Stock Exchange), giving RIM, a company of five hundred employees, a market value of $11 billion (C$16 billion).

When soaring BlackBerry sales pushed RIM's revenues to $85 million for its fiscal year starting March 1, 1999, Balsillie saw an opportunity to harness U.S. investor enthusiasm. In October 1999, RIM raised $172 million by selling 5.6 million shares on NASDAQ. Martha Stewart and World Wrestling

Federation impresario Vince McMahon were taking their companies public at the same time, and during one day of meetings with investors in Boston, Balsillie and Kavelman kept running into menacing wrestlers and women in crisp blouses and gray pleated skirts brandishing cookies as the deal teams crossed paths. "This was my first exposure to raising money in the United States," says Balsillie. "Funny world."

Merrill Lynch led the RIM offer—and announced an order for 1,500 BlackBerrys. That day, Patrick Spence got a call from Ken LeVine, a senior IT executive at Citigroup. "You just made my life hell," LeVine told him. Spence had already seeded about fifty devices into Citi's Salomon Smith Barney investment banking unit. When they learned of the Merrill order, hundreds more executives bombarded LeVine with calls and e-mails, demanding their own BlackBerry. Four months later, Salomon placed an order for 2,500 devices, and LeVine later came to work for RIM.

To outsiders, Balsillie and Lazaridis, now paper billionaires, were the new princes of the dot-com age. Lazaridis declared BlackBerry "the first addictive application since the video game."[9] RIM's success won Balsillie access to business luminaries. If the son of an electrician was fazed by business celebrities, he never let it show. When he met Michael Dell in 1999 at New York's Four Seasons Hotel for breakfast, heads turned as they walked through the lobby. As they neared their table, Balsillie deadpanned to Dell: "I hope it doesn't make you uncomfortable having everyone look at me."

/ / /

RIM's successful fall 1999 U.S. stock offering earned the company a place of honor at one of Wall Street's most exclusive rituals—the closing dinner. The event is a longstanding celebration hosted by bankers grateful for clients showering them with multimillion-dollar fees. The dinners were traditionally staid private club affairs involving dull speeches and expensive cigars. At the height of the tech boom, however, revelries had grown exotic and feverish. Parties were staged at elite Manhattan restaurants and clubs. Occasionally, advisers and executives were ferried on private jets to Las Vegas or Monaco. Merrill Lynch approached Lazaridis and Balsillie with plans to fete NASDAQ's new tech darling. But their night would be unlike any the Wall Street firm had hosted. Having battled to survive for sixteen years, RIM's cautious bosses were conditioned for adversity, not success. There had never been any room for self-congratulation because the company had always been on guard for the next challenge. How would they celebrate their coming-out party?

Instead of flying to a distant pleasure palace, Balsillie and Lazaridis stayed true to their roots by celebrating Waterloo and Canadian culture. If the underwriters wanted to bankroll a celebration, the CEOs decided it should be for all RIM employees, which is why on a cold January in 2000 Wall Street technology bankers and lawyers found themselves at Lulu's Roadhouse, a Kmart-turned-music hall on the outskirts of Kitchener-Waterloo, that had been drawing both students and middle-aged suburban revelers since the 1980s. The club had a sunken, tennis court–sized dance floor and a sprawling wood and brick bar that Guinness World Records deemed the world's longest. As the bar filled up, some two thousand guests, including hundreds of engineering students from University of Waterloo, noticed the stage being readied with microphones. But they were not for corporate speeches.

"I personally felt it was a party and our success and the event spoke for themselves, so no need to grab the microphone and talk about it," Balsillie says. When the lights went up a group of men walked to the front of the stage. The crowd roared as they recognized one of Canada's best known bands, the Barenaked Ladies. The playful group started off with impromptu songs about two things the hometown crowd held dear: beer and BlackBerrys. Their signature song, "If I Had a Million Dollars," was the hit of the night. For many in the audience who were on their way to being paper millionaires that was no longer a hypothetical question. "We wandered around looking at each other saying, 'Wow, this is really happening,' " says Perry Jarmuszewski.

6 / / / TOP THIS

Lazaridis stole a glance at Balsillie. He knew his co-CEO was thinking the same thing: *Can you believe this guy?* Seated across the table, talking endlessly, hands wild in the air, was Carl Yankowski, CEO of Palm Inc. Yankowski had invited the RIM chiefs to dinner in New York in the spring of 2000 to initiate takeover talks. Going into the meal, Balsillie and Lazaridis understood their host considered them the main course. An MIT-trained engineer, Yankowski had breezed through a series of senior marketing posts with Sony, PepsiCo, and Reebok. He had hit the jackpot a few months earlier upon taking the helm at Palm.

Palm's parent, 3Com[1], was about to capitalize on dot-com mania when Yankowski joined by selling a stake in its popular personal digital assistant maker through an initial public offering. On its first day of trading in March 2000, Palm's stock soared from its offering price of $38 a share to more than $95 at closing. The score gave Palm a stock market valuation of more than $50 billion, making its new CEO $1 billion richer on paper and handing Palm a powerful currency for stock-based takeover offers.[2]

Palm's overpriced stock inflated Yankowski's ego. During media interviews on Palm's first day of trading, he showed up in a $3,000 wool suit shimmering with pinstripes woven from 14-karat gold thread. The man with the golden suit carried himself like he believed in his own Midas touch. "He couldn't be in a room with you for thirty minutes without taking credit for at least three big moments in computing history," says Andrea Butter, a former Palm executive and company biographer.

As the night unfolded, there wasn't a thing about Palm's inner workings Yankowski wouldn't share with his two guests, as if it didn't matter that they knew. He talked and talked. Then the conversation turned to personal pursuits. Yankowski wanted to know where they went to school, what jets they flew, what cars they drove.

When he discovered the RIM executives flew in a used Westwind jet, Yankowski declared he was certified to pilot dozens of planes. When the Palm CEO enquired about Lazaridis's impressive home theater, Yankowski bragged about his $250,000 Nantucket home stereo system, custom-built by Sony engineers. Learning that Lazaridis drove a new BMW M5, Yankowski leaned in. "Mike," he said. "I have an M6." There was no stopping Yankowski. "Whatever you said, he had to be better," Balsillie says.

Yankowski recalls the one-upmanship as "the kind of light discussion we were having over dinner." What the Palm CEO didn't realize was that his two guests, who were so in synch they could practically finish each other's sentences, subtly used their two-man advantage to amuse themselves at the expense of their unsuspecting suitor as the night went on.

The RIM duo turned his boasting into a sport. They began fibbing about their own accomplishments to see if he'd try to top them—and he took the bait every time. "We were just making shit up," says Balsillie. The CEO crowing contest took a turn for the ridiculous when Balsillie falsely told Yankowski he'd won an Olympic gold medal playing for Canada's national hockey team. *Top that!* As Balsillie recalls, Yankowski volleyed back that he'd won several medals. Balsillie felt his BlackBerry buzz. He looked down. It was a message from Lazaridis, sitting next to him. "1–0 for you." The RIM bosses quietly exchanged scores through the rest of dinner. After this evening, Balsillie and Lazaridis referred to Yankowski as "Topper," a nod to the fictional *Dilbert* comic strip character who routinely interrupts office conversations with cries of "That's nothing," followed by implausible claims that he insulated his house with cheese or swallowed insects to spin silk.

There was a bigger game under way. Though they flattered Yankowski with attention, RIM's partners had no interest in selling their company. They took Yankowski's calls, showed up for meetings, and swapped boasts to keep him off guard. "Most people's instincts tell them to seek clarity in business dealings, but ambiguity is more powerful in my view," Balsillie explains. "You'd be surprised how long you can string competitors along without ever showing your cards." An unsuspecting Yankowski pursued a takeover of RIM for months. Throughout Yankowski's courtship of RIM, Balsillie down-played his own company's abilities and ambitions—flashing what he calls the "Aw, shucks card." BlackBerry, he told Yankowski, was a small niche device lacking the global appeal of Palm. He talked of licensing Palm's operating system and continually asked what RIM should do next. "That seemed to be his primary preoccupation," Yankowski says. That's exactly what RIM wanted him to think. "My objective," comments Balsillie, "was to get him to under-estimate RIM."

When Balsillie joined Yankowski in San Francisco for dinner later in 2000, the RIM chief pulled out a prototype of an upgraded BlackBerry, called the 957, which shared many of the features of the latest Palm device, including a large, square screen. He handed the model to Yankowski, who was suddenly full of questions:

"What network will RIM use for this BlackBerry?"

"We haven't told anybody yet," Balsillie replied.

Eyeing the screen, Yankowski flashed Balsillie a big grin. "That's okay. I already know."

"What do you mean?"

"It says right here." Yankowski pointed to the letters CDPD in the top right corner of the screen. CDPD, short for cellular digital packet data, was a wireless data network technology heavily promoted by its creator, AT&T. So that's what RIM's up to: dumping Mobitex for CDPD, Yankowski figured. Palm was already testing its next device on the CDPD data net-work.

Balsillie was still giddy when he caught up with David Yach, a Canadian engineer who had been recently hired away from California software maker Sybase as RIM's chief technology officer. Joining Yach in RIM's jet, Balsillie blurted out: "He fell for it!" In fact, what he showed Yankowski earlier in the evening was a decoy with the screen changed to read CDPD by one of Yach's engineers, with the specific intent of fooling the Palm boss. RIM had no inter-est in CDPD. Lazaridis viewed it as technically inferior technology, correctly predicting it would soon be dead. If Palm wanted to jump to CDPD, that was fine with Balsillie. For now, RIM was sticking with Mobitex, a slower but more reliable messaging highway.

Yankowski has no recollection of the San Francisco dinner, but he remem-bers what happened soon afterward. Takeover talks broke off abruptly when Balsillie said he would have no part of a deal that did not hand him full executive control of the merged company. The petulant demand by a firm with one-twelfth the revenues of Palm seemed preposterous to Yankowski, who recalled Balsillie "throwing a hissy fit." Once again, the Palm CEO misread the RIM bosses. That was just Balsillie's way of saying "game over."

/ / /

Palm was one of several mobile device makers courting corporate alliances around the turn of the new millennium. Cellphone, direct paging, and computer manufacturers were all looking for partners as increasingly sophisticated network technology made it possible for users to browse the Web, send messages, and phone on a single pocket-sized device. Blurring technology boundaries, coupled with rapid growth in consumer demand for mobile products, sparked a global race by software, cellphone, and handset makers to launch all-in-one devices, soon to be called smartphones.[3] Accelerating this rush was the dot-com frenzy. Soaring technology share prices provided large publicly traded companies with robust takeover currencies to spend on stock-based mergers with competitors. Many companies were on the prowl.

The player everyone in the handset business feared was Microsoft. The Redmond, Washington, giant had already conquered the personal computing market. Many believed the global cellular market, which was fast approaching 1 billion subscribers in 2000, was its next target. Microsoft made its first move in 1998, approaching the world's largest cellular phone maker, Nokia, to explore a joint venture to develop enhanced phone software. Even though Nokia dominated the global cellular market with a 30 percent share, it saw Microsoft as an aggressor that needed to be contained. Microsoft had crushed early computing and Internet partners in its quest to dominate desktop applications with what regulators would later call an "embrace, extend, and extinguish" strategy that sometimes put allies out of business.[4] Mobile device makers were determined not to make the same mistake. Months after Microsoft's overture, Nokia joined forces with rivals Ericsson and Motorola to create a new mobile operating system called Symbian. Microsoft responded by teaming with South Korea's Samsung Electronics Co. to launch Stinger, a software package for cellphones.

RIM decided to sit out the convergence dance. Lazaridis didn't buy into the idea that the handset race would be won by smartphones combining computing, phone, and Internet services. To him, that made no sense. All-purpose operating systems sucked batteries dry, hogged wireless bandwidth, and were awkward to use with their tap-and-write touch screens or full, shrunken desktop keyboards. He and his engineers had spent years creating the world's most efficient handheld device, focusing on a single, perfect application: wireless e-mail. It was light on battery use and e-mails were dispatched so efficiently that an average month of messages consumed less network spectrum than one local telephone call.[5]

It was one thing to buck an industry fad. The bigger danger was that some global mammoth would simply smash the small Waterloo upstart. The rival Balsillie and Lazaridis worried about most was Microsoft after it signaled an interest in wireless e-mail by joining a short-lived venture with semiconductor maker Qualcomm in the late 1990s. At the same time Microsoft executives, including CEO Steve Ballmer, began asking RIM staff questions at trade shows about how BlackBerry worked. Microsoft's combative generals would not be thrown off by the playful ruses that kept Yankowski at bay. Nor was Balsillie inclined to mess with them. "I had an expression: Never moon the gorilla," Balsillie says. "Microsoft was the gorilla. We cut them by far the widest berth of anyone."

Balsillie's strategy for dealing with Microsoft was to undersell RIM's potential. Upon launching BlackBerry, he pitched the device to Microsoft as a pager-like service to promote the software giant's corporate e-mail software, Exchange. Little was made of BlackBerry's e-mail potential. Microsoft was so taken with the device it installed one of the first BlackBerry servers at its headquarters. Before long, RIM was invited to set up booths at Microsoft conferences; no one objected when the Waterloo firm signed up attendees for BlackBerrys.

The friendly, casual alliance deteriorated in 2000 following RIM's decision to make its e-mail service compatible with Lotus, Microsoft's software rival. Another affront was the launch of the 957 BlackBerry. RIM's first big-screen device abandoned the pager-like shape of the Leapfrog; now it looked more like a Palm Pilot and other competing PDAs that used Microsoft's mobile operating system. Microsoft stopped inviting RIM to conferences. The BlackBerry server was even yanked out of its Redmond headquarters.

Lazaridis wanted to continue nurturing the Microsoft relationship, but Balsillie steered him away. He was worried Microsoft would exploit the relationship to RIM's disadvantage. "[Bill] Gates was superpredatory, and nothing good would come from trying to form a relationship back then," says

Balsillie. In fact, Microsoft turned out to be less threatening than Balsillie feared. Distracted by its battle with Apple, Microsoft was a halfhearted competitor in the wireless e-mail and smartphone race. It jumped in and out of alliances with various manufacturers, including Qualcomm, Palm, Motorola, Nokia, and South Korea's LG Corp.,[6] but none of the initiatives vaulted Microsoft to the front of the smartphone pack.

When RIM began selling BlackBerry, Palm dominated the wireless handheld device business. Its 1999 launch of Palm VII, combining e-mail with the handset's popular calendar and contact functions, was an instant hit. It sold more than a hundred thousand Palm VII devices during its first year, four times as many as BlackBerry. The lead was short-lived, however, once customers realized that e-mails were instantaneous on RIM's device. Using e-mail on a Palm VII was a two-step process that involved flipping open an external antenna and waiting for messages to download. Also, unlike BlackBerry, Palm e-mails couldn't be synched with corporate e-mail in-boxes. BlackBerry grabbed the lead in 2000, outselling Palm VII by about 40 percent and backed by its first marketing campaign, running print ads in business and trade publications touting its new PDA-sized 957 as "Berry Amazing." By the end of 2001, Palm was in trouble. Its stock plunged more than 90 percent and Yankowski left. The handset maker tried in vain to recover with the launch of Palm i705 in 2002. Technology tastemaker Walt Mossberg dismissed its e-mail interface as "clumsy and inefficient," chastising Palm for sticking with its trademark stylus and touch screen instead of adding a keyboard. "It amazes me that the company took 18 months to develop this device and yet failed to match some of the key things that made the RIM so popular," he wrote in early 2002.[7] The California company returned to its roots in 2003, acquiring an inventive smartphone start-up called Handspring, which happened to be owned by Jeff Hawkins and Donna Dubinsky, Palm's founder and former CEO, respectively.

The major rival in the 2000 mobile data market was Motorola. The Chicago two-way radio maker had grown into a diversified global communications company with $38 billion in annual sales. It ranked second behind Nokia in global cellphone sales and was a formidable force in semiconductor, paging, walkie-talkie, and network equipment markets. Its PageWriter 2000, the world's first two-way pager, launched in 1998, was the player BlackBerry had to beat. Like RIM, Motorola saw the need for a mobile communicator that could receive and send text messages. Unlike RIM, however, Motorola did not have the benefit of the BellSouth's national Mobitex data network. Instead, it relayed messages through the smaller ReFLEX network, which had limited capacity and reach. Messages were restricted to about five hundred characters and were often dropped or delayed. Active users were saddled with expensive monthly fees if they exceeded tight monthly text limits of six thousand characters, or twelve full-length e-mails. BlackBerry's sturdier network and packet-sending capabilities allowed users to send messages as long as sixteen thousand characters and there were no limits on monthly e-mail volume.

Motorola had the resources to out-engineer BlackBerry. But the communications giant was preoccupied with corporate restructuring and lost interest in what it considered a niche messaging market. Also, Motorola was convinced the future of wireless communications lay in outer space, investing heavily in a consortium of satellites called Iridium to provide global wireless phone service. The project was plagued with challenges. Satellite phones were too expensive at $3,000 each and service was spotty.[8] Iridium filed for bankruptcy in 1999, and Motorola wrote off billions of dollars it had invested in the company. With competitors preoccupied or looking elsewhere, the longshot from Waterloo moved into the lead of a race for mobile data business that everyone had underestimated.

/ / /

From the voice on the other end of the line, Lisa Garrard knew this wouldn't be a pleasant call. It was another chief information officer from a Wall Street bank, thundering for one of RIM's bosses—*It doesn't matter which one*. The executive assistant to Balsillie and Lazaridis, Garrard called out from her hallway desk, midway between the two CEOs' offices. "Mike, Jim, there's another call for you. It's the CIO of—"

"I'm not here, but I'm pretty sure Mike is!" Balsillie called out from his office.

"I'm not here either!" Lazaridis replied.

"Guys . . ." Garrard said. Peering into Balsillie's office she saw him slide under his desk. "I saw your head!"

"That's not my head," Balsillie giggled. "There's nobody here but us chickens!"

Everyone at RIM was diving for cover in 2001. BlackBerry was selling faster than anyone predicted, and the Waterloo company was feeling the strain of its success. RIM's BlackBerry user base rocketed from 25,000 in fiscal 2000 to 165,000 the following year. There was no time to pop champagne. If the company couldn't keep pace with demands, prosperity would be short-lived. RIM raced to keep up by hiring an average of two people a day, more than doubling its workforce to 1,260 inside a year. The company scrambled to find room for everyone, buying or leasing buildings around the Waterloo region. No matter where they landed, new employees were greeted with confusion. Without a fully functional back office, billing for the BlackBerry service was a nightmare; RIM didn't even have a proper billing system to charge customers until months after the device was launched.

RIM's evangelists had done an effective job of converting people to BlackBerrys, but some sales people didn't initially keep track of who received the product. When RIM's controller Harvey Taylor complained to sales vice president Don McMurtry that hundreds of customers weren't paying monthly service charges he was unprepared for the response. "Who cares," McMurtry replied. "Losing a few hundred to get tens of thousands of orders is an acceptable cost." Although the company tried to track down freeloaders, product manager Dave Castell says "we ended up paying monthly airtime for BlackBerrys used by God-knows-who for years." Balsillie says the company was able smoke out some of the non-paying customers by cutting off service on some accounts. Customers were outraged, Balsillie says. "We asked for forgiveness, but we also asked for money."

A bigger issue was the rickety network shuttling e-mail messages. Delays and system crashes were daily headaches. E-mails were often twenty minutes late. Sometimes they would arrive five hours late. Occasionally, they disappeared altogether, lost in space. The situation made a mockery of RIM's claim that BlackBerry was "Always On, Always Connected."

Suffice to say, RIM's customers weren't the patient types. Senior executives who couldn't live without BlackBerrys came down hard on their chief information officers; when the yelling stopped, the CIOs turned the heat up on Lazaridis and Balsillie. John McKinley, Merrill Lynch's chief technology officer and an early BlackBerry champion, was a frequent caller and he wasn't happy. The conversations were "adrenaline-filled," he says. "It was a very direct dialogue, letting them know we viewed this as really critical, and when there were repeated instances, our patience wasn't unlimited."

When RIM's chickens came out from under their desks, feathers flew. "We hated those calls so much," says Balsillie. "They'd threaten everything.

They'd say, 'I don't care, just make it fucking work.' It [was] like root canal without anesthetic." RIM salesman Patrick Spence missed his sister's university graduation reception—which he was hosting at his home—spending most of the celebration on a conference call with a RIM engineer and an incensed Salomon Smith Barney's IT specialist Ken LeVine, who was himself under fire from bankers unable to communicate with their team during crucial deal negotiations.

There was no quick fix for RIM's network issues. The problems resided at both BellSouth and RIM. Each side blamed the other. When managers from the two companies sat down in New Jersey to solve the crisis in the latter part of 2000, the meeting deteriorated into a shouting match between RIM's irreverent young engineers and the carrier's graying executives.

Both sides had a point. BellSouth was adding base stations to accommodate expanded Mobitex traffic, particularly in Manhattan, but not fast enough. To prevent the clogged network from collapsing, BellSouth's engineers sometimes delayed the flow of messages into the pipeline, drawing accusations from RIM that the carrier was "throttling" traffic. For its part, BellSouth had plenty to complain about. RIM activated new Wall Street customers without giving BellSouth notice. The added traffic quickly overwhelmed the nearest BellSouth Mobitex base stations. A senior Morgan Stanley executive went to the top at BellSouth, calling chairman John Clendenin to complain that a new shipment of BlackBerrys wasn't working. As tensions rose, flustered BellSouth executives insisted RIM give the carrier four to six months' notice before a new customer was brought online. The edict was greeted with howls of laughter in Waterloo.

RIM engineers were loath to concede problems could be traced to Waterloo. RIM's initial Relay system may have been ingenious, but it was a makeshift wonder. It was located in a modestly sized server room, and it occasionally ran over a laptop belonging to one of the system's architects, Allan Lewis, when it needed to be debugged. The server room was sometimes used as a thoroughfare; the network once went down after an employee tripped over a power cord. Lewis and his colleagues always figured the Relay system was a preliminary, temporary setup that would be replaced with a more powerful system to accommodate tomorrow's increased traffic. What he and everyone else at RIM failed to anticipate was how fast tomorrow would come. Once, the Relay crashed when Lewis was visiting Disney World in Florida with his family. The only person in Waterloo who could fix it was warming a bar seat. When the engineer arrived at RIM's offices, Lewis patiently communicated with the woozy engineer over his BlackBerry as they worked together to fix the server.

As RIM's engineers raced to work out bugs in a network upgrade called Relay 2, the outages got worse—one left BlackBerry users in the United States without e-mails for hours during Thanksgiving. "You [always] felt like you were a thread away from the thing just crashing," says sales VP Justin Fabian. In early 2001, the company successfully switched the network over to Relay 2, the first of many upgrades needed to cope with a mounting daily avalanche of e-mails.

/ / /

BlackBerry's long-term success wouldn't have been possible without the support of conservative executives who were trained skeptics about new technology. Chief information officers began appearing in major North American companies in the 1980s as computers assumed a key role in corporate back rooms.[9] When businesses purchased mainframe computers in the 1960s, data processing supervisors handled accounting and financial reporting. As computing powers expanded with the arrival of desktops and powerful software programs, technology expertise became an essential business tool. Big companies allocated hundreds of millions of dollars to hardware and software purchases and they needed senior executives to take charge. As the pace of automation accelerated in the 2000s, technology investments become high-stake decisions. Computing, software, and hardware start-ups jockeyed with technology giants for lucrative corporate accounts. In this fevered market, CIOs operated with caution. Would the technology last? Might it overburden existing systems or expose the company to hackers? Would the supplier survive? Inevitably, many big companies preferred to stick with the likes of Oracle, Microsoft, or IBM, blue-chip technology suppliers that wouldn't embarrass the CIO.

Balsillie's original plan was to infiltrate Fortune 1000 companies by bypassing CIOs. If RIM's evangelists seeded BlackBerrys with enough top executives, they would force the CIO to embrace RIM, he thought. What this plan didn't anticipate, however, were the anxieties triggered by an e-mail system that called for companies to install RIM's Business Enterprise Server (BES) software in their internal computing systems. There was no way a Black-Berry server would be allowed behind fiercely guarded corporate network firewalls unless CIOs were convinced the RIM system was secure and dependable.

"I knew we had a gap that was impeding the sales process," says sales VP Don McMurtry. His answer was to recruit veteran IT consultants experienced with large-scale corporate technology applications. They understood CIO preoccupations with security and won them over by explaining unique protections invisible to most BlackBerry users. RIM's in-house network gave the company the ability to guarantee the safe passage of every message. Using an advanced encryption standard similar to one used by the U.S. military for internal communications, RIM designed its BlackBerry system to ensure every e-mail was automatically protected by an encryption code when sent. On arrival the message was decoded before appearing in the recipient's in-box. Every company or organization that acquired a RIM server received customized encryption keys that authenticated and decoded e-mails. The keys were unique to every customer and the system was so protected that even RIM could not unscramble messages traveling through its relay system.

Once it could demonstrate and fully explain BlackBerry's security features, RIM's relationship with the CIO community changed. Before long, CIOs were allies, not enemies. And the United States' biggest companies threw open their doors and wallets to a company that was virtually unknown a year earlier.

As RIM's business gained momentum, its stock became the plaything of speculators. After the stock's enormous rise in the dot-com bubble, it took a hit along with every other tech company whose value had inflated beyond reason. Less than three months after topping $156 in March 2000, the stock had dropped by more than 75 percent, and analysts began to fret about its rising sales and marketing costs. But as RIM's revenues continued to soar—rising more than 45 percent from quarter to quarter through the latter part of 2000—its stock rebounded and was back over $100 by October.

Balsillie, who kept his finance team poised to take advantage of hot equity markets, put out the word that RIM was ready to do its second U.S. stock offering in a year. He and Kavelman had cultivated interest among U.S. investors and Wall Street underwriters, and demand among investment bankers was so intense to join the offering that RIM hired three "bulge firms"—tier one Wall Street banks Merrill Lynch, Credit Suisse First Boston, and Goldman Sachs—to lead an offering of 6 million shares for $102 each in late October. Because of RIM's dual U.S. and Canadian stock exchange listings, it was able to clear its prospectus with less onerous Canadian regulators within days rather than the weeks it would have taken with the Securities and Exchange Commission. "We caught the market window by the skinniest of margins," Balsillie says.

Almost immediately after the offering, RIM shares fell as tech stocks overall headed into a prolonged slump. RIM now had a war chest few early-stage companies could dream of. It would guarantee the company's safe passage through the challenging industry conditions that lay ahead. Large tech stock offerings on Wall Street would be scarce for the next few years—until RIM again came to market in early 2004 to sell $945 million worth of stock.

/ / /

BellSouth Wireless Data president Bill Lenahan had been right about RIM: it was better suited to making devices than building its own wireless service for thousands of customers. "It's one thing to develop stuff like this," says Lenahan. "It's another to deliver and bill and support it. They didn't have that capability."

But another thing was clear to Lenahan by 2000: the little wireless e-mail device was a huge hit with powerful customers and had substantial growth prospects, while two-way paging's moment in the spotlight would be fleeting. With two-way paging, customers could trade messages, check stock quotes, and send text messages to phones, "but that wasn't what people wanted to do," says former BellSouth executive Neale Hightower. What worked was putting corporate e-mail in their hands. The point was driven home in Atlanta, where BellSouth executives, including CEO Duane Ackerman, were among the first users to receive free BlackBerrys. Before long, they were so addicted that Ackerman forced them to place their devices on the desk during meetings to ensure nobody was distracted. "I think that was kind of the closer," says Hightower.

Inside BellSouth, discussions ensued about when and how the carrier would start distributing BlackBerry directly. "After the product came out and we saw the performance and sell-on, we put our own plan together," said Lenahan. "It was what the customer wanted in corporate America. And it became what the individual users wanted, what they needed once they understood the power of it. I think it was a very natural extension to move away from the airtime deal for both companies."

Balsillie and Lazaridis knew they were not well suited to running their own service. "We were just barely holding stuff together," says Balsillie. RIM lacked the staff and experience to manage the billing and service needs of its booming customer base. But while it made sense to hand the back office administration over to BellSouth, Balsillie wasn't going to yield everything. RIM's airtime deal with the carrier enabled the Waterloo company to operate an in-house e-mail network, a unique right not enjoyed by other handset makers. Of the $40 RIM was charging each BlackBerry customer monthly, $10 went to BellSouth. If the carrier was going to take over billing and service, Balsillie insisted RIM would hold on to a share of the monthly fee. The carrier would have to pay what he called a "service access fee" of $10 a month for each customer. It was a brash demand, but Balsillie knew RIM had leverage. BellSouth was desperate to pocket a bigger share of BlackBerry's profitable growth and RIM could reasonably argue it had to cover the costs of running its internal e-mail Relay system. "Sometimes in negotiations you have to find something stupid to hold onto and wave your hands madly," Balsillie says. "I fought like crazy to get $10." BellSouth capitulated, handing Balsillie the clout he needed to wrestle similar fees from other carriers eager to sell BlackBerrys. ARDIS followed, as did Canada's Rogers and Bell, which ran similar data networks. Lenahan and his carrier counterparts didn't like sharing any of their service revenues with RIM. If they wanted to get in on the gusher of revenues from wireless e-mail to feed their still-struggling data networks, they had no choice.

7 / / / EL CAMINO

Nearly three hundred RIM engineers were on the move. A caravan of buses, cars, and bikes were traveling northeast from the company's offices to the Waterloo Inn on the edge of town. Filing into a large conference room just before 4:00 p.m. on March 1, 2001, engineers spied Larry Conlee at the podium. He was hard to miss. The imposing Texan stood six feet tall and weighed more than three hundred pounds. Until two months earlier, Conlee had been an enemy commander, overseeing Motorola's paging division. While working for BlackBerry's chief competitor, he wanted to turn Motorola's big guns on the Waterloo upstart. But when Motorola sidelined its paging business, Conlee decided he'd rather switch than fight.

Lazaridis and Balsillie hired Conlee as one of two chief operating officers they hoped might bring order to RIM's chaotic growth. Their first hire, Don Morrison, joined the company in late 2000 to oversee sales and marketing. He reported to Balsillie. Morrison brought years of experience as an AT&T and Bell Canada executive. A soothing, nurturing executive, he also carried a passion for religious studies. Balsillie took to calling Morrison, eight years his senior, "Father Time." If Morrison was the good-cop hire, that left Conlee with an obvious role to fill. It wouldn't be hard for the Texan to play the bad cop. At Motorola, his nickname was "Silent Thunder."

Rumbling in a deep southern drawl, Conlee made it clear to the room of engineers that RIM's new product sheriff wasn't happy. He'd been hired by Lazaridis to keep RIM's products on schedule, and the company was late. RIM was gearing up to ship a big order to a British carrier, BT Cellnet, for a new

BlackBerry model, called 5820, adding voice-calling to the device's signature e-mail service for the first time. The code name for the new phone was Project Tachyon. Like many confidential RIM projects the name came from the world of subatomic particles: tachyon is the hypothetical particle scientists believe can travel faster than the speed of light. RIM's Tachyon was not breaking any speed records, unfortunately. The already-delayed June shipping deadline had recently been pushed out to August. RIM couldn't risk further delays, Conlee warned. The dot-com bubble had imploded, sales were down, and new players were entering the mobile data device business. "If we don't deliver on time, there is no need to deliver," he told the room. Conlee's oft-repeated mantra was "Today's peacock is tomorrow's feather duster."

The son of a sweet potato farmer from Clyde, Texas, Conlee quickly grasped that success at Motorola involved hard work and a relentless attention to designing, making, and marketing products. Product management was an iron discipline at the Chicago company. Accountability was an absolute priority. Managers and engineers signed their names to product books listing delivery schedules and budgets and faced tough questions if they didn't meet projections. Nor were product demonstrations for the fainthearted. Conlee once watched a senior Motorola executive impale a Phillips screwdriver into a walkie-talkie prototype after a manager bragged that it was indestructible. "It's not that perfect," the executive said as the device exploded across the table.

"That's what I grew up with," said Conlee. "I did not expect any less of myself."

Overambitious expansion had eroded Motorola's once formidable culture of discipline and accountability by the time Conlee resigned after twenty-eight years with the company. Product failures and division rivalries opened such deep rifts within Motorola that employees called it a "loose confederation of warring tribes."[1] He was determined to prevent the same fate at RIM. When he arrived in Waterloo, Conlee found a technically advanced company made vulnerable by poor discipline and coordination. Despite BlackBerry's success, RIM was managed like a small start-up, with one executive hub coordinating an expanding circle of spokes. By 2001, the company was adding so many spokes, doubling staff annually, while management remained unchanged. Lazaridis and Balsillie drove most decisions, which is why both agreed to select their own chief operating officers. "They could not take care of everybody," says Conlee.

Conlee and Morrison were astonished to find a company devoid of the practices that shaped modern corporate life. Forget about a five-year plan. The company with $221 million of revenues in its 2001 fiscal year didn't even have a one-year goal. When Conlee requested a report on the company's strategic objectives, all he got was a forecast of the next quarter's sales and expenses. He was told there were no profit-and-loss projections for the next year, no budgets for the company's divisions. Lazaridis or Balsillie signed off on spending. When Conlee asked for a manufacturing cost breakdown, he got a blank stare. When he asked engineers to estimate delivery times for Project Tachyon phones, the answers ranged from six months to two years. In fact, RIM did have a corporate strategy, but as the new senior executives discovered, it was a loose collection of short-term plans discussed privately between Balsillie and Lazaridis. "There were things that Mike and Jim got involved with that they didn't share," says Morrison. "It took me eighteen months to get RIM."

One thing Morrison didn't get was Balsillie's objections to talking about the company's stock price, a ritual in most executive suites. Anyone caught talking about RIM's share value was penalized. Balsillie didn't want staff becoming complacent or distracted about company or personal fortunes. When Morrison sent Balsillie a congratulatory e-mail about RIM's soaring stock price, he had to buy hundreds of donuts for RIM employees. Stock prices and quarterly results were precisely what Conlee believed needed more attention. He'd been hired to expand RIM "from millions to billions." The company wasn't going to get there unless it paid more respect to commercial details. That, the Texan knew, called for "a different culture." Conlee invited RIM's engineers to the Waterloo Inn to explain new marching orders. He introduced a detailed schedule of product milestones for Project Tachyon's 5820 Black-Berrys, goals that would be enforced by a new product management office. Going forward, deadlines would be short and inflexible. All software features on the 5820 had to be completed within two weeks; for hardware design and beta-testing, the deadline was six weeks.

RIM's engineers listened to Conlee in shocked silence. Software and hardware teams were working flat out to solve reliability issues with the 5820, struggling to adapt BlackBerry's first voice-and-e-mail device to BT Cellnet's more powerful cellular network. The smartphone was far from ready. Conlee's deadlines were unrealistic, radio software designer Matthias Wandel would later vent in a private journal entry about the meeting: "The whole idea was probably to change RIM's culture to be something more along the line of something stable, like Motorola, instead of the wild and unstable entrepreneurial company. This could alienate the people that helped create the company. . . . RIM could no longer rely on star performers. Instead, the company would rely on procedures and policies to get things done." Many engineers, Wandel wrote, were asking the same question: *How could Mike let him do this?*

/ / /

RIM had arrived at the bridge every high-tech start-up must cross in the pursuit of long-term success. It's the point at which a product triumph forces a fledgling company to shift from unfettered free-form innovation to the steely commercial discipline required to foster sustainable growth. In Silicon Valley, founders often fall by the wayside after innovations take off. Creative entrepreneurs are often poorly suited to managing business success. Venture capitalists have the upper hand because they typically demand major or controlling stakes when betting on risky start-ups. This wasn't the case in Waterloo. Balsillie had rebuffed venture capitalists, carefully raising cash through public stock offerings that did not overly dilute its founders' clout. Lazaridis was the company's largest shareholder, with an 11.2 percent holding in 2001, followed by Balsillie, with 9.3 percent, and Lazaridis's childhood friend Doug Fregin, with 3.5 percent. Combined, their stakes would make hostile advances difficult.

RIM had another advantage: unlike many competitors in the high-risk technology sector, Balsillie and Lazaridis had forged a highly functioning partnership between an audacious and outgoing businessman and a trailblazing engineer. The unlikely duo had balanced the competing motives of profit and invention for a decade. At first they were braided together by a desire to keep RIM alive in the face of assaults. By 2001, their shared ambition was to grab a large piece of the competitive global market. The partnership was founded on the understanding the company would make no major decision unless both agreed. They also committed to present a united face to staff and customers. "We didn't contradict each other in front of anybody. It was pretty much the understanding we had. We could close the door and talk, but we made sure we were a unified force in the organization," says Lazaridis.

The two CEOs were so aligned that they often sketched out each other's roles before meetings. They had secret signals, including an under-the-table nudge when a private chat was needed and crinkling of paper to indicate it was time to stop talking. Nudges were seldom necessary, however, because each anticipated where the other was headed. "They were in such amazing synch," says Patrick Spence, RIM's U.S. salesman. "It was absolutely incredible to watch them work in that kind of an environment, sitting right beside each other, where you think they're almost connected in their brains."

Paradoxically, the two had little in common other than RIM and the fact that they both drove black Eagle Vision sedans. Lazaridis was the chief innovator who drove software and hardware advances; Balsillie was the in-house financier who wielded products like hammers to pound more favorable terms from powerful carrier clients. Lazaridis found financial and corporate confrontations so stressful he often left the room when Balsillie was in full Sun Tzu mode. Balsillie, meanwhile, never set foot in RIM's product labs and deferred entirely to his partner on technology decisions.

Outside business, their differences were profound. When Lazaridis left the office late at night, he headed home to Ophelia and their son and daughter, with armloads of patent filings, product manuals, and textbooks. His hobbies included music, movies, and collecting vintage editions of *Scientific American*. One of his favorite pastimes was driving to Cape Canaveral with his childhood friend Doug Fregin to watch spaceship launches. Another was religious study. He frequently hosted groups to discuss the Bible and other spiritual readings.

Lazaridis was an admirer of the writings of Emmet Fox, the popular Depression-era New York minister who drew thousands to his church with sermons about the mystic powers people possess to transform lives of misery and despair. His book *Sermon on the Mount* was a staple for Alcoholics Anonymous members. Lazaridis was also a follower of the religious writings of Mary Baker Eddy, the flinty American journalist who founded the Christian Science movement in the late 1800s. "He has a deep spirituality and deep belief in the eternity of the spirit. . . . There is a constancy of his belief, he generally marvels at the wonders of the planet," says his friend and former Rogers executive David Neale.

When Balsillie left the office, it was often to get on an airplane with an entourage of RIM staffers and suppliers to meet clients. Some of Balsillie's fellow travelers, like their boss, carried pocket-sized copies of Sun Tzu's *The Art of War*. When not working, Balsillie chased victories on golf courses, hockey arenas, basketball courts, and cycling trips. During the 2002 Olympics, he bought tickets for a large crew that included veteran Canadian hockey players from the 1950s to watch Canada's hockey team seize the gold medal in

Salt Lake City. When Canada's captain Mario Lemieux skated triumphantly around the arena after the game, he waved a Canadian flag tossed over the glass by Balsillie. "What Jim is trying to do is squeeze as much electricity from every living moment that he possibly can," said Morrison, who joined the Olympic pilgrimage.

Off the corporate battleground Balsillie seemed incapable of relaxing, even for a leisurely game of basketball. "He was the most competitive person on the court, bar none," says Patrick Spence of their weekly pickup basketball games. When others goofed around, Balsillie called time-out to plot winning moves. "Jim has one gear, which is the full on gear of 'We're going to win this,'" Spence says.

Balsillie also sought the company of business legends who bucked the system. One close friend was George Soros, the New York speculator who made a fortune betting against the British currency in the 1990s. Another role model companion was the Quebec billionaire Paul Desmarais, the scrappy founder of the global financial conglomerate Power Corporation of Canada, a man who overcame humble beginnings in the small Ontario city of Sudbury.[2] As the demands of managing RIM's growth intensified, Balsillie spent more time away from the modest suburban Waterloo home he shared with his wife Heidi and their son and daughter.

Morrison, a fan of workplace socializing, sought to pull RIM's diverse senior executives closer with outside activities. Before RIM, he was one of many AT&T executives who resided in Basking Ridge, a leafy New Jersey suburb. There, coworkers belonged to the same clubs and churches. Morrison wanted to duplicate the experience in Waterloo. Several days after he made overtures to socialize with the families of other RIM executives, Balsillie appeared in his office. He was agitated.

"Cut it out," Balsillie warned.

"What do you mean?"

"We don't do that here. We don't hang out together."

Morrison was shocked by his boss's abrupt warning. As a newcomer, he assumed Balsillie and Lazaridis were inseparable. The two CEOs were in constant touch, e-mailing and meeting constantly to feed each other product, market, and sales news. There were no harsh words, only mutual enthusiasm for RIM's successes. Eventually, Morrison realized that work was the only language the two men shared. When he wasn't talking about RIM, Lazaridis was rhapsodic about technology breakthroughs and quantum physics. Balsillie's enthusiasms were sports, traveling, and business celebrities who were starting to pay attention to BlackBerry's founders. They were a poor match for any social outing.

/ / /

BlackBerry's success was a validation of Lazaridis's counterintuitive bet that professionals wanted less, not more, from a mobile communicator. His high school teacher John Micsinszki was proved right: the proper combination of computing and radio would be transformational. Like many innovators experiencing belated success, Lazaridis was enchanted with his creation. He carried a bag of BlackBerrys with him on trips to show off the latest models. On an office desk cluttered with family photos and his high school oscilloscope, he made room for a few BlackBerry models encased in Lucite. The device was his baby and he rigorously opposed the addition of emerging smartphone features such as color screens, Web browsers, and video. These enhancements drained batteries and clogged networks, he explained to staffers who suggested the additions. Part of his reluctance reflected his belief that engineers built useful things, not toys. RIM's clients also informed his views. Conservative carriers worried incessantly about heavy data loads and network crashes, while large clients didn't want to risk exposing secrets by allowing cameras in the workplace. "The carriers were absolutely terrified of a bandwidth-hogging application. So they didn't like browsers; they didn't like streaming video," Lazaridis says.

In the summer of 2000, RIM's director of product management, Steve Eros, urged Lazaridis to add a universal serial bus connection to BlackBerry. USB cables, which connect mobile devices to computers, were gaining popularity as a convenient way to charge mobile devices while simultaneously synching data. Lazaridis was against the idea. It cost too much time and money to replace the existing connection technology. Days later, Lazaridis called an urgent meeting to chide engineers for failing to anticipate the need for a BlackBerry USB. Lazaridis rarely acknowledged his change of heart, but such shifts became a familiar pattern. His first response to proposed BlackBerry enhancements was typically negative. After days, sometimes weeks of research, he would often embrace the new idea, forcing difficult deadlines on engineers.

"He wouldn't adopt new technologies when they came out. He would adopt them when they made sense . . . when it made his devices better," says Eros.

Lazaridis would add to the confusion by visiting engineering teams with shopping lists of ideas. He became so enthusiastic about some design concepts that when he intoned, "This is important," his engineers often mistook his passion for marching orders. When Lazaridis's chief lieutenant, Larry Conlee, noticed engineers working on unauthorized parts or software, he quickly realized his boss had paid a visit. Mindful of pressing delivery dates, he asked Lazaridis to choose his words more carefully. Don't use the word "important," he warned, because there were too many people "saluting and clicking their heels." RIM's engineers learned to be more cautious about embracing Lazaridis's ideas. It soon became accepted wisdom that no one was to follow Lazaridis's orders unless he issued the command three separate times.

The shifts marked what some engineers believed were discouraging changes in RIM's collegial culture. The company that inspired staff to experiment and think outside industry conventions was taking fewer chances with its products. More troubling, its chief innovator, Lazaridis, was harder to read and less accessible after Conlee's arrival. "We started acting like a big company," says Perry Jarmuszewski, a RIM radio designer. "It felt like we had lost some of the innovative team feeling where everyone worked together to solve problems."

Change was also evident in Balsillie's domain: sales and marketing. Success was not a relief to the ambitious executive; rather it was a new stress point. Like a seasoned general who had just won an important skirmish, Balsillie worried about the next battles. "You can't imagine how much personal pressure I felt," he remembers. "That personal pressure increased each time RIM doubled in size, so that pressure didn't really allow me to sit back and think 'We made it.'" Inevitably, there were explosive, General Patton–like outbursts with RIM's expanding sales troops. He could be particularly testy with fresh recruits. It fell to Rick Costanzo, hired as a sales manager in 1999, to coach incoming employees on how to survive their first meeting with Balsillie.

"Be brief and don't look him directly in the eyes," Costanzo warned hires. "You don't know if he's going to hug you or . . . maul you. So lie down on the ground in the fetal position and let him do whatever the hell he's going to do." Costanzo made light of his boss's temper but hoped newcomers paid attention. They had to watch their step. If Balsillie began rubbing his forehead, Costanzo advised, it was a bad sign. If he asked a question requiring a yes or no answer, the answer had to be one or the other. If recruits gave rambling or confusing replies, Balsillie cut them off. "Just stop. You've forgotten the question I asked you, haven't you? Because you're *not* listening to me," Balsillie would seethe as his face grew red with rage in a typical interaction. "Why you're not prepared coming into this meeting is beyond me. I need to be working on other things." It's a message few needed to hear twice. Sometimes, his fury was calculated. If Balsillie grew angry in a meeting, he checked after with managers to see how staff responded. "I wanted to keep the organization on its toes," he says. "I think having a level of nervousness, installing an oh-my-god-ness in the organization, is not a bad idea. I'm not perfect. Sometimes you go too far."

/ / /

Mobitex, the rickety Swedish radio highway that carried BlackBerry into the world, was near the end of the road. Its rudimentary technology wasn't up to the task of managing increasing data traffic. Lazaridis and Balsillie could see that if they wanted to continue developing the company, they would need a new network home for their wireless e-mail service.

RIM wasn't the only communications company in need of a new wireless network. Second-generation, or 2G, wireless networks launched in the 1990s only had limited capacity for mobile data. Carriers were under pressure to invest in new systems and technology to a newer, faster generation of networks, called 3G, to satisfy a widely expected boom in wireless data traffic. They spent tens of billions of dollars to acquire 3G licenses from their governments. Building the networks would cost billions more.

Across the industry, many believed the era of 3G was just around the corner. But Lazaridis was convinced the expensive 3G revolution would arrive later rather than sooner and set his sights on what many industry experts dismissed as a pale alternative. For a fraction of the cost of implementing 3G, carriers could make minor upgrades to their existing 2G networks, adding speed and bandwidth. The fix wouldn't deliver the full benefits of 3G, but it would provide enough capacity to handle a rising tide of data. Network suppliers called this semi-upgrade 2.5G.

Many device makers and carriers dismissed 2.5G: why waste money on a temporary measure when a more powerful third generation was imminent? For RIM's thrifty bosses, however, 2.5G was the perfect choice. It provided all the bandwidth they needed for BlackBerry to thrive and expand. European carriers were the first to invest in 2.5G in 2000, which is why BlackBerry sold its first voice and data phone, the 5820, to Britain's BT Cellnet.

RIM wouldn't succeed with 2.5G cellular, however, unless it won the blessing of its key CIO customers. In late 2000, Balsillie took RIM's case to a fraternity of chief information officers from the world's largest corporations. This elite group, known as the Research Board, was preparing a report on the future of wireless. The report's author, Jim Roche, was convinced, like others, that the future of wireless was all about 3G. But when Balsillie met Roche and later a gathering of Research Board members, the RIM chief convinced them that 3G was far enough away that companies should instead opt for devices that consumed less bandwidth on more limited 2.5G networks that were being deployed. "Jim's view was spot-on—you have to respect scarcity," says Roche, whose report to Research Board members in February 2001 largely articulated the RIM party line. Corporate support for 2.5G handsets cleared the way for RIM to join the smartphone race, and opened the door for the likes of Johnson & Johnson and Caterpillar to order thousands of BlackBerrys instead of hundreds.

Building a product for 2.5G was a bigger challenge: RIM would need a new battery, a new radio, and a new operating system, essentially replacing the guts of its BlackBerry 957 to produce the similar-looking 5820. It also needed a new chipmaker, Britain's ARM, after Intel showed no interest in doing a mobile version of its Pentium chip for RIM, ending what had been a successful relationship. The big difference with the 2.5G device was voice: products that ran on cellular networks had to be able to handle voice calls. Cellphone makers Nokia, Ericsson, and Motorola had been moving into RIM's backyard for years by adding text and e-mail message applications to mobile phones. Balsillie and Lazaridis mocked their efforts. Mobile phones were getting smaller and more stylish, while utilitarian data devices needed big screens and keyboards. Balsillie figured jamming a phone into a Black-Berry would be as ungainly as Chevrolet's 1959 El Camino, the boat-sized vehicle with the front of a sporty coupe and the rear end of a pickup truck. The first El Camino was parked after two years of anemic sales. Any time someone pushed for a BlackBerry phone, Balsillie waved them off with two words: "El Camino."

RIM's bosses did a U-turn with the 5820, or Project Tachyon, or, if Balsillie and Lazaridis would admit it, their own El Camino. Conlees's tight deadlines and the office of product management did succeed in getting the hybrid phone and e-mail device out the door in August 2001 to its British customer BT Cellnet. The final product, however, was as awkward as the mutant Chevy. In the rush to deliver, RIM's engineers had no time to fully integrate phone hardware. Instead, the 5820 came with a headset that had to be plugged into the device in order for users to make calls. The phone had another bug: it froze so frequently early on that RIM's British staff and BT Cellnet salespeople had to keep paper clips handy to insert into the device's small reset hole when needed.

/   /   /

Looking out the window from his Jersey City office, Louis Gutilla rattled off an e-mail on his BlackBerry at 8:58 a.m. to friends under the subject line "Holy Shit":

"A plane just crashed into the World Trade Center. The building is on fire, I'm staring right at it. I pray to God no one is hurt, but it appears as if the top floors are all on fire."[3]

An office worker, identified as Craig, worked his BlackBerry minutes after emerging from the PATH station in lower Manhattan. At 9:13 a.m. he sent a frantic message to his wife:

"It was a huge [Boeing] that crashed right into the wtc, then a second explosion caused something to hit the second tower and its now on fire too!! E-mail is my only form of contact."[4]

Bill Kelley, a Bloomberg employee, waited minutes before replying on his BlackBerry to a relative asking: "Bill, are you OK?" At 9:23 a.m. Kelley sent the last message of his life from the Windows on the World restaurant on top of the World Trade Center.

"So far . . . we're trapped on the 106th floor, but apparently [the] fire department is almost here."[5]

These messages are a sample of a vast collection of e-mails sent on September 11, 2001, and later shared with news media or stored in a 9/11 digital archive owned by the Library of Congress. Many of the e-mails were dispatched by BlackBerrys. For trapped or fleeing workers, BlackBerrys were the only reliable communication link in lower Manhattan. After the first plane knocked out cell towers on top of the World Trade Center, cell and landline circuits were overwhelmed. Paging companies lost many of their frequencies, and phone lines went dead for hundreds of thousands of Verizon customers[6] when a call-switching center, several cell towers, and fiber-optic links were smashed by debris from a collapsed building.[7]

Mobile e-mails got through because data messages required significantly less bandwidth and BlackBerry had largely fixed its network problems of the previous year. In addition, the Mobitex network had several base stations— radio towers with transceivers for relaying data—throughout Manhattan and nearby New Jersey. Unable to call home, Wall Street workers hammered out messages on BlackBerrys, sending reassuring e-mails to worried family and friends under such subject lines as "I'm alive," or "I'm okay." Others used the devices to share information about missing colleagues, arrange meetings in safer locations, or negotiate transportation and lodgings in a paralyzed city. "I had my cellphone in one hand, and it was useless, and my BlackBerry in the other and it was my lifeline that day," Lynne Federman, a lawyer working three blocks from Ground Zero told the *New York Times*.[8]

While BlackBerrys kept Wall Street online during 9/11, in the U.S. capital it was a different story. RIM had been knocking on Washington's door for years with little to show for its efforts. The company made headway in 2000 after hiring Anthony LeBlanc, a specialist in government sales hired from the Ottawa-based software company Corel. His big break came in mid-2000 when he targeted Al Gore during his presidential race against George W. Bush. Gore's staff rebuffed LeBlanc, explaining the candidate was a Palm Pilot user. When LeBlanc proposed a free trial, a staffer returned with terms: Gore would only accept a BlackBerry if RIM made the same offer to Bush. It was no obstacle. Bush's staff explained he wasn't big on technology, declining the offer. Two days after dropping the device off at Gore's New York campaign office, LeBlanc received a call from a campaign staffer: Gore wouldn't put his Black-Berry down. By the spring of 2001 LeBlanc had made enough headway elsewhere in Washington to start BlackBerry trials at high-profile government departments such as the U.S. Air Force and National Institutes of Health.

Despite the inroads, Washington was in disarray after the World Trade Center attacks. President George Bush, visiting schoolchildren in Florida, and Vice President Dick Cheney, in the White House, were both whisked away to secret locations. Neither man had BlackBerrys. When a third plane attacked the Pentagon, knocking out most cellular and landline phones, communications down the chain of command went dead. Senators and congressional representatives were evacuated with no marching orders. A few talked their way back into their offices; others drove home or visited nearby friends to watch televised news. "[We were] without direction, without purpose," Democratic senator Jay Rockefeller told the Capital Hill newspaper *Roll Call* two days after the attack.[9]

In a town where information is power, some of the most potent players that day were the few politicians who owned BlackBerrys. After Democratic congressman Rob Andrews was barred from his office, he set up shop on a park bench, communicating on his BlackBerry throughout the morning.[10] Republican congressman Dick Armey retreated to his car to fire off BlackBerry e-mails.[11] When he learned House Speaker Dennis Hastert was headed to Andrews Air Force Base, Armey joined him in time to be helicoptered to a Virginia mountain bunker, well ahead of House and Senate leaders. The isolated leaders arranged conference calls with far-flung party members, but many were shut out by inaccurate calling codes. It would be more than ten hours after the first terrorist attack before federal politicians were able to fully communicate. This time they did it the old-fashioned way: in person. At 7:30 p.m. hundreds of senators and congressmen gathered in front of the Capitol building for a televised message to a devastated nation. "We stand together," Hastert told the television audience. Shoulder to shoulder, Democrats and GOP approved in the following days a number of initiatives. One was a plan for a modernized communications system. One of the first upgrades came weeks later when the House issued BlackBerrys to all 435 representatives.

Another enhancement took place behind closed doors. The National Security Agency dispatched a team to work with RIM on a device that became known as "CryptoBerry." RIM and government officials have said little about the CryptoBerry. Balsillie lifted the veil slightly during a December 2003 quarterly conference call with investors and financial analysts. RIM had worked "intimately" with the United States, Canada, and other countries to design special encryption codes for CryptoBerrys, he said. The system was so bulletproof that even IT managers couldn't decipher e-mails traveling through government networks. Government demand "popped" for the devices in 2003, Balsillie says. That same year the United States launched Operation Iraqi Freedom to topple Saddam Hussein's regime. A Department of Defense manager let it slip in an interview with the trade publication *Government Computer News* that NSA personnel were armed with CryptoBerrys during the invasion.[12] BlackBerry was no longer an outsider in the Beltway. It was an official pipeline of Washington's most closely guarded secrets.

8 / / / GAME OF PHONES

Balsillie hurried past the elegant boutiques, chic apartments, and palm trees lining Cannes's famed Boulevard de la Croisette. It was a cold, wet, and windy evening in February 2003, little better than winter-bound Waterloo but typical of the reception Balsillie was getting on the French Riviera. Balsillie hoped that was about to change as he ducked into the white art deco splendor of Cannes's flagship Hôtel Martinez.

The RIM chief was in town to steal a few minutes with some of Europe's most powerful wireless carrier CEOs at the global industry's annual conference. His goal was to convince them to offer BlackBerry smartphones to their customers. So far, he'd had little luck.

Securing face time was a hopeless endeavor at the cavernous Palais des Festivals et des Congrès, where more than twenty thousand people from 150 countries hobnobbed. Balsillie came across as a pushy promoter, pestering conference organizers to add more panel discussions on wireless data and begging his contact at Lehman Brothers, Greg Feller, to introduce him around the investment bank's cocktail reception. "He never missed a trick" to promote RIM, Feller says. "He didn't want to go into the room and be a nobody. Jim had a unique story and he was going to be pretty loud about it."

Balsillie's name tag may as well have read Mr. Nobody as he entered the Martinez. He'd come to crash a gala for the industry who's who, but Balsillie navigated hopelessly around the cocktail reception unable to break through crowds of hangers-on flanking the CEOs he badly wanted to meet.

Balsillie was getting desperate. How would he get their attention? He left the reception to clear his head. Nearby, he saw the grand ballroom where dinner would be served. He decided to check it out.

The room was empty save for waiters in white jackets and black ties making final preparations. Balsillie wandered by a table at the front of the room and read the place cards. René Obermann, a top executive of Deutsche Telekom, Boris Nemsic, CEO of central European carrier A1 Telekom, Gilles Pélisson of France's Bouygues Télécom—they were all seated at the table, all of the people he wanted to meet.

Balsillie had an idea. He approached the nearest waiter. "*Monsieur*, there's supposed to be another setting here," he said, pointing to the table. The waiter returned moments later with a chair and setting, gingerly moving the other dishes and cutlery around to accommodate one more person. Balsillie thanked him as though channeling the full authority of the conference organizers.

Balsillie pulled a business card from his pocket and folded it in two. He studied the calligraphy on the other place cards and did what he thought was a passable forgery of his own name on his improvised place card. Voilà! He admired his work for a moment: his card was smaller than the others and the ink was blue, not black. But it didn't look that bad. *Not bad at all*, he thought.

He placed it on the new setting. Then he rearranged the other cards at the table. He placed TurkCell CEO Muzaffer Akpinar to his right and Nemsic to his left. The two he really wanted to talk to were Obermann and Pélisson, but he placed them one over on each side. He didn't want to be too obvious.

Balsillie returned to the reception and waited until all guests had taken their seats. He walked into the ballroom, pretending to look hither and yonder for his seat. *Wherever could it be? Ah, there it is!* "I guess this is my seat," he said as he approached the table, mustering an expression of nonchalance mixed with a sense of good fortune.

As the banter turned to shoptalk, Balsillie pitched his tablemates. Black-Berry was no longer just an e-mail device; it was a full smartphone with an integrated speaker and microphone. The big American networks—including Verizon, AT&T, and T-Mobile—had all signed on in the past eighteen months, he explained. Their big multinational clients, including Johnson & Johnson, Goldman Sachs, and GE—loved the product so much they wanted to roll it out by the thousands to their employees in Europe. "They just want to know who to call," Balsillie said.

By the end of the meal Balsillie had pocketed business cards from all the senior executives at his table and the names of their lieutenants he should contact next. Within months, talks were under way with all of the carriers. Balsillie had finagled the European entrée he badly coveted.

/ / /

RIM's close relationship with major U.S. customers gave it a powerful lever with European carriers who were indifferent to BlackBerry's North American success. Overseas carriers generated the bulk of their revenues from cellular voice calls and simple text messages. They purchased most of their phones primarily from the "MENS Club," the world's biggest cellphone makers Motorola, Ericsson, Nokia, and Siemens. Their limited e-mail services paled against BlackBerry offerings, and the promise of wireless e-mail traffic was not something European carriers embraced as eagerly as their North American counterparts.

Unable to break through fortress Europe, Balsillie and his sales team looked for a smaller player that had more to gain by expanding traffic with BlackBerrys. That led them to Britain's BT Cellnet, a more adventurous carrier that was among the first to upgrade its network to increase data capacity. RIM's contract with BT Cellnet opened the door for U.S. multinationals to deploy BlackBerrys to Europe. When RIM and BT Cellnet sales teams began pitching BlackBerrys to Britain's leading businesses, large European carriers paid closer attention to the Waterloo upstart. One of the first to notice was Ivan Donn, director of mobile applications for Vodafone, Britain's dominant carrier. When Donn talked to business clients about the Canadian device, the message was clear: "There were three reasons they liked it: It. Fucking. Works," says Donn. Wireless data was becoming a lucrative business and Vodafone, its very name a contraction of the words voice, data, and phone, risked losing market share if it focused too narrowly on cellphone voice services.

Expanding data traffic made sense to Donn's colleagues at Vodafone. What didn't were RIM's expensive service fees. The monthly $10 service access fee that RIM charged carriers for each BlackBerry customer was as unpopular in Europe as it was in the United States. "It was alien and counterintuitive to a mobile operator," says Donn. "A lot of people thought it was unacceptable." When Donn took a closer look at the fee math, he saw an opportunity.

Multinational corporate customers were willing to pay about thirty times more for BlackBerry e-mail service than Vodafone was charging at the time for equivalent data usage. RIM's service access fees would be a small price to pay for a potentially substantial increase in revenues.

Vodafone held its nose, swallowed RIM's service access fees, and placed orders for BlackBerrys. At first, however, the devices idled in warehouses. Vodafone's salespeople were trained to sell voice phones, not data. Sales teams were so handicapped that when they called on customers they were unable to offer a basic BlackBerry demonstration because Vodafone had not installed BlackBerry servers in its own systems. Without a server connection, the demo phones were little more than paperweights. Frustrated with Vodafone's slow progress, RIM sales crews leaned on the British carrier to purchase more BlackBerrys. If relations between RIM and Vodafone didn't improve, the smartphone maker's European charge would falter.

The fraying relationship between the carrier and the device maker began to shift when RIM hired British sales veteran Mary Grundy to manage the Vodafone account. At first Grundy couldn't get past the front door. Her initial meeting with the head of Vodafone UK's enterprise business, Kyle Whitehill, took place in the carrier's lobby. Whitehill gave her an earful: unless Grundy could help Vodafone expand phone sales, the relationship wasn't going anywhere, he said. Grundy's strategy was to win Vodafone over by embedding herself in the British carrier. She was given a desk at Vodafone, created BlackBerry training manuals, accompanied the carrier's sales staff on customer calls, and secured RIM's backing for special phone discounts and promotions. Inventory started moving after she convinced Vodafone to launch a two-for-one BlackBerry sales campaign called "Juice It Up." Within a year, Vodafone was squeezing fresh profits with BlackBerry sales exceeding thirty thousand devices a month.

RIM's enterprising sales rep grew so close to Vodafone's sales team that Grundy once appeared in a skit at a Vodafone sales conference. A Vodafone executive wearing a bowler hat portrayed RIM in the pantomime, but it was Grundy who stole the show when she appeared onstage disguised as a wolf to mimic the carrier's competitor BT Cellnet devouring customers. When the Waterloo company moved to the next sales stage, RIM would be wearing the wolf mask.

/ / /

BlackBerry pushed so far ahead of other smartphone makers with its e-mail and voice services that corporate clients and carriers began worrying RIM was effectively becoming a monopoly. They didn't want to see it turn into the next Microsoft or Nokia, dominant industry players that threw their weight around with customers. One of the earliest answers to these complaints was Good Technology, a California start-up selling e-mail software that could be loaded onto any mobile device. Quietly backed by a few U.S. carriers, Good Technology signed hundreds of U.S. business clients. The new competitor didn't come close to matching RIM's full-service offerings, but Balsillie saw long-term dangers. By creating agnostic software for any mobile device, the California rival was giving businesses and carriers more choice. They could now pick from a variety of devices, some cheaper than BlackBerrys, which were not taxed with RIM's expensive service access fees.

RIM capitulated to pressure for more choice by opening its e-mail system to other handset makers. They would design keyboard phones, and RIM would supply software and links to connect the phones to its data network. In exchange RIM charged licensing fees. RIM called this new program Black-Berry Connect. Many employees couldn't understand why RIM was rushing to aid competitors. It wasn't. Like some Balsillie strategies, appearances were deceiving.

Balsillie and a small team of executives had other ambitions for Connect. This was more than a licensing program; it was a Trojan horse. RIM's long-term game was to buy time. Competitors who signed up with RIM would be preoccupied making BlackBerry Connect phones rather than creating their own rival e-mail service. RIM gained an inside peek at rivals' long-term development plans and opened the door to new customers. Every enterprise customer signed up under the program represented another stream of service access fees for RIM. It wasn't empowering competitors at all; it was locking in its lead. "Sometimes you have to disguise yourself as another animal in the forest," says Tyler Nelson, a RIM vice president who ran the program.

Lazaridis was initially concerned that Connect would distract RIM's engineers and designers at a time when RIM was racing to keep up with demand and introduce new BlackBerrys. He never worried, however, that corporate customers would abandon RIM for the Connect phones offered by other handset makers. Their Connect phones could not hope to match the security and encryption protections that made BlackBerry such a valuable business communications tool. "We knew ultimately that the enterprise customer . . . was never going to go for it, because it was not a verifiably secure solution," he says. "It was our advantage. It wasn't hidden; it was in plain sight."

Unaware of RIM's hidden agenda, phone makers in Europe and Asia flocked to the program to strengthen their presence in North America with BlackBerry-enabled phones. Samsung was so keen to make a Connect phone that one of its employees idled for weeks at a Waterloo hotel waiting for RIM to grant him a meeting with Balsillie. Finally the visitor appeared at the company's offices in a distraught state. Samsung, he explained, would not let him return home to his family and job in South Korea unless he secured a Connect deal. RIM opened Connect discussions with Samsung, and the manager was free to fly home.

RIM's most dedicated Connect partner was Nokia. The Finnish phone maker had been trying to break into the U.S. wireless business market for years, and Connect looked like an easy shortcut. Nokia's executives did not worry about dancing with a competitor because Balsillie played down RIM's ambitions during initial discussions in 2002. "He emphasized he didn't believe RIM would be able to compete in the hardware business [and] might even give up their hardware business," says Panu Kuusisto, who managed Nokia's Connect agreement with RIM.

Nokia spent two years and millions of dollars on research and development and manufacturing of the BlackBerry Connect phones to fulfill its part of the bargain. RIM, however, seemed less committed. It delayed software deliveries, and when they finally shipped, the programs often lacked the latest BlackBerry features. Nokia grew so infuriated with the slow progress that it summoned Nelson and RIM's chief legal officer, Karima Bawa, to a meeting in 2004 at its Helsinki headquarters. Marko Luhtala, an enterprise sales executive with the Finnish company, stood in front of an oversized map of the world as he complained to the RIM duo about the heavy costs of software delays. Pointing to the map, he fumed: "These dots are ships full of parts heading to our manufacturing facilities. When they arrive I own the inventory on them. You've just cost me because that [software] code isn't in the plant." Luhtala continued to wait. The slow pace was deliberate. "We'd find all sorts of ways to credibly slow down their engineering process for as long as possible," says Nelson. "We told Nokia it was a series of unfortunate delays."

By the summer of 2004, Nokia was in a panic. One week before Nokia was finally about to launch its BlackBerry phone with Spanish carrier Telefónica, Nokia discovered RIM had not negotiated an agreement with the carrier to deploy the product. Without a deal, Telefónica wouldn't let Nokia BlackBerry phones onto its network. Instead the Spanish carrier opted to buy conventional BlackBerrys directly from RIM. Not a single Nokia Connect phone had been activated by September 1, a huge disappointment for a handset maker that planned to sell 150,000 of the phones that year. Kuusito finally understood the Waterloo company's game. "At that point, nearly two years after signing the Connect deal, we really started to think maybe the whole BlackBerry Connect program was a plot and Nokia was being abused by RIM," he says. "We were so ignorant that they must have been just laughing at us," he says.

Nokia would not start developing in-house e-mail programs for its smartphones for at least another year. In 2006, Kuusisto bumped into Nelson at an industry conference. Nelson, who no longer worked at RIM, confirmed Kuusisto's suspicions about RIM's ulterior motives. "I was glad he confessed what was going on," says Kuusisto, who saw his career at Nokia stall after the fiasco. Nelson apologized for the rough play. "I did feel bad about the impact on him. I knew it would have cost him a great deal of career harm," he says. Other BlackBerry Connect partners did not fare much better. About forty different Connect phones were designed and none sold well.

For its part, RIM accomplished what it wanted from Connect. It distracted big competitors at a time when they might have bypassed BlackBerry. It also validated Lazaridis's prediction that the Connect phones could not come close to matching BlackBerry security and reliability. Balsillie makes no apologies for a strategy he agrees "was a complete, pure bum steer." It was the kind of "stealth tactic, pure *Art of War*," he says that RIM needed to protect its core business. His tactics, he says, were no different than the cold-blooded maneuvers of Silicon Valley giants. "Show me how else you build a $20 billion company."

/ / /

Employees at RIM's Waterloo offices had stopped working to watch an American Thanksgiving television tradition. It was November 24, 2003, and one of the world's most influential consumers was about to reveal her shopping picks for the Christmas season. Oprah Winfrey's staff had worked her audience into a frenzy in her Chicago studio. There was hooting, bouncing, and, on some faces, tears. Every guest would walk away with gifts that the queen of daytime television was about to unveil during her annual *Oprah's Favorite Things* special. Winfrey's annual endorsements carried so much weight that stores often emptied of products she trumpeted.

"I've done your holiday shopping for you," Winfrey announced as she walked into the boisterous studio. The audience grew so excited when she arrived that Winfrey had a crowd control problem. "Okay. Okay. Okay. Let me get your attention. Okay. Everybody, everybody, let's just all breathe together. Take a deep breath."

Finally the moment arrived that RIM's executives had been alerted about days earlier: "My new favorite thing . . . oh, I love this so much," Winfrey said. "I cannot live without this. It's with me everywhere I go. It's called a Black-Berry. It's literally changed my life." Back in Waterloo, the cheers were almost as exuberant as those in Chicago. "There was a lot of cheering, smiles, and excitement," says sales vice president Patrick Spence. "It was awesome," he says, the "flashpoint" at which RIM branched from corporate and government customers to the broader consumer market.

RIM had been eyeing the lucrative consumer market ever since it launched BlackBerry in 1999. At first, the small company was overwhelmed with corporate demand for the device. When it had more time and resources to focus on small businesses and consumers in the early 2000s, it faced another obstacle. BlackBerry e-mails operated on Windows and Lotus programs, expensive software that few individuals or small businesses used. Most consumers used free Web-based e-mail services such as Hotmail and AOL Mail. RIM did not have the same capacity to replicate these e-mail services on BlackBerrys as it did with Windows and Lotus programs. It solved the problem in 2002 by acquiring TeamOn.com. The Seattle-based start-up had developed software RIM needed to allow phone users to fully access a variety of Web-based e-mail, calendar, and contacts accounts.

The BlackBerry Quark model that Winfrey applauded on her show was the first BlackBerry to carry TeamOn.com software. The handset was also more stylish than the boxy, no-nonsense BlackBerrys so popular with business professionals. Sharp corners on previous devices gave way to curves, new colors replaced the solemn black case, and the device came with a color screen. Thanks to improvements in the technology, the Quark performed twice as fast and had twice the memory of previous BlackBerrys. An improved production process meant it was also faster and cheaper to make than its predecessors.

But while the new-generation BlackBerrys had full voice capabilities, few customers were using them for phone calls, and carriers stuck the devices at the back of their stores with other data products. There was a simple reason: people were embarrassed to use BlackBerrys as phones. "The form factor was weird," says Jason Griffin, RIM's chief product designer. "It was a calculator, a piece of toast. You'd hear these comments in our research. People didn't feel comfortable drawing attention to themselves holding up a device that was so wide. But they loved the BlackBerry. There was a huge difference between holding it in front of you and typing and holding it to your head."

Internally, a debate had raged for a couple of years: was the BlackBerry a phone or not? The customer insights prompted "a mental shift" inside RIM, says Griffin. Of course it was a phone. Now it had to look more like one to gain acceptance from customers, says Dave Castell, who was now in charge of RIM's fledgling retail business.

Once again, Griffin realized he'd have to strip keys from the BlackBerry so it could fit its new form and function. Griffin dusted off a concept he had tinkered with years earlier: squeezing two letters onto a single key and cutting the keyboard's size in half. To make the design work, RIM developed a "predictive" software program that could guess which of the two letters on any key a user intended to type. The idea initially met with resistance internally, Griffin says, but the program worked surprisingly well. More importantly, Lazaridis embraced it. "It would have died if Mike hadn't pushed it through," says Griffin.

The new BlackBerry was called Charm. It was about 20 percent thinner than the Quark and a bit longer. With only five keys across the top and numbers positioned prominently in the middle of the keyboard it still looked like a BlackBerry—but much more like a phone. That convinced carriers to place the new BlackBerry at the front of its stores, next to the Nokias and Motorolas.

With more consumer-friendly BlackBerrys, RIM's sales began to soar. RIM logged its millionth BlackBerry subscriber in February 2004. It hit 2 million nine months later, and 3 million six months after that.

/ / /

RIM's consumer ambitions opened a new line of conflict with carriers. They balked at paying RIM the same $10 monthly service for consumers that it charged business users. RIM struck a compromise by lowering the monthly fee to $8.50 for corporate customers and pushing consumer fees to as low as $5. Another point of friction was RIM's push to add new services for consumer BlackBerrys. Smartphone makers sought deeper ties with retail buyers by adding ring tones, games, Web browsers, and other applications to their phones. Carriers, however, wanted this business to themselves. If they couldn't sell applications within their "walled gardens," carriers worried they would be reduced to mere utilities or "dumb pipes" carrying data and voice traffic.

Nokia learned the hard way just how ferociously carriers could defend their turf. In the late 1990s the Finnish phone maker launched Club Nokia, a Web-based portal that allowed customers to buy and download ring tones. It expanded the club in 2000 by partnering with Amazon.com so Nokia customers could shop online for phones. Nokia's mobile phone president, Matti Alahuhta, predicted Club Nokia was at the forefront of a wireless shift so seismic that by "as early as 2003 the number of mobile devices capable of Internet access will exceed the number of personal computers connected to the Internet."[1] Alahuhta was right about the shift, but it would take years longer and Nokia would not be leading the way. So many carriers balked at allowing Nokia to offer the service on their networks that the phone maker backed off and shuttered Club Nokia. The carriers' iron grip prompted technology columnist Walter Mossberg to liken them to Soviet ministries.[2] They limited choice, stifled consumer services, and stalled mobile commerce.

RIM had an advantage that Nokia and other phone makers lacked: its own data network. BlackBerry messages traveled through RIM's in-house network, which was plugged directly into the carriers. The unique connection gave RIM a back door to sneak in services carriers wouldn't allow. In the mid-2000s RIM began shipping BlackBerrys secretly loaded with sleeper applications. Carriers and customers had no idea the applications existed until RIM sent an alert to BlackBerry users about a software upgrade. Hidden within the digital transmission was a file that unlocked the applications on the device—a Web browser and links to popular instant messaging services. Icons immediately popped onto BlackBerry home screens around the world. By the time carriers realized what was happening, millions of customers were using the Internet and exchanging instant messages on their BlackBerrys.

Initially carriers were furious. Verizon threatened to pull BlackBerry from all retail channels. "I had to speak with probably twenty different carriers about this," says Aaron Brown, then a director of services in RIM's product management group. "But at that point, they realized the truth": carriers were powerless to turn off the browsing or messaging services. Brown reminded his angry callers about the fine print in service contracts that gave RIM the right to change features and services on its phones "without permission or notice." After a while carriers stopped complaining. Lucrative data traffic was becoming a multibillion-dollar business for the carriers thanks to the growing popularity of e-mails and instant messaging. "The key was stealthily leveraging and launching, then asking for forgiveness," Balsillie says.

/ / /

By 2005, everyone wanted BlackBerry. Carriers who wouldn't give RIM the time of day two years earlier were lining up; the company had one hundred carriers in the pipeline, and at the rate RIM was going it would take years to sign them all up. Balsillie wanted them all selling BlackBerry within twelve months. For Balsillie it was important to keep everyone happy. If he couldn't, somebody else would. Balsillie did not want to leave a void in an unserved market for a rival to fill. To speed up the recruitment process, he hired Frenny Bawa, a banking and high-technology executive and sister of RIM's chief legal officer Karima Bawa. She scaled back the company's onerous carrier contract process and paperwork; contract implementation times dropped to four weeks from thirteen months. RIM added all one hundred carriers in just over a year, and even more the year after that.

As the company added new customers, it began to lose familiar faces. Long-time RIM employees who had been key to the company's early success struggled to find their place in a much larger company. Some, like early sales VPs Don McMurtry and Justin Fabian and programmers Gary Mousseau and Matthias Wandel, felt lost and disenfranchised inside a growing multinational machine, removed from or at odds with the CEOs with whom they had once worked so closely. They began to leave, spent and anguished after living through such an all-consuming experience. Some veered into entirely different careers; Fabian, the expert salesman, became a nature photographer, while Wandel got into woodworking. "Over the years, the company has changed itself into a large telecom company, and I was only willing to follow this so far," Wandel wrote on his LinkedIn page, summing up his fourteen years with the company.[3]

Having muscled its way into the MENS Club, RIM, the small new player, easily outsmarted its bigger, less agile competitors. By late 2005, rivals such as Nokia, Motorola, Siemens, and Palm were working on wireless e-mail-enabled smartphones to stop the march of BlackBerry. They were hopelessly behind, and their latest offerings showed they still had a lot of catching up to do. "None of these devices represented a breakthrough in terms of user experience," says John McKinley, who was now AOL's chief technology officer. "They lacked any compelling case to enterprises why they would be a better value proposition to the entrenched BlackBerry user bases."

BlackBerry's popularity introduced a new compulsiveness to modern communications. The corporate world had been the first to succumb: Intel chairman Andy Grove told USA Today in May 2001 that BlackBerry "should be reported to the DEA" it was so addictive, while Salesforce.com CEO Marc Benioff called it "the heroin of mobile computing."[4]

Users were becoming so attached to BlackBerrys they couldn't put them down. Lazaridis once admitted that he, his wife, and their two school-aged children preferred to chat at the dinner table through BlackBerry e-mails.[5] British actress Mischa Barton was tabloid prey after she reportedly ignored her dinner host Lord Frederick Windsor at Kensington Palace to catch up on BlackBerry messages.[6] But RIM also counted royals, cardinals, and world leaders among their most dedicated users. The American political drama *The West Wing* captured the zeitgeist in a 2006 episode when deputy White House chief of staff Joshua Lyman, played by Bradley Whitford, misplaced his Black-Berry for ten minutes. "Why would you think it would be okay for me to be cut off from the world like that?" he barked at an assistant. "Electronically stranded for ten minutes—it feels like an hour!"[7]

Twitchy BlackBerry fans predictably drew critics and withdrawal strategies. A 2006 study by researchers from MIT's Sloan School of Management warned that chronic BlackBerry users were developing "an inability to disengage from work." Etiquette experts called for BlackBerry-free zones.[8] One Toronto advertising agency penalized employees who overused their devices.[9] In Chicago, the Sheraton Hotel offered to store handhelds for guests to allow them to "reconnect with the hotel experience."[10]

It was as pointless as commanding the tide to roll back. Many users couldn't even go to the bathroom without pulling out their BlackBerrys, sometimes with disastrous results. A repair service in Houston received a hundred Black-Berrys a week that had been dropped in the toilet. One of the worst offenders was Balsillie himself. Three of his handsets were flushed out of action after they tumbled into toilets. One of the porcelain drops occurred shortly before he was due to board a transatlantic flight. RIM's support staff "went nuts," Balsillie says, loading a new phone before he stepped on the plane. "Boy, was I scolded for that."

/ / /

In fourteen short years Lazaridis and Balsillie had steered RIM from the obscurity of a small Ontario city to claim the title as the new kings of technology with an inventive smartphone that was a must-have status symbol for professionals. Through a mix of innovation and brazen tactics the duo had outsmarted bigger competitors and skated around wolfish carriers. Most remarkable of all, the unlikely pairing of the bookish innovator and abrasive business strategist had thrived. Contrasting personalities that might have driven Lazaridis and Balsillie apart during the stressful fight to survive instead united them into a stronger force against RIM's adversaries. They understood each other's strengths and weaknesses, presented a unified front to their staff and the outside world, and never yielded their shared ambition to transform RIM into a technology powerhouse. And RIM's financial condition was catching up with their aspirations. By its 2006 fiscal year, the company's revenue exceeded $2 billion, a milestone that would soon be passed with the release of a new BlackBerry smartphone.

Lazaridis and his close friend, Doug Fregin, spent most of the Christmas holidays in 2005 perfecting RIM's first smartphone squarely aimed at consumers, a handset that combined e-mail and phone service with a music player, memory card, and camera. Fregin, the gifted circuit board designer, had the difficult challenge: fitting the new applications and internal circuitry into a slim new phone that would be called the Pearl. The challenge was so complex that Lazaridis found Fregin in the office alone on Christmas Day tinkering with a circuit board. He rewarded his oldest friend that day by driving to a nearby Harvey's fast-food restaurant to pick up a hamburger and french fries. By the end of the holidays, "We got it all to fit," Lazaridis says.

The following September, RIM invited dozens of journalists and bloggers to a theater in New York's Times Square to watch a video presentation of Lazaridis speaking a new language. There was the father of battery and bandwidth conservation in a black V-neck sweater describing the Pearl as a "sleek" and "stylish" phone. This, Lazaridis said, was a "way different BlackBerry," delivering music and home videos. RIM was also talking to customers a different way. For years it had relied on carriers to market its products to their customers. Now, RIM was starting its own branding campaign, aimed for the first time at consumers. It tapped TV actress Mariska Hargitay, author Douglas Coupland, and Martin Eberhard, CEO of Tesla Motors, to appear in advertisements talking about how the Pearl had changed their lives.

The showstopper was a new trackball in the middle of the device, a rubber ball that users rolled to navigate around the screen like a mouse, replacing the trackwheel that had been a feature on all previous BlackBerrys. Reviewers were smitten. *Computerworld* columnist Mike Elgan declared the slim phone a "ground-breaking, genre-killing, trend-setting device." With its fluid trackball, Internet navigation was so easy that Elgin wrote and filed his lengthy column from the Pearl.

"The trackball will become the dominant navigational device for mobile devices within two years," he wrote. "Welcome to the future."[11]

PART TWO

EVERYBODY HAS PLANS UNTIL THEY GET HIT.

—MIKE TYSON

9 / / / ROCKET DOCKET

Jim Balsillie was fighting a losing battle against an unfamiliar adversary. He slept and ate so fitfully that he dropped twenty pounds. In November 2005 he booked a room in a Toronto hotel to confront a bigger loss: his confidence. RIM's dogged dealmaker was paralyzed with fear. He retreated to the hotel to come to grips with his crisis. Alone in his room he sobbed uncontrollably. "I know what depression feels like. You're bawling your eyes out at night for hours. You can't function," Balsillie says. "I had never been in this position before. I never felt dread like that before."

His crisis was triggered by a tiny slip of a company with only a fistful of patents to its name. Balsillie and Lazaridis had underestimated NTP Inc. ever since the Virginia-based shell company sued RIM in 2001 for infringing on its wireless e-mail patents. Don't worry, RIM's lawyers reassured him; it's a nuisance claim. But it didn't play out that way. RIM badly underestimated NTP's case and the risks of fighting a patent dispute in a U.S. court, where the odds did not favor defendants. RIM suffered a humiliating court defeat in 2002, multiple appeals failed, and settlement talks foundered. Now a Virginia judge was threatening to take the company to the brink by enforcing an injunction to bar BlackBerry service in the U.S.

Unless RIM quickly forged a settlement it would be locked out of its most lucrative market. Peace talks, however, were going nowhere because NTP insisted on a rich royalty that would sap RIM's profits for years. Balsillie balked at the terms. While the standoff dragged on, BlackBerry U.S. subscription growth began to fall short of expectations. Balsillie's days were filled with insistent calls from the country's most powerful carriers, businesses, and government agencies. *What was the backup plan for BlackBerry e-mail service? Why hadn't RIM solved the crisis?*

For the first time in his life, Balsillie was confronted with a problem he could not fix. He always had a solution, a cunning ploy or two to gain the advantage. After three years of fighting he'd been backed into a corner without ammunition. It was a place Sun Tzu called the "death ground." According to the ancient military guide he had two choices: succumb or advance. Moving forward did not seem like an option that evening as fear and panic overwhelmed Balsillie.

"I never thought of killing myself, but it didn't seem like a bad idea."

/ / /

NTP's lawsuit began with a talented engineer whose early life closely mirrored that of Mike Lazaridis. Thomas Campana was born fourteen years before Lazaridis in a working-class neighborhood on the south side of Chicago. He shared more than a humble upbringing with the Canadian. Campana was a mechanical prodigy, inspired by his father, a radio operator who had flown bombing missions in World War II.[1] He showed an early affinity for machines, repairing radios, and building a family television from scrounged parts. He earned an engineering degree from the University of Illinois, served in the air force's communications branch, and landed a job building a wireless communications system for the Chicago police.

Like Lazaridis, Campana took a leap and founded a wireless business, Electronic Services Associates. Unlike Lazaridis, Campana had no Jim Balsillie lassoing deals and money to keep the business afloat. "He was not the greatest businessman in the world," his father, Tom Campana Sr., told the *Globe and Mail*.[2] Campana's prospects improved in the late 1980s when he helped a fledgling Miami paging company, Telefind, develop a breakthrough pager that worked on multiple frequencies across the United States. The innovation attracted AT&T, which asked Telefind and Campana to develop a wireless e-mail service for a new line of laptop computers. Campana designed a system connecting AT&T laptops to Telefind's paging network. But rather than striking it rich, the venture ran aground: Telefind's paging system proved unreliable and AT&T walked away in 1991. Telefind filed for bankruptcy, owing one of its biggest creditors, Campana, half a million dollars.[3]

One of the few things Campana salvaged from Telefind's collapse was the legal right to a set of patents for the wireless message technology he helped develop. The other was a business relationship with Telefind's lawyer, Donald Stout, a former government patent examiner based in Arlington, Virginia, who liked to hunt in his spare time. Stout saw an opportunity to parlay Campana's patent rights into a revenue stream of licensing fees at a time wireless data was taking off. The two men formed NTP to hold the stranded patents. The skeletal company was part of a growing breed of patent trolls whose primary business was to sue businesses allegedly infringing on their rights. Lawyers represented trolls on the contingency they would share a portion of any court awards. It was a booming business. U.S. lawsuits filed by patent trolls rose sharply to 428 in 2007 and 2,750 just five years later, by which point they accounted for nearly 60 percent of all U.S. patent lawsuits, double the level of five years earlier.[4]

Stout started the hunt for licensing fees by writing letters to dozens of communications companies suggesting they were infringing on its technology. One of the last letters was sent in January 2000 to RIM. NTP received no replies from most of the targets, including RIM. In May 2001, Stout noticed a story in the *Wall Street Journal* about U.S. patents granted to the Waterloo company for its BlackBerry wireless e-mail system. Calling it a "huge day for RIM," Balsillie put copycats on notice. "BlackBerry knockoffs will now need a license from us," Balsillie told the newspaper. "The amateurs out there have to stop."[5] Balsillie had hoped to warn off patent violators, but instead he put a target on RIM's back. The more Stout read about BlackBerry, the more he thought it sounded like NTP's technology.[6] "That certainly made our choice easy," Stout says.

Within a day, Stout and Campana lined up $2 million, from several investors including other lawyers, to finance a patent infringement lawsuit against RIM. He didn't have to go far to find an accommodating jurisdiction for his case. Stout lived in one of the friendliest U.S. court districts for patent plaintiffs. The Eastern District Court of Virginia propelled cases so quickly through its courts it was known as the Rocket Docket. The district's motto summed up its priorities: justice delayed is justice denied. A median case in the district took barely nine months to move from claim to trial in the early 2000s, less than half the national equivalent.[7] Time was the friend of patent plaintiffs. The faster complex cases traveled through courts, the less time defendants had to prepare, and to educate and convince a judge and jury that they had not breached the patents.

"Fast justice is what you want," says Stout.

/ / /

Patent disputes are as old as ancient Greece. Local politicians granted primitive patent rights to favored cooks to protect culinary inventions from kitchen pirates. Medieval kings and queens solved disputes by selling lucrative long-term patents for everything from farm equipment to playing cards. The rudimentary system was not up to the task of policing innovations during the Industrial Revolution. Machines transformed everyday life in so many ways that the boundary between inventions and copycats grew blurry. Breakthroughs were dogged by so many ownership disputes that new patent laws and rights were imposed to referee the idea wars.

Patent fights snowballed in the Information Age. Computing and communication advances arrived with such velocity that U.S. patent applications increased fourfold in the decade ending in 2010.[8] Leading the way was the mobile phone business, accounting for nearly 25 percent of total U.S. patents granted in 2013, up from 5 percent in 2001.[9] Many breakthroughs were based on software concepts, opening a new front in the patent wars involving a labyrinth of algorithms and code. These feuds became high-stakes battlegrounds when U.S. courts began handing out rich awards for patent infringements. The case that would define these damaging patent crusades began in November 2001, when NTP filed its claim against RIM for patent infringement.

NTP's legal assault on RIM's chief witness began under stormy skies in Richmond, Virginia, in the second week of November 2002.[10] The city's massive granite federal courthouse was impervious to the violent winds and lightning dancing above the century-old building. The same could not be said for the witness who took the stand on November 11. Before long Mike Lazaridis was reeling.

NTP's lawyers were veterans of the Rocket Docket. In an impatient court district and before an untrained jury, they understood that cases were seldom won or lost by launching into weighty technology examinations. There wasn't enough time and the risks of jury confusion were high. A more effective tactic was attacking the credibility of defense witnesses. If they could rattle RIM's founder they might win over the jury.

Lazaridis took the stand for only half a day. Under questioning from NTP's lawyer, Jim Wallace, he was defensive and easily flustered. When he testified that RIM had thoroughly researched whether RIM had infringed on NTP's patent rights, Wallace cited contradictory sworn evidence from another RIM employee. When Lazaridis cast RIM as a struggling company, Wallace brandished a rosy newspaper account of the company's prospects and internal RIM e-mails about the company's prosperity. The failed attempt to poormouth RIM's condition hurt Lazaridis's credibility with jurors. "We didn't really buy that," says Rose Ann Janis, one of the jurors. "He kept talking about how poorly they were doing financially . . . and it was really hard to believe. BlackBerry was the new, cool thing."[11]

With the credibility of its chief witness under attack, RIM's legal team had to convincingly demonstrate to the jury that the company had not infringed on NTP's patents. This meant RIM had to prove that similar wireless e-mail technology preceded Campana's patents, rendering them invalid. To win that point, RIM's legal team from Jones Day Reavis & Pogue decided to demonstrate another company's wireless e-mail system. It was a risky strategy. Old technology was often so unreliable that RIM's case could collapse if the system didn't work. The other challenge was the presiding judge. Federal judge James Spencer was a formidable and sometimes impatient judge who was known to rebuke lawyers, witnesses, and even jurors. He once cut off a windy witness, blurting: "I can't take another second of this."[12] RIM did not want to be on Judge Spencer's bad side.

To prove his case that wireless e-mail existed prior to Campana's patents, a Jones Day lawyer called the founder of Arizona-based TekNow as a witness. David Keeney told the court his company had designed a wireless messaging system in the late 1980s, well before Campana filed his patent applications. To drive home the point, Keeney sent a message on a computer he rigged up in the courtroom to a modem and paging transmitter. When his message, "Tommy, the deal is closed," arrived on a pager, another lawyer on the defense team triumphantly carried it across the room to the jury.

NTP's lawyers noticed something wrong when examining background documents for the TekNow demonstration. According to materials RIM gave the court, the successful demo operated on computer programs dated in 1994 and 1997, years *after* Campana filed his patents. When NTP cross-examined Keeney he explained the dates referred only to the last time the files had been saved on a computer. The program was in fact created years earlier. When asked why the original program wasn't used, Keeney gave NTP what it was looking for. He said that a RIM engineer who helped put the demonstration together "couldn't get it to work" with the older files supplied by TekNow. The testimony crippled RIM's case. Even worse, it was vulnerable to accusations that it had misled the court.

After ushering the jury out of the courtroom, Judge Spencer could barely contain his fury when addressing RIM's legal team. "It is just not going to cut it," he fumed. "Please. I'll count to ten. I don't want to yell at you. . . . I'm going to strike the entire demonstration and any discussion of it." When RIM's lawyers asked to test the correct version of the program in court, Judge Spencer refused. RIM would not recover from the setback. "Up to that point I had total confidence we were going to win it," Lazaridis says. "It became a completely different trial. He threw out our whole case."

The legal water torture lasted for twelve days. As the trial dragged on Lazaridis called Balsillie with grim updates.

"This is going really, really bad," Lazaridis said.

"Just do your best," Balsillie said, "We'll find a way through. Don't worry."

"This is killing me, Jim. It's like a nightmare that won't end."

/ / /

It took the jury less than five hours to reach its verdict. RIM, they concluded, infringed on all of NTP's five patents. Judge Spencer lowered his gavel six months later in a written decision that awarded NTP $53.7 million in damages and a royalty of 8.55 percent on RIM's annual U.S. sales, then more than $250 million. Judge Spencer's scathing decision accused the Waterloo company of "egregious" behavior for attempting to "confuse and mislead the jury" with the "fraudulent" TekNow demonstration. "This was not a close case," he wrote.[13]

Devastated by the jury's decision, Lazaridis returned to Waterloo in frail health. He doesn't recall what happened next, but colleagues remember he disappeared from the office for two weeks. "That whole [period] was like a blank," he says. "It was post-traumatic stress. You're about to lose the company, about to lose everything." His second-in-command, Larry Conlee, says the defeat was more than a business setback. "What I sensed from Mike was a lot of pain. Here's the founder of the company being told he's cheating these people and his technology is wrong. He was personally hurt by it."

After the defeat, Balsillie assumed responsibility for managing the case. He told investors RIM would appeal the verdict and push to invalidate NTP's patents. After dropping Jones Day he hired Howrey Simon Arnold & White, a firm that specialized in intellectual property cases. Howrey and RIM's board agreed to keep fighting. Outraged by the idea of handing nearly a tenth of RIM's sales to NTP, Balsillie dispatched lawyers, lobbyists, and former Canadian prime minister Brian Mulroney to Washington to neuter the impact of the court ruling. Eventually, appeal courts upheld the jury's decision. A review by the U.S. Patent and Trademark Office took three years. As the wait dragged on and political pressure and media attention intensified, Judge Spencer grew incensed. "I've spent enough of my life and my time" on the case, he told a hearing in early November 2005, adding there would be no more waiting for the Patent Office's review of Campana's patents. Unless RIM struck a settlement with NTP, the company would be slapped with an injunction barring BlackBerry from the U.S. market, the source of more than 80 percent of its revenues.

As the cataclysm approached, Balsillie became consumed with dread. He kept his fragile state from colleagues because, in his words, "I knew they looked to me as a rock of stability." A crack in his tough-guy exterior was hardly what the troops needed now. On the advice of friends, he booked a Toronto hotel room that November to meet with a man whose job was staring down defeat. Hearing a knock on the door, Balsillie came face-to-face with Donn Smith. Balsillie had heard about Smith from sports friends. The lantern-jawed guru had helped prominent golfers overcome the yips, nervous hands on the putting green. Hockey stars such as Jarome Iginla, Doug Weight, and Bill Guerin turned to Smith to crawl out of slumps. Often their problems weren't physical. Players had to get their head back in the game and Smith knew how to get them there.

Once Balsillie explained his circumstances, Smith shared his own story. He was one of ten children born into a hard-luck family in Prince Edward Island. According to Smith's book, *Internal Perfection,* his parents lacked money for such basic necessities as indoor plumbing or electricity.[14] As a young man, Smith battled a drinking problem, moved to Alberta to work as a pipe fitter, corked his alcohol dependency, and parlayed his redemption into a new career as a high-end personal life coach. Smith shared past traumas with clients to put them at ease. Anything bad they were going through had already happened to him.

Smith helped clients cage their fears. The trick, he told Balsillie, was summoning a joyful experience. RIM's chief was comforted that night by the memory of carefree childhood swims in a lake near the family home in Peterborough. Balsillie didn't want to let go of the dreamy recollection when Smith pulled him back to reality after a minute. In that short time, Smith had shown him he had the ability to push away fears and think about something other than the NTP fiasco. By the end of his first session, Balsillie was able to hold his happy memory for several minutes. "He taught me how to put my nervousness in a box," he says. "You understand this is about choice. You know you can get out of it. It gives you your power back." To Balsillie the athlete, it was no different than working a weak muscle with a trainer. "He knew how to shut the nervousness out. It worked, it was what I needed," he says. "It shifted the dread feeling out of me, and I started sleeping and eating properly. The sense of relief was remarkable."

As Balsillie continued to meet with Smith over the next weeks and months, he recovered enough energy to confront the NTP nightmare. If RIM could delay Judge Spencer's injunction until the U.S. Patent office finished its review of NTP's patents, it might have a chance. The injunction was stalled, and in February 2006, the Patent Office announced what RIM had waited three years to hear. NTP's wireless e-mail patents were invalidated.[15] The messy war, however, was not over. NTP vowed to challenge the patent invalidation, opening another maze of hearings and rulings. Judge Spencer, furious with RIM's blitzkrieg of appeals and lobbying, dug in his heels. The Patent Office had no legal authority over his court, he said. As he once told RIM, "This is still probably one of the few places left where money and power and political influence don't mean a damn thing."

RIM was out of options. If RIM and NTP did not strike a settlement within thirty days, Judge Spencer would enforce the injunction. Both sides were ready to settle. RIM could not risk losing customers and NTP's legal position had weakened. It could take years of appeals to resolve the ongoing patent validity, and RIM had strengthened its bargaining position by developing an e-mail detour on its U.S. BlackBerry service that did not trip over NTP's patents.

RIM dispatched a team of lawyers to a New York law office to meet with NTP's Stout and an arbitrator to end the five-year legal odyssey. Within a few days, they struck a preliminary agreement. With the end finally in sight, Balsillie did not want to make the decision alone. He turned to Lazaridis and

RIM's board, which rarely disagreed with the CEOs, asking them what they would do in his shoes. By the end of the meeting, everyone was behind him. In March the two sides announced a settlement. NTP's persistent demand for royalties was off the table. Instead RIM would pay NTP a lump sum of $612.5 million. Thomas Campana did not live to see his case validated. The heavy smoker died of cancer in 2004. NTP's law firm, Wiley Rein, pocketed $245 million of the settlement, the largest contingency fee earned by any U.S. law firm that year.[16] Campana's widow, Stout, and other investors shared the rest of RIM's payment. Stout marked the victory with a three-week hunting trip to New Zealand, where, with a crossbow, he bagged another icon, a majestic red stag known locally as the trophy of kings. In Waterloo, there were no celebrations. "It's not a good feeling to write this kind of check," Balsillie told reporters. Privately he believed the outcome was an important financial win because NTP's royalty demand would have drained RIM's cash flow for years. RIM restored its profits within a year of writing the NTP check. What was harder to recover, however, was the personal damage.

Few people knew of the emotional toll the case took on RIM's chiefs. Lazaridis looked for solace in his faith, and Balsillie in his new guru. The humiliating legal spectacle had unnerved the company's leaders and diverted their attention from emerging competitors. "We lost some of who we were through that," says Patrick Spence. "That's ultimately the cost to the company. It's not the $612 million. It's what that cost us in terms of taking focus away from where we needed to go."

10 / / / THE JESUS PHONE

Steve Jobs walked onto the stage of a San Francisco conference center to announce a revolution his competitors would regret underestimating.

Dressed in his signature black mock turtleneck and faded jeans on the morning of January 9, 2007, Apple's founder announced he would "change everything." He had three firsts to proclaim: a touch-screen iPod, a mobile phone, and an Internet communications device. Turning to more than four thousand tech reporters, bloggers, and cheering employees in the room he asked: "Are you getting it? These are not three separate devices. This is one device and we are calling it iPhone. Today Apple is going to reinvent the phone."

For the next eighty minutes Jobs trumpeted the iPhone by comparing it with "not so smart" smartphones, leaving no doubt that BlackBerry, the runaway market leader, was his target. Apple's iPhone, he promised, wouldn't come with the frustrating "fixed" or "plastic" keyboards that made Internet navigation so cumbersome. "We are going to . . . get rid of all these buttons and use this giant screen," he said waving an iPhone at his audience. Poking, pinching, and swiping across the glass surface, he scrolled music files, played Beatles songs, screened a clip of the hit TV series *The Office,* and listened to a voice mail from Al Gore. This wasn't the "baby Internet," he said, dismissing the limited Web browsers of BlackBerry and other smartphone makers; this was "the Internet in your pocket." The only thing bolder than iPhone's design was its price tag: $499, twice the price of the latest BlackBerry.

Jobs had something else in his pocket. At the presentation's end, he invited a guest onstage. The room fell quiet when Stanley Sigman, the stocky CEO of Cingular Wireless, emerged from the wings. It was an appearance few would have imagined. Jobs had been a vocal critic of the nation's powerful carriers. He resisted entering the phone business for years because of the stifling control exerted by big wireless carriers, whom he once called "the four orifices."[1] Ironically, Sigman now represented the biggest orifice of them all. Days earlier, Cingular was devoured by AT&T as part of a $67 billion takeover of RIM's earliest U.S. carrier, BellSouth. AT&T was now the world's preeminent telecom operator.

"We come from two different worlds," Jobs said of Sigman, looking stiff beside him in a navy blue jacket, clutching white cue cards. Despite their differences, he and Sigman "worked wonderfully together," Jobs added. Sigman agreed, following his notes. Two years earlier, the Cingular executive said, the carrier signed a contract to sell an Apple phone it hadn't seen, an unheard-of concession by any carrier. Apple was also given carte blanche and unlimited bandwidth to develop services BlackBerry was denied by carriers— video downloads, map searches, and full Internet browsing. This was market disruption Silicon Valley style: Apple aimed to win by ignoring the established rules. In exchange for the unusual freedoms, Apple granted Cingular a multiyear contract to sell iPhones exclusively in the United States. "Ours is a unique relationship that lets Apple be Apple and Cingular be Cingular," Sigman said.

Jobs finished his presentation by making one more announcement. From now on, Apple Computer, Inc. would be Apple Inc. Gesturing to an overhead chart, he pointed out that in 2006 almost 200 million personal computers were sold globally. One billion mobile phones were sold during the same period. Silicon Valley could no longer afford to ignore the smartphone market that BlackBerry had created. Apple, Jobs boasted, would grab 1 percent of the mobile phone market by selling 10 million iPhones in the following year. Apple was pivoting from its computing roots to grab a share of the world's fastest-growing technology market. Jobs rationalized the shift by reaching north to BlackBerry country to quote Canadian ice hockey legend Wayne Gretzky: "I skate to where the puck is going to be, not where it has been."

/ / /

Standing in a tightly secured office about forty miles south of San Francisco, engineers watched a webcast of Jobs's iPhone presentation with growing dread. The fretting took place in Building 44,[2] one of scores of structures at Googleplex, the Mountain View headquarters of Google. For the previous fifteen months Google had been secretly working on a smartphone. Like Jobs, Google founders Sergey Brin and Larry Page had their eyes fixed on the exploding mobile phone market. What Jobs hadn't said in San Francisco was that the fastest-growing, most lucrative segment of the mobile phone market was the wireless data boom RIM had detonated five years earlier. U.S. carriers were projected to more than double 2005 wireless data revenues to above $27 billion that year.[3] Data was Google's DNA. Its search engine delivered websites, media, and maps to the digital world. If the world was going mobile, Google had to be there in a much bigger way.

Google got into the game in 2005 by acquiring Android, a mobile device start-up co-founded by Silicon Valley innovator Andy Rubin. The acquisition was followed by the launch of two projects known to only a few Google executives. The first, code-named Dream, was a long-term effort by Rubin to build a touch-screen phone. It was nowhere near the finish line when Jobs strode onstage that day. The second project, Sooner, was in the final stages of development: it was to be a BlackBerry-like phone with a keyboard and advanced applications, including a full Internet browser and Google Maps.[4] Sooner's team understood immediately what Jobs's virtuoso iPhone demo meant: Project Sooner was a goner. If Google wanted its phone to make it, the keyboard had to go. Rubin's Dream touch-screen phone was moved into the fast lane.[5] Fred Vogelstein summed up iPhone's impact that day in his book *Dogfight* with a quote by Google engineer Chris DeSalvo: "We're going to have to start over."[6]

/ / /

Mike Lazaridis was home on his treadmill when he saw a TV report about Apple's news. He soon forgot about exercise. There was Steve Jobs waving a small glass object, downloading music, videos, and maps from the Internet onto a phone. "How did they do that?" Lazaridis wondered. His curiosity turned to disbelief when Sigman took the stage to announce Cingular's deal to sell Apple's phone. What was its parent, AT&T, thinking? "It's going to collapse the network," he thought.

The next day Lazaridis grabbed Balsillie at the office and pulled him in front of a computer.

"Jim, I want you to watch this," he said, linking to a Webcast of the iPhone unveiling. "They put a full Web browser on that thing. The carriers aren't letting us put a full browser on our products."

Balsillie's first thought was RIM was losing AT&T as a customer.

"Apple's got a better deal," Balsillie said. 'We were never allowed that. The U.S. market is going to be tougher."

"These guys are really, really good," Lazaridis replied. "This is different."

"It's okay—we'll be fine."

RIM's chiefs didn't give much additional thought to Apple for months. "It wasn't a threat to RIM's core business," says Lazaridis's top lieutenant, Larry Conlee. "It wasn't secure. It had rapid battery drain and a lousy [digital] keyboard." If the iPhone gained traction, RIM's senior executives believed, it would be with consumers who cared more about YouTube and other Internet escapes than efficiency and security. Offering mobile access to broader Internet content, says Conlee, "was not a space where we parked our business."

Lazaridis and Balsillie had more urgent concerns than Apple's new phone. They were scrambling to feed a world hungry for BlackBerrys. By 2007, RIM was adding more than a million BlackBerry subscribers a quarter and split its stock, three for one, following a two-for-one split three years earlier. Anyone who had bought in early 1999 for $13 a share and held on would have seen their investment rise forty-fold in value in eight years. Its new consumer phone, the Pearl, was a sensation, with sales leaping 59 percent, to 6.4 million handsets in fiscal 2007. Balsillie's global ambitions were another strain. Lawyers and marketing staff were racing to fulfill his plan to sign up a hundred foreign carriers from Venezeula to Vietnam within a year. Conlee grew concerned that emerging market carrier customers were not generating sufficient profits to justify extra work for RIM's stretched staff. "You never have the luxury of being able to say yes to everything," Conlee says. "We had to commit dollars and hours we didn't have."

There weren't enough manufacturing facilities or employees to keep up with the growth. For instance, the company's practice of holding new-hire Monday gatherings was becoming a logistical nightmare. Sometimes there were so many recruits that buses were hired to ferry new hires to hotel conference rooms. Senior executives were so busy they only appeared on pretaped video presentations. RIM was building so many new offices that it soon became Waterloo's largest landlord, owning an estimated 30 percent of the city's commercial real estate. Unlike Silicon Valley, where corporate headquarters are playful and futuristic monuments to their founders' visions, RIM's was a testament to the founder's fiscal and engineering restraint. In a hurry to keep up with demand, there was little time for creativity. Virtually all of the Waterloo offices were dull gray glass-and-cement structures, with cookie-cutter offices furnished with the same utilitarian brand of chairs, wood desks, and tables.

A more complex challenge was manufacturing. RIM built its Waterloo plant in 2002 so that its research and development teams could work closely with production and quality control could be managed locally. With snowballing sales, those ambitions were no longer sustainable in 2007. The factory was already working at full capacity. The solution, Conlee decided, was tapping manufacturing partners in Mexico, United States, and Europe. When he met with a consultant to draft a proposal, he was immediately warned off. Outsourcing such complex technology would endanger quality control, the consultant said. When Conlee said his priority was keeping up with sales that were expanding 25 percent from each quarter to the next, the consultant replied such a growth rate was impossible.

"Welcome to the problem," Conlee said.

/ / /

The iPhone had a cult following before a single phone was sold. In a year filled with breaking news about the U.S. military surge in Iraq and Paris Hilton's jail sentence, media couldn't write enough advance stories about the coming of a smartphone that gadget blog Gizmodo dubbed the "true Jesus Phone." Apple followed through with a publicity campaign leading up to the launch that was filled with spiritual overtones. "Touching is believing" was the slogan of print and TV ads featuring a finger reaching out of the darkness to touch the phone. Journalists happily played along, comparing the image to Michelangelo's Sistine Chapel painting of God stretching to touch the finger of Adam. The iPhone's retail debut day, or "iDay," as it was dubbed, June 29, 2007, was also the date of the Roman holiday celebrating the feast of the martyred apostles St. Peter and St. Paul. By that day, it had already inspired more than 11,000 print articles and generated 69 million Google hits.[7]

No one understood consumers' digital desires better than Steve Jobs. A generation earlier Apple's elegant Macintosh took desktop computers mainstream. Six years before the iPhone launch, Apple reinvented the music business in the face of industry skepticism by making portable music easy and fun with the iPod digital music player and its iTunes online music service. Computer and music industry executives dismissed iTunes as a pipe dream. Record labels would not initially yield to Apple the right to control the online distribution of music purchases, but eventually relented.[8] They were wrong. Apple offered a lifeline to a drowning business, and Jobs appealed personally to artists hurt by Internet music pirates, including Bob Dylan, who agreed to let iTunes prerelease his new album *Modern Times*.[9] For the first time in thirty years, a Dylan album ranked number one on the *Billboard* chart. Other music celebrities and music labels soon followed Mr. Tambourine Man.

Now Apple was reinventing another industry. It had convinced one of the world's most powerful carriers to promote the type of device the industry had resisted for years: a phone that allowed users to carry the Internet in their pockets. Eight years after RIM had unseated Motorola with its mobile e-mail service, the iPhone was challenging BlackBerry as the new standard of wireless communications. Gizmodo's editor-in-chief, Brian Lam, who coined the phrase "Jesus phone," says iPhone's success was preordained. BlackBerry and other smartphones were dull, utilitarian tools meant for corporate types who lacked imagination. The iPhone, with its elegant design and hypnotic zoom and pinch touch interface, he says, was for "everyday people." In its first three months, more than 1 million iPhones were sold, matching the quarterly sales volume of the RIM's Pearl, only months earlier hailed by critics as the phone of the future.

To rivals such as RIM, Nokia, and Motorola, the iPhone's popularity was illogical. Its battery lasted less than eight hours, it operated on an older, slower second-generation network, and, as Lazaridis predicted, music, video, and other downloads strained AT&T's network. RIM now faced an adversary it didn't understand. "By all rights the product should have failed, but it did not," said David Yach, RIM's chief technology officer. To Yach and other senior RIM executives, Apple changed the competitive landscape by shifting the raison d'être of smartphones from something that was functional to a product that was beautiful. "I learned that beauty matters. . . . RIM was caught incredulous that people wanted to buy this thing."

/ / /

John Richardson started RIM's board meeting on March 2, 2007, with a somber update no one wanted to hear. This would not be a discussion about Apple or the iPhone. No, this was a pressing emergency jeopardizing the reputation of the company and its senior executives. Richardson, a retired accounting and insurance company executive, headed a special committee of the board appointed in 2006 to investigate RIM's stock option practices. The company alerted shareholders months earlier of a potential $25 million to $45 million charge relating to employee option grants. The committee's investigation revealed a bigger problem than anticipated. Guided by Toronto securities lawyer Rob Staley, Richardson discussed the findings of a report by Staley's firm, Bennett Jones. RIM, the report concluded, had improperly backdated hundreds of option grants to more than sixty managers and senior executives, including Balsillie and Lazaridis, to inflate the value of the benefits over nearly a decade ending in 2006.

RIM was one of dozens of companies, most in the technology sector, involved in a spreading options backdating scandal. Publicly traded businesses typically compensate employees with options, allowing them to buy company stock at a fixed price over a set period of time. The more share prices rose, the more profit employees pocketed when exercising their right to buy shares at the discounted option price. During the tech boom and bust, stock prices were so volatile that some employees were left holding worthless options. Many companies remedied the problem by backdating option grants to a time when stocks traded at lower prices, thus increasing the potential for profit. Altering fixed dates on stock options is legal as long as changes are communicated to shareholders. RIM failed to follow the rule for years. Even worse, RIM's chief financial officer, Dennis Kavelman, publicly denied company options were backdated when questioned at the company's annual meeting the previous summer. RIM had an accounting problem and a regulatory disclosure issue.

Richardson advised the board that his committee had alerted the U.S. Securities and Exchange Commission and the Ontario Securities Commission about its findings. RIM was now under investigation by both regulators. At the same time, Richardson explained that his committee had found no evidence of intentional misconduct. Mistakes were made, he said, because of "sloppy administration." His committee strongly recommended that Balsillie and Lazaridis remain as co-CEOs, but changes were needed. The new order was revealed when Balsillie told the meeting he was stepping down as chairman of the board. The next to go were Kendall Cork and Douglas Wright, directors responsible for overseeing stock options as members of the compensation committee. The board accepted their resignations but took the unusual step of naming each honorary director emeritus, "in recognition of their special contributions to RIM." There would also be changes in the finance department: Kavelman stepped down as CFO, moving into a senior administration job; his lieutenant, Angelo Loberto, transferred out of finance to operations.

RIM announced the moves three days later along with news that it was appointing former Toronto Stock Exchange CEO Barbara Stymiest and former IBM Canada CEO John Wetmore to the board. Two months later, on May 17, RIM announced it was restating all financial statements between 1999 and 2006 to reflect additional stock option compensation charges totaling nearly $250 million. The stock market shrugged off the financial hit. The share price of one of North America's fastest growing companies was still on a tear. One week after RIM's bad news about the multimillion-dollar charge, RIM's stock closed at $166, a 22 percent leap from its closing price the day of the board's March meeting.

What appeared to be a small financial setback was in fact a far more damaging blow than anyone, except a small circle of insiders, appreciated. Behind the scenes, the fifteen-year-old business marriage of Jim Balsillie and Mike Lazaridis was coming unglued. The co-CEOs, the pioneering mobile e-mailers who communicated incessantly on their BlackBerrys, handed regulators a paper trail that traced improper option practices to the highest level of the company. For many difficult days in the spring of 2007, SEC investigators and U.S. Justice Department officials in New York and OSC staff in Toronto grilled Balsillie, Lazaridis, and several senior RIM officials about hundreds of e-mails. According to regulatory documents, Balsillie and, on occasion, Lazaridis made e-mail requests to backdate options for recent hires and executives to improve their value. Loberto grew so concerned about the volume of backdating requests that he warned his supervisor in an e-mail obtained by regulators: "I can NOT continually change history." Balsillie told U.S. and Canadian regulators from the beginning that he was directly involved in the backdating, but that he had not intended violating securities rules and did not realize he was doing so.

The inquisition was much harder on Lazaridis. He told regulators he had no knowledge the practice was improper; his job was engineering and innovation, not securities laws, finance, and stock options. He didn't understand why regulators dragged him into a mess Balsillie, his finance team, and the overseeing directors had failed to prevent. Less than a year after the conclusion of the NTP fiasco, his reputation and RIM's credibility were again under assault. The prospect of a scandal and regulatory discipline devastated Lazaridis. "We had just gotten over NTP [which] was a nightmare," he says. "Then it was the stock options. That literally knocked the wind out of my sails." His friend, David Neale, said Lazaridis felt "completely humiliated" by the regulatory investigation. "I think it sickened him to his heart," he says.

Larry Conlee says Lazaridis lost more than his zeal. The founder's faith in Balsillie was badly shaken. "I think Mike felt betrayed," Conlee says. Lazaridis declines to discuss his personal response to the scandal other than to say he was "blindsided" by the investigation and extra work required "to protect the company and protect ourselves personally." He says he did not discuss the options crisis with Balsillie because lawyers warned the co-CEOs against discussing the case while they were under investigation. Lazaridis says he was also in no shape to confront his partner. "It was painful. I was frightened. I didn't understand it." Running a global company that he and Balsillie had built in the face of so many obstacles was no longer where he wanted to be.

"You name all the great things that RIM was able to do, this thing just sucked it all out. I mean, why bother building a great organization if this can happen to it?"

11 / / / STORM

Mike Lazaridis, ever the boy electrician, liked to relax by tearing apart small machines in his spare time. Just as he once opened radios in his basement lab for fun, Lazaridis lifted hoods on competitors' phones. Staff visiting his third-floor office in a building called RIM 4 grew accustomed to disemboweled phones with chipsets, antennas, and wires strewn across his desk. Usually the desktop autopsies confirmed Lazaridis's faith that BlackBerry was the smartest phone on the market.

In the summer of 2007, however, Lazaridis cracked open a phone that gave him pause. "They've put a Mac in this thing," he marveled after peering inside one of the new iPhones. Ever since Apple's phone went on sale in June, critics and consumers were effusive about the sleek phone's playful touch screen, elegant graphics, and high-resolution images. Lazaridis saw much more. This was no ordinary smartphone. It was a small mobile Apple computer whose operating system used 700 megabytes of memory—more than twenty-two times the computing power of the BlackBerry. The iPhone had a full Safari browser that traveled everywhere on the Internet. With AT&T's backing, he could see, Apple was changing the direction of the industry.

Lazaridis shared the revelation with his handset engineers, who had been pushing to expand BlackBerry's Internet reach for years. Before, Lazaridis had waved them off. Carriers wouldn't allow RIM to include more than a simple browser because it would crash their networks. After his iPhone autopsy, however, he realized the smartphone race was in danger of shifting. If consumers and carriers continued to embrace the iPhone, BlackBerry would need more than its efficient e-mail and battery to lead the market. "If this thing catches on, we're competing with a Mac, not a Nokia," he said. The new battleground was mobile computing. Lazaridis figured RIM's core corporate market was safe because the iPhone couldn't match BlackBerry's reliable keyboard and in-house network delivery of secure e-mails. But in the consumer market, where the Pearl phone was competing, RIM needed a full Web browser. BlackBerry was a sensation because it put e-mail in people's pockets. Now, iPhone was offering the full Internet. If BlackBerry was to prevail, he told RIM's engineers, "We have to fix everything that's wrong with the iPhone."

While Lazaridis pushed internally for a response to the iPhone, publicly he and Balsillie dismissed their new rival. Companies often ignore competitors' triumphs, but by downplaying a consumer sensation, RIM suddenly seemed out of touch. "I haven't seen one," Balsillie told the *Toronto Star* after the iPhone went on sale in June.[1] Months later, when the iPhone grabbed a fifth of the U.S. smartphone market, Lazaridis complained to the *New York Times* about its keyboard: "I couldn't type on it and I still can't type on it, and a lot of my friends can't type on it. . . . It's hard to type on a piece of glass."[2]

/ / /

With every click of his PowerPoint presentation, Lazaridis felt his audience grow slack and bored. It was late August 2007 and RIM's boss was making a pitch in a Manhattan hotel meeting room to a team of senior executives from Verizon and its British affiliate Vodafone. Lazaridis and Conlee had been invited to New York by the carriers to propose new phone ideas. Although the iPhone wasn't mentioned, there was no doubt Verizon and Vodafone were looking for a device that might supplant what was now America's fastest-selling smartphone.

Judging by the drooping faces of John Stratton, Verizon's chief marketing officer, his colleagues, and the executives from Vodafone, Lazaridis was losing the room.

RIM's co-CEO had started with a pitch for BlackBerry Bold, due to launch in 2008. Clicking from slide to slide, Lazaridis extolled Bold's improved keyboard, with an innovative track pad to replace the trackball, and large screen. This, he told the room, was the best phone RIM ever designed. But to Stratton and company, Bold failed to live up to its name. Up against AT&T and its exclusive multiyear deal to sell the iPhone, Verizon had little interest in another keyboard phone, nor did Vodafone. "The whole atmosphere was, AT&T has the iPhone and we don't, so what do we do?" remembers Conlee. "Neither of those carriers likes to lose. It's a religious war."

Verizon had been caught off guard by iPhone's ascendency. Two years earlier, Verizon rejected an overture from Steve Jobs to partner with Apple on its plans for a new phone.[3] A stickler for bandwidth reliability, the New York–based carrier wouldn't relinquish control of its network to an unseen phone Jobs wanted complete authority to design. Like Lazaridis, Verizon executives correctly predicted iPhone traffic would create gridlock on AT&T's network. What they didn't anticipate was that consumers didn't care. A multibillion-dollar market in carrier revenue was opening up and AT&T had a lock on the hottest device. RIM's Bold was no match for the iPhone.

Sensing the audience's mood, Lazaridis hurried to plan B. Up on the screen, surrounded by lightning, shone an ebony glass-covered phone. That, Lazaridis explained, was Storm. Phone and computer companies had experimented with touch-screen devices for years. None, he said, could match the magic touch of Storm. Pulling out a prototype, Lazaridis pressed a finger on the glass screen. There would be no sweeping fingers, no clumsy iPhone typos on this device. To make the point, his finger hovered like a computer mouse over a digital version of BlackBerry's signature keyboard on the phone's touch screen. When he pressed on a digital key, the entire screen clicked down like a giant button, replicating the tactile feel of tapping a BlackBerry keyboard. RIM had combined the navigation feel of a computer mouse with the secure handling of a BlackBerry keyboard. Under the hood, the ingenious floating Storm screen was designed to activate existing BlackBerry software every time it was clicked. This was how RIM would outsmart Apple, by combining the best of BlackBerry with the seductive lure of a touch screen. His old swagger returning, Lazaridis hailed the next smartphone wave. No one disagreed. Superlatives followed as Verizon and Vodaphone executives passed around the prototype. "They were over the moon," Lazaridis would remember. "They loved the prototype. They called it revolutionary."

RIM had its own reasons for backing the kind of touch phone that Lazaridis had initially and so publicly disdained. Verizon and Vodafone were two of the world's biggest carriers with deep ties into the U.S. and European consumer phone market. Their endorsement of Storm came with an estimated $100 million marketing budget and thousands of retail stores to promote the phone. If Storm took off, the two carriers could potentially sell millions of phones. RIM could stand toe-to-toe with Apple. This was the biggest break in RIM's history. When Lazaridis and Conlee returned to Waterloo, Balsillie had only one reservation about the Verizon contract. RIM had to make the transformative phone in nine months. Was it possible for RIM to deliver in such a short time frame? The answer, Lazaridis and Conlee agreed, was yes.

Conlee broke the news about RIM's ambitious deal to a select group of engineering executives shortly after the Manhattan meeting. In a room located adjacent to his office in RIM 4, Conlee outlined the secret project for the company's first touch phone. The code name for the product was Project Storm, a nod to the disruptive impact RIM hoped the phone would have on the market. But that day the name captured a blizzard of objections from the company's engineers.

RIM was racing to roll out Bold phones for 2008; now it wanted to shift gears and create a new phone in nine months! It took eighteen months to create a new BlackBerry. A touch phone was something else. Although Storm would use BlackBerry's existing operating system, it would need new hardware, radio and antenna configurations, and additional software. RIM products were reliable, never this rushed. There would be no time for proper "soak-testing"—engineering talk for working bugs out of software. Waving off protests, Conlee, RIM's product enforcer, asked each engineer to explain what he or she needed to make the touch phone happen. The room of problem solvers reluctantly itemized the parts, software, and staff they would need, *immediately*. Conlee then turned to Perry Jarmuszewski, a soft-spoken radio engineer who had been with RIM for more than a decade. "Perry I guess you're good to go. You haven't said anything," Conlee offered.

Jarmuszewski, who preferred solving problems to making them, had deliberately held his tongue. Prodded by Conlee, he pushed back. "On a scale of 0 to 10, if 10 means no way, then this project is an 11," he said. "It's impossible. It's something I would not be able to deliver." Conlee shrugged and gave his marching orders: "Well, you guys are the heads of our engineering groups. You are paid accordingly. I expect you to get it done. Verizon wants an answer to the iPhone. We have to do it."

As engineers filed out, they looked anxiously at RIM's chief technology officer, David Yach. He'd just returned from a short holiday ready to devote the next months to fine-tuning the Bold phone. Now this. Yach would later say he and his colleagues understood the importance of the touch-phone contract. "But the importance didn't mean we could get it done any faster than we'd ever built a phone before," says Yach.

"Did we push the teams too hard?" says Lazaridis. "Probably. Can you show me a company that doesn't? I'd be hard-pressed to believe you. The pressure Jobs put his iPhone team through was worse than anything I ever put on my team. The fact is, that's how business runs."

/ / /

After years of flying below the radar, RIM's chiefs were in the limelight as Lazaridis and Balsillie won awards and mainstream media attention. In March 2008, Wall Street's weekly financial bible, *Barron's,* called RIM's co-CEOs "underappreciated northern lights," adding both to its annual list of the world's best CEOs.[4] Also on the list was Steve Jobs. After Mac computers, iTunes, and the iPhone, Jobs was Silicon Valley's undisputed king of cool. By comparison, Lazaridis and Balsillie were bright but awkward public speakers. When Jobs spoke, his fans cheered. When Lazaridis and Balsillie stepped onstage, people sometimes scratched their heads.

For all his confidence, Balsillie could be a surprisingly baffling public speaker. The executive who carefully rehearsed scripts for customer presentations preferred a let's-see-what-happens approach to interviews. He once explained his speaking strategy to university students: "The great thing is, when I talk, nobody knows what I'm going to say, including me."[5] On April Fools Day, 2008, Balsillie gave the kind of spontaneous interview that gives publicists coronaries. Wearing a tan jacket and a blue T-shirt, Balsillie sat down with George Stroumboulopoulos, host of a popular Canadian Broadcasting Corporation TV show. Referencing the popular iPhone, Stroumboulopoulos asked if it was time to add to RIM's lineup: "Do you ever look at it and go, 'What are we going to do if this isn't our primary business, growing RIM beyond . . . a BlackBerry?'"

"Um, no," Balsillie laughed, "we're a very poorly diversified portfolio."

"You're just going to focus on one thing!" said Stroumboulopoulos.

"It either goes to the moon or it crashes to Earth," Balsillie replied.

In the spring of 2008, no one believed RIM would flame out. Its stock market value was more than $70 billion, quarterly revenues were up 100 percent from the previous year, and the company sold sixty thousand BlackBerrys daily. Still, the company couldn't afford to be arrogant. The iPhone had grabbed a 17 percent share of the U.S. smartphone market, while RIM's share slipped from 45 to 40 percent.[6] This was more than a battle of dueling devices. Apple and RIM were competing to capture consumer imagination. When Jobs promoted the iPhone he talked about tangible pleasures—the ability to search Paris maps, listen to Bob Dylan, play video games, and tap cameras that captured the world. When Lazaridis talked about RIM's phones, you needed an engineering degree to parse his words. Unveiling RIM's Bold phone at a conference in Orlando, Florida, in May 2008, he began with a spiel ripped from a product manual: "3G tri-band HSDPA. Quad band Edge. Wi-Fi A, B, and G. GPS. 624 megahertz strong-armed with MMX. Powerhouse processing. Bold. Brilliant, strong color display. The best keyboard we've ever made."

Translation? RIM was launching a third-generation phone that came with Wi-Fi, GPS, and a more powerful processor. To technology wonks in the theater, corporate IT managers, and CIOs, Lazaridis made perfect sense. He was announcing the smartest new smartphone for business customers. But to investors, journalists, and nonengineers, Lazaridis might as well have been reciting algorithms.

In other public appearances that spring, Lazaridis fretted about the very thing iPhone users considered irrelevant: network capacity. One of the great strengths of RIM's internal network system was its ability to compress large amounts of data, a service that reduced bandwidth use and data charges for big customers. When he was presented with a global leadership award by the Computerworld honors program, Lazaridis, the practical engineer, lectured an interviewer about the wireless industry's long history of preserving limited bandwidth: "We have to keep that same way of reasoning, that same conservative conserving mind-set going forward as we apply more and more applications to the wireless spectrum."[7]

Three months later, in July 2008, Apple smashed the networks Lazaridis wanted to conserve by launching the App Store. The online outlet was stocked with software applications that iPhone users, then numbering 6 million, could download. A finger swipe could race cars through video games, book hotel rooms, and order food. Apple sold more than 10 million apps in three days. The number rose to 60 million in a month.[8] By 2011, the App store was stocked with half a million apps and had registered more than 15 billion downloads.[9] Bandwidth conservation was yesterday's priority. AT&T's networks were so clogged that customers began suing Apple and the carrier for dropped calls and other transmission headaches. The message was clear: wireless data traffic was only going to get bigger. The answer was not conservation, rather, it was bigger, faster wireless highways.

/ / /

While Lazaridis chased a new path with Project Storm, Balsillie pursued a once unthinkable opportunity in a northwest Chicago suburb. Schaumburg, Illinois, had been Motorola's home base since 1976, to accommodate its expansion into communications equipment, pagers, semiconductors, and Quasar televisions. Its greatest success came in the 1980s and 1990s when it parlayed its pioneering cellphone technology into a global powerhouse, earning dominant market shares in North America, Asia, and Europe. By 2006 cellphones accounted for two-thirds of Motorola's $43 billion in revenues. The glory days, however, didn't last. Preoccupied with internal turf battles, Motorola's "warring tribes" had missed threats posed by BlackBerry and iPhone. It had focused most of its attention on sleek phone designs, such as the ultra-thin Razr, failing to grasp that software-powered smartphones were the future. Motorola "didn't have the DNA or the people" to understand the software, former CEO Ed Zander told *Chicago Magazine*.[10] By the time Balsillie came calling in the spring of 2008, Motorola was under seige.

Motorola's core mobile device sales were rapidly shrinking, tumbling nearly 40 percent in 2008 from the year before to $12.1 billion. Operating losses in the group, nearly doubled to $2.2 billion in the year, a humbling decline that prompted cantankerous shareholder activist Carl Icahn to wage a noisy battle to dismantle the company. Motorola's misfortunes, Icahn complained in a public letter to shareholders, were the legacy of "blunders" by management. Under pressure, CEO Zander left the company, and its new chief, Greg Brown, was directed by Motorola's board to explore a sale of its mobility business. When RIM got an overture from the U.S. company's investment bankers, Balsillie and RIM's senior executives jumped at the chance to acquire the struggling mobile division. Despite its market woes, Motorola had a treasure chest of assets. Its cellphone operations and global market channels could help RIM keep pace with runaway BlackBerry demand. Motorola phone hardware could be repurposed with BlackBerry operating systems and software. If a deal could be worked out, RIM would have more clout to face Silicon Valley rivals.

What Balsillie prized most of all was Motorola's vast arsenal of intellectual property rights. There were an estimated seventeen thousand issued mobile patents, most of them for dated cellphone technology that was more valuable in the legal arena, where RIM and its competitors faced a constant onslaught of patent lawsuits. RIM's dealmaker was obsessed with intellectual property after the emotionally scarring NTP war. He lobbied governments on both sides of the border and spoke to business groups to push for reforms that might prevent the legal brinksmanship that nearly flattened RIM. Washington and Ottawa were receptive, but progress was slow. In this vacuum, tech companies strengthened their legal rights by acquiring patent collections from struggling rivals. With Motorola's patent chest, RIM would hold a much stronger hand against patent trolls and competitors alike.

Balsillie and senior RIM executives and bankers met frequently in Schaumburg with Brown and his team during the spring and summer of 2008. Balsillie initially believed the takeover would happen. Motorola was under enormous pressure from investors to sell its mobility business. Motorola's weakened condition did not prevent it from slapping a rich price tag on its mobility unit. Brown, according to people familiar with the talks, wanted $10 billion for the money-losing division. The asking price, billions more than RIM was willing to pay, didn't include patents. All Motorola put on the table were dated factories, weak phone products, and a bloated staff. After studying Motorola's books, RIM concluded the division could only survive if thousands of jobs were eliminated, a mass execution that would be left to RIM. "We didn't want all these people, but they said, 'That's your problem,'" remembers Balsillie, who, in the end, opposed shouldering what he considered "a hell of a burden."

After six months of negotiations, talks ended in August. For Motorola, the missed opportunity was devastating. With no buyers and a deepening global financial crisis, Motorola went into a tailspin. Mobility sales tumbled further and the company cut another 10,000 employees, reducing Motorola's total employee count to 60,000 from a peak of 150,000 in the late 1990s. Balsillie walked away believing Motorola Mobility was worth little more than its patents. He would later regret undestimating RIM's long-standing adversary.

/ / /

There is a small white building on Columbia Street, close to the University of Waterloo, where BlackBerrys were sent to be tortured. Beatings took place in a concrete-floored lab with a white, corrugated-steel ceiling, from which pipes, wires, and row after row of high-voltage lights hung. This was where RIM's quality assurance team tested the limits of new BlackBerry models. Phones were thrown in swirling industrial tumblers, shaken by robotic arms, dropped on cement, and subjected to extreme temperatures. Afterward, a confidential report on phone flaws was circulated to product managers and executives. The meticulous attention to quality resulted in a low phone return rate, just 3 percent.

In the summer of 2008, the quality assurance team was itself a target of abuse. RIM had to ship hundreds of thousands of Storm phones to Verizon and Vodafone. That was a problem because the new phone kept getting failing test grades. The floor of the quality assurance lab offered grim proof of Storm's fragility: shards of glass and parts everywhere. The phone's hardware engineers rejected the test findings, however. The problem, they insisted, was the quality assurance team. The pneumatic pistons that repeatedly poked Storm touch screens were too rough. These phones were not traditional Black-Berrys encased in hardy metal and plastic—they were glass-covered. Storm had to be tested by humans, the engineers insisted. So they pulled in University of Waterloo students to test the phones in the quality lab. The dazed students sat in chairs repeatedly poking the glass screens of test phones for hours. The screens survived the rhythm of human touch, but other problems soon became evident.

Storms frequently crashed. The touch screen, which hovered over a hidden dome to allow digital menus, icons, and a keyboard to be poked and clicked, was stiff, cumbersome, and unreliable. Storm was specifically designed to overcome the iPhone keyboard's biggest flaw. Millions of Americans dispatched botched, often comical messages because of iPhone's unreliable, seemingly subversive autocorrect function. Type the word "pens" and "penis" might appear. "Your dad and I are going to Disney" might turn into "Your dad and I are going to Divorce." Storm was designed to eliminate this annoyance with a glass screen that activated BlackBerry software only when a user clicked down on the screen. The floating screen, however, became less reliable the farther a user's finger moved from the center. Poke the letters *a* or *l*, letters at the opposite end of the keyboard's home row, and the activation signal grew so weak that the phone's software sometimes misunderstood the command and responded with the wrong letter. "It needed work," Craig Mc-Lennan, a RIM sales vice president who oversaw the Verizon relationship, recalls thinking when he got his hands on the device for the first time in summer 2008. "It wasn't ready for game time."

RIM insiders weren't the only ones to find fault with Storm. RIM hand-picked a few loyal customers to give the company feedback after testing early versions of the phone. One was Alexander Trewby, a vice president of mobile development with one of RIM's largest clients, Morgan Stanley. The Storm phone Trewby received in the spring of 2008 lasted an hour. "It just turned off and then we could never turn it on again," he says. When he finally got a Storm that worked he was surprised how much he disliked it. "From a hardware perspective, it was an automatic fail," says Trewby. "With the iPhone, where you tapped the screen, it was just a much more elegant solution, as opposed to physically pressing something and waiting for the click. The Storm felt a lot more machine-like, more mechanical, as if it was less electronic, less done by sensors. It was very much about hardware. It wasn't about software. We knew straight away it felt it was a wannabe. It was not as visionary, modern, as fun to use as an iPhone was. The device was dead on arrival."

More shocking to Trewby was Lazaridis's reaction when Trewby raised concerns about Storm at a private event for corporate customers during a Black-Berry conference in Orlando in May 2008. Lazaridis glared at Trewby, whom he knew, and then turned to an aide and complained: "I thought there weren't going to be any press in here." The *Wall Street Journal* that day had broken the story of Storm's impending arrival, enraging Lazaridis, who hated seeing BlackBerry product details routinely leaked to tech blog sites. But his response was as troubling to Trewby as Storm's faults. Lazaridis had turned to Trewby in the past for his thoughts on new BlackBerry features, and now he was treating him like a stranger. Lazaridis seemed to be in such denial about Storm's flaws that he was shooting the messenger. A RIM executive wrote Trewby to apologize for the CEO's reaction, but the damage was done. A huge Black-Berry fan, the London executive began doubting the Canadian company. "It gets you scared because you realize they're slipping," he says. "His back was obviously up."

RIM's founder worked closely with software and hardware teams to oversee the integration of the new touch screen with the company's existing software. It had been a problematic marriage from the beginning because the poke-and-click touch screen was so unreliable that it activated the wrong responses unless its software was in good working order and various components were assembled with care. While Conlee pushed far-flung foreign and domestic parts suppliers and contracted manufacturing companies to stay on schedule, Lazaridis fended off complaints from company veterans begging for more time. Quality shortcomings forced RIM to delay delivery four months past the initial June deadline. Problems persisted and soon the October ship date looked impossible.

The first phones rolling off production lines suffered from what RIM engineers called "high infant mortality rates," a greater chance of failing in early life. The problems persisted as the Christmas selling season approached. If the phones were not shipped before late November, there was a good chance Verizon would walk from the contract. RIM senior executives agreed it was better to ship a flawed product than no product at all. To engineers, Lazaridis repeated the same mantra: "We've bet the company on this. It's critically important. We have to get this done." When problems persisted, Yach says Lazaridis grew frustrated. "He was almost incredulous that it couldn't be done," he says.

Lazaridis's conviction that RIM could deliver a new phone within a year came down to faith, a deep abiding confidence in himself and his company. A follower of the Christian Science movement and Emmet Fox's sermons on the transformative power of human will, Lazaridis believed people could, if sufficiently determined and talented, shape their own destiny. The fabulous success of BlackBerry only cemented that belief. Where would RIM be if not for his and Balsillie's persistence in the face of countless near-fatal reversals and product challenges? BlackBerry lived because Lazaridis and Balsillie never gave up. Ever. "Mike believes that the mind can will things to happen," Balsillie says. And Lazaridis always aimed high. He didn't just want to catch up to Apple. Storm had to be better than the iPhone. "Mike thought of himself as Canada's Bill Gates. He wanted to beat Steve Jobs," Balsillie says.

For his part, Lazaridis says the rush with Storm was unavoidable: RIM couldn't afford to say no to the biggest contract in its history. Besides, RIM's engineers had done the impossible before, pushing out the Pearl in less than a year while juggling other phone launches. He was confident the magic would work again with Storm. "This is a team that prides itself on pulling off miracles, pulling all-nighters, working hard, solving the most complex problems, getting things done on time, getting things done under the wire. This is a team with a can-do spirit," he says. At first Lazaridis's faith appeared to pay off. RIM had assigned a team to hand-assemble Storm phones before they moved to mass production, and the results were impressive. Under expert hands, the movable screen had been carefully calibrated to react to user clicks. The phones worked flawlessly and Verizon's executives, according to RIM officials, loved the early samples. It was a different story when the phones were mass-produced by RIM's manufacturing partners in Mexico and Europe.

Racing by what Balsillie calls "the seat of our pants," the company pushed Storm out the door in time for Black Friday, November 28, the busiest shopping day of the year in the United States. Verizon and Vodafone had tested and approved the phone, but RIM knew they were shipping an unfinished product. Balsillie remembers the weeks before the launch as a nervous time. After years of high-speed typing on BlackBerry keys, Balsillie was dismayed at Storm's delayed response to touch-screen clicks. "It was slow," he says, like someone walking with ten-pound bags tied to each leg. When he took his concerns to Lazaridis, Balsillie says: "Mike said he'll fix it. You trust him." Other employees were not so optimistic, some privately referring to their new product as a "shit storm."

Critics were merciless about RIM's new offering. "Head-bangingly frustrating," said *New York Times* columnist David Pogue in a scathing critique two days after Storm went on sale.[11] "Storm had more bugs than a summer picnic," he wrote, going on to list a litany of complaints: "Freezes, abrupt reboots, nonresponsive controls, cosmetic glitches." Raising a question quietly asked by numerous RIM employees, the *Times* reviewer concluded, "How did this thing ever reach the market? Was everyone involved just too terrified to pull the emergency brake on this train?"

British actor and gadget reviewer Stephen Fry was similarly caustic. A fan of Apple products and BlackBerry's Bold, Fry complained about the absence of wi-fi, a free local network application available on iPhone. As for Storm's touch screen, he described the "judder, lag and jerk" of the click-screen keyboard as "a painful horror."[12] He compared typing an e-mail to "an antelope trying to open a packet of cigarettes." Storm, Fry concluded, "is the Edsel of smartphones, an absolute smeller from top to bottom."

Slamming any technology device backed by Silicon Valley's forceful public relations armies was rare in 2007. Twitter, today's social media venting platform of choice, was just a year old and technology bloggers sometimes pulled their punches out of fear of being cut off from future interviews and product events. When the British celebrity took a sledgehammer to the admired BlackBerry brand, his comments went viral. Was he trying to sabotage BlackBerry, a BBC reporter asked? Unrepentant, Fry replied, "Honestly:

play with the Storm for two days as I have and you will admire my patience at not throwing it out the window."[13]

Although reviews were devastating, BlackBerry's fans had faith in RIM's record of producing reliable phones. Borrowing a page from AT&T's Apple promotions, Verizon lubricated sales by heavily subsidizing Storm phone purchases for any customer signing up for a two-year phone contract. After rebates, the touch BlackBerry sold for $200. The low price, combined with BlackBerry's reputation for quality and innovation, attracted hundreds of thousands of customers early on. While sales soared, RIM's engineers worked feverishly to repair software glitches with upgrades. The more phones sold, the more time RIM had to clean up after its Storm. By the end of January 2009 hope grew within the company that Storm might lift off. The company's chief promoter, Balsillie, told the *Wall Street Journal* RIM was producing 250,000 phones a week to keep up with demand.[14] In a bullish forecast he pronounced that Storm was "an overwhelming success."

12 / / / OFFSIDE

On a frigid February morning in 2009 Mike Lazaridis and Jim Balsillie walked from a downtown hotel toward Toronto's city hall. News they had been dreading for years had hit the papers the day before. There was no more hiding it. The CEOs and former chief financial officer of Canada's most celebrated business had agreed to collectively pay more than C$90 million to settle allegations that RIM backdated stock options to enrich themselves and others. Now, RIM's bosses were on their way to a public hearing, a firing squad, really; penalties, sanctions, and reprimands from the Ontario Securities Commission awaited them. Restrained by lawyers from discussing the case, they said little about what lay ahead. Even if they could, the conversation would be painful. The three-year investigation into improper stock option grants had driven a wedge between them. The business partners who once finished each other's sentences were now finding it difficult to start conversations. Lazaridis and Balsillie still called and e-mailed regularly to discuss business, but it wasn't the same. When they reached a mirrored glass-and-steel office tower near city hall, the humbled executives glanced at each other. "Let's get this over with," was the best Balsillie could manage.

There was barely room for Balsillie and Lazaridis to maneuver when the elevator opened onto the twentieth floor. The hallway was crammed shoulder-to-shoulder with media. Swallowed by TV crews inching backward with rolling cameras, RIM's founders were forced to do the walk of shame. Slowly moving toward a large hearing room, the two CEOs, as always, marched to different rhythms. Lazaridis, wearing a stately blue suit with an Order of Canada pin in his lapel, moved as if in a trance, face frozen, eyes downcast. He might have been in a funeral procession. Balsillie, meanwhile, grinned maniacally into the cameras, eyes merrily alive. Light from whirring cameras picked up his flashing aqua tie. There was no shame here. RIM's chief promoter could have been ambling up a red carpet to grab an award.

The cocky smile certainly didn't play with OSC staff—men and women who had spent difficult years investigating and negotiating the forthcoming settlement. When the three members of the presiding OSC panel walked onto a raised dais at the front of the hearing room, Jim Douglas, Balsillie's lawyer, noticed some of the staff were staring with irritation at his beaming client. "Jim, you've got to stop smiling," he whispered. Balsillie turned off his movie premiere grin, but he'd made his point. He'd been through this before. When his Trinity College elders punished him for blowing his own horn too loud at dinner, the trick, he'd learned back then, was to hang tight and smile right into his accusers' faces. "They wanted to bring me down," Balsillie would later recall of the OSC hearing. Smiling, he says, was his way of saying: "I'm giving you nothing. I'm not letting you break my spirit." Lazaridis's wooden face told a different story. Sitting next to the man he blamed for the regulatory nightmare, he had the look of a defeated general.

Jim Turner, the OSC's vice chairman and head of the panel, told the crowded hearing room that the case against RIM involved "shocking" corporate misconduct and governance failures.[1] For nearly a decade RIM improperly enriched the compensation of more than sixty executives and managers by switching stock option grants to more lucrative dates. The scheme was not properly disclosed to the company's shareholders. Practices were so lax that directors never reviewed or approved many RIM option grants. Four company directors had been among the lucky recipients of backdated options. The biggest winners in the deception were the company's top executives. Options changed to more lucrative dates for Balsillie, Lazaridis, and the company's chief financial officer, Dennis Kavelman, resulted in $66 million worth of excess profits. Most of the gains were generated by a remarkable run-up in the company's stock price, but lower option prices obtained through backdating amplified the rewards.

RIM's executives and officers didn't dispute the OSC allegations. What they bitterly contested, in negotiations leading to a settlement, were the proposed penalties. One initial OSC demand, according to those familiar with discussions, was for Balsillie, who accepted responsibility for the backdating, to step down as CEO and director of the company. The OSC retreated from the requirement after RIM's lawyers argued that the loss of the company's strategic, financial, and sales chief would send the stock price of one of Canada's leading companies into a tailspin. With no successor in the wings, RIM's shareholders would suffer if Balsillie was pushed out. The other flashpoint, known only to a small circle, was Lazaridis. In the fall of 2008 his lawyers made a request for lighter penalties. His lawyers, according to people familiar with negotiations, argued Lazaridis was unaware of the scale or impropriety of the practices and therefore should not be subjected to significant regulatory sanctions.

When details of the settlement were revealed at the OSC hearing, Balsillie was the primary target. He had agreed to step down as a RIM director for a year and pay a $5 million penalty to the commission. Lazaridis remained a director and suffered a $1.5 million penalty. Together, the CEOs and Kavelman agreed to pay the commission a combined $83 million, one of the largest set of sanctions ever paid by officers of a Canadian company. The four directors during the time of the backdating, Lazaridis's childhood friend Doug Fregin and long-standing board members Kendall Cork, Douglas Wright, and James Estill, who received backdated options, were ordered to attend a directors-training course, while RIM agreed to hire an outside consultant to address boardroom failings.[2]

Once the OSC panel approved the sanctions and penalties, Balsillie's grin was back firmly in place. His next challenge was a swarm of reporters waiting in the lobby of the office tower. With a glum Lazaridis standing behind him, Balsillie, who had just yielded his board seat and a substantial fortune, faced the pack with an oddly triumphant smile. "We are very pleased to put this behind us," he told reporters. Surprised by an evident lack of contrition, a reporter asked if he wanted to apologize to shareholders. "Absolutely," Balsillie said. "We take full responsibility and accept that we've made mistakes. . . . We don't duck it one bit."[3]

When the impromptu press conference ended, Balsillie and Lazaridis left the building to drive back to Waterloo. "We just went back to work," Balsillie later recalls. Work, however, would never be the same. Several weeks after the OSC hearing, Balsillie appeared in Lazaridis's office in RIM 4 to confront his longtime partner. The two CEOs were finally free to discuss the case because the SEC had followed the OSC with a separate settlement agreement involving minor penalties of only $1.4 million. The securities investigations were over and the two CEOs were finally free to discuss the case. Agitated and emotional, Balsillie uncorked months of suppressed resentment. In his mind, Lazaridis had betrayed their partnership by going behind his back to ask for leniency from the OSC. "I was shocked and very hurt by his action," Balsillie recalls. He reminded Lazaridis of the big messes he mopped up during their fifteen-year partnership. When U.S. Robotics balked at paying for RIM's faulty modem cards in the late 1990s, it was Balsillie and his sales team that saved the company by selling thousands of the devices to Korean buyers. When Lazaridis was devastated by the NTP patent defeat, Balsillie took the reins and the emotional beating during the tortured legal odyssey. Why hadn't Lazaridis stood with Balsillie during the settlement talks? "I'm so hurt," Balsillie said.

For Balsillie, it was all out on the table. But Lazaridis did not open up the same way. Ever reserved, he didn't share with Balsillie his own disappointments. He'd told close confidants he felt betrayed by Balsillie's failure to prevent a decade of reckless backdating—and had lost his passion for a business he loved. But he didn't go there with his partner of seventeen years. Instead, he coolly informed Balsillie the securities scandal was different from previous difficulties. The U.S. Robotics and NTP crises were "business," Balsillie recalls him saying. The backdating scandal was "personal" because his reputation had been dragged through the mud. Staring evenly at a distraught Balsillie, Lazaridis said simply: "I'm sorry you feel this way." Lazaridis disputes Balsillie's account of the difficult meeting. He denies that he described the options scandal as personally damaging. He also disagrees that his discussions with securities regulators were aimed to damage Balsillie. In a written response to questions about the meeting, a spokesman for Lazaridis said: "Although Mike's lawyers obviously took necessary and appropriate steps to defend him in this matter, to the best of our knowledge this was done in cooperation with the other parties and their counsel. Mike did not instruct his counsel to take any steps that were intended to prejudice Jim or any other of the parties."

After the unresolved emotional encounter, Balsillie says he and Lazaridis "carried on" with the business of running a still rapidly growing company, but he concedes their relationship was damaged. As far as Balsillie was concerned, it was Lazaridis's actions with regulators that amounted to a "betrayal" that damaged his trust in his long-time partner. Despite the falling out, Basillie and Lazaridis insist, RIM's senior partnership remained effective in managing the business. Lazaridis continued to oversee product development, while Balsillie drove sales and services. They communicated daily, consulted regularly on major decisions, and remained respectful in meetings. Few of RIM's senior executives or directors were aware of the falling out, but in time it became apparent that, like an estranged married couple, Balsillie and Lazaridis were drifting apart and fault lines would open within the company.

One executive who became concerned about the internal divide was Larry Conlee. Aware of the options falling out, Conlee hoped the rift could be healed if Lazaridis and Balsillie spent more time together. For most of their partnership, the co-CEOs were only footsteps from each other's desks. In the mid-2000s Lazaridis moved to RIM 4 to keep close to engineering teams and the network operating center that oversaw the company's data relay network. Balsillie was blocks away in RIM 10 with the company's sales and administrative staff. Sticking together wasn't easy in Waterloo because the city's building height restrictions limited the company's ability to assemble large groups of staff under one roof. When a new building was under construction, Conlee proposed assembling all senior executives in one wing. From his experience at Motorola and earlier at RIM, Conlee felt senior executives could get a lot more accomplished chatting in hallways and over car hoods when they were in close quarters. Balsillie strongly disagreed. He wanted nothing to do with a "mahogany row" of stately offices that detached top executives from the expanding ranks. "No way would we have stayed with the level of intimacy that we had with the teams if we were all in this cordoned zone," Balsillie says. To this day, Conlee believes it was a mistake to keep the CEOs apart. "I talked to Mike and Jim about it quite often," he says. "I thought it was a problem."

/ / /

Away from the smartphone wars, Balsillie was fighting a different battle against a powerful adversary. The devoted hockey fan had been trying for years to spend some of his RIM fortune on a National Hockey League team. Two previous deals had fallen through, a 2006 agreement to buy the Pittsburgh Penguins and a 2007 deal for the Nashville Predators. Now, on July 29, 2009, he was in Chicago to face the league for a new bid. The RIM boss, who had brought along his legal pit bull, Richard Rodier, was one of three bidders for the bankrupt Phoenix Coyotes. Balsillie had signed a $212.5 million deal in May 2009 to purchase the struggling team from owner Jerry Moyes on one condition: the Coyotes would have to move to Hamilton, Ontario, an hour's drive southeast of Waterloo. To do so, he would have to get through the NHL's top brass, commissioner Gary Bettman, deputy commissioner William

Daly, and the executive committee of the league's board of governors. Bettman had a reputation as a ferocious defender of the league's corporate interests.

Balsillie had wanted this face-off for years. The boy goalie from Peterborough who once dreamed of winning a Stanley Cup could now afford a bigger fantasy, thanks to RIM's plush stock price. With a personal net worth exceeding $2 billion in RIM stock alone, Balsillie could try to win a championship trophy that was first awarded to Canadian amateurs in 1893 but which had not been won by a Canadian franchise since 1993. "I thought it would be a great thing to do," Balsillie says. For all his noble intentions, however, he appeared so unpredictable during two previous attempts to acquire troubled U.S. hockey teams that all he'd earned for his money and trouble was the contempt of a powerful professional sports league.

The backstory wasn't pretty. In 2006, Balsillie abruptly tore up a $175 million agreement to buy the struggling Pittsburgh Penguins, he would later tell a court, after the NHL insisted at the last moment he could not switch the team to Hamilton.[4] Balsillie's sudden retreat embarrassed NHL officials and Pittsburgh's hockey royalty, which supported his bid. Canadian hockey legend and Penguins part-owner Mario Lemieux told reporters he was "shocked and offended" by the about-face of a man he considered a friend.[5] Balsillie's next move to buy the Nashville Predators collapsed in 2007 amid recriminations about combative tactics to move the team north. The Phoenix Coyotes would be different, Balsillie was convinced, because the future ownership of the bankrupt team would not be decided by Bettman or NHL officials. In bankruptcy court, Balsillie believed the league would be a neutered force because the presiding judge was obligated to accept the best available deal for creditors. Once again, the Sun Tzu warrior thought he had a better chance at a victory on uneven ground. "I thought it would be decided by a judge, not the NHL," Balsillie says.

Balsillie's confidence disappeared, however, shortly after he and Rodier stepped into a large meeting room that July day in Chicago. Seated there with league officials was Craig Leipold, a Wisconsin businessman and sports investor who owned the Minnesota Wild franchise. He was also the former owner of the Nashville Predators, the man who angrily turned his back at the last minute on Balsillie's acquisition offer in 2007. As Leipold would later state in a court declaration, he had requested time with the NHL's executive committee to read a five-page statement about "surreptitious" and "bad faith" efforts by Balsillie and Rodier to devalue the Predators.[6] "I simply don't trust Jim," Leipold told the governors.[7]

Like an NHL referee standing by the penalty box, Leipold read off a list of alleged misconducts by Balsillie and his advisers. There was the time Balsillie's lawyer Rodier threatened to file an anti-competition complaint against the NHL if Leipold didn't close the Predators sale.[8] Then in May 2007 Balsillie agreed to terms that included a commitment "to make the franchise work in Nashville," Leipold said. One month later, Balsillie's advisers were negotiating an arena lease in Hamilton and selling thousands of reservations for season tickets to Hamilton Predators games. That morning, in Chicago, Leipold looked directly at Balsillie and asked how selling tickets to Hamilton fans could have possibly helped Nashville's interests. "Mr. Balsillie had the gall to say that by selling tickets for the Predators in Hamilton he had helped me by leading to a resurgence of fan interest for the franchise in Nashville," the Wisconsin millionaire later said in a court declaration.[9] According to Leipold, there was a "palpable feeling of stunned disbelief throughout the room," after Basillie spoke.[10]

By the end of the day, the NHL announced it had voted 26–0 to reject Balsillie's bid, citing an obscure bylaw requiring owners to be of "good character and integrity." In a memorandum later filed in court, the league said Balsillie failed the character test because of his conduct with the Penguins and the Predators and his "wrongdoing at RIM related to the backdating of options."

Balsillie, who knew more than a little about NHL history, was stunned by the decision. The NHL's roster of past officials is loaded with rogues and fraudsters. LA Kings owner Bruce McNall, who later would serve time in jail for defrauding banks, had recruited Bettman to the NHL in 1993. The NHL's Norris Trophy, handed out annually to the league's top defender, is named after the father of former Chicago Blackhawks owner James D. Norris, a one-time associate of mobster Frankie Carbo. Former Toronto Maple Leafs owner Harold Ballard was jailed in the 1970s for fraud and tax evasion, but he got to keep the team. Former NHL president Clarence Campbell, the Bettman of his day, was convicted in 1980 for bribing a Canadian senator. More recently, Silicon Valley entrepreneur and San Jose Sharks part-owner Gregory Reyes kept his stake in the team after being sentenced in 2008 to twenty-one months in prison for securities fraud related to one of the same types of offenses for which the NHL had red-circled Balsillie—options backdating.[11] Why the hard line on Balsillie? The league defended its unusual decision in a biting personal attack filed weeks later in court:

There is something sad . . . about Mr. Balsillie's inability to grasp the plain fact that it is his conduct, insensitivity, perceived lack of trustworthiness and unwillingness to accept responsibility for his own actions over several years that has caused the NHL Board of Governors to wish to not be associated with him in the business of professional hockey.[12]

To many hockey observers, Balsillie had bungled the opportunity to gain an NHL franchise. He had lots of money and celebrity, but he tried to strong-arm the league as if he was still outfoxing the likes of Nokia and Palm. He apparently didn't appreciate that he was seeking membership in an exclusive, tightly held country club where members were expected to play by club rules and show proper deference.

Balsillie attributes the bad blood with the NHL to the league's initial evasiveness about moving money-losing U.S. teams to Canada. He says the league had surprised him in Pittsburgh with a last-minute restriction on moving the team. The same thing happened in Nashville. "The commissioner played the 'Let's get you in and then we'll see' card to me many times, but I wanted clarity before closing any deal because I didn't trust vague future promises," says Balsillie. None of the friction, however, justified the personal attacks, he says. "I learned these guys play dirty. This is a dirty game. I learned this wasn't a place to go."

RIM's chief had solid legal grounds for thinking the NHL couldn't thwart him in an Arizona bankruptcy court. What he underestimated, however, was how much he'd angered the league. Balsillie pushed the boundaries in business because that was the way the game was played. No matter how many times he provoked customers such as BellSouth or pulled a fast one on Black-Berry Connect partners such as Nokia, customers were always clamoring for BlackBerrys. NHL owners had to be seduced, not conquered. Flattered, not flattened. "He went down this path exactly the wrong way," says a senior executive with an NHL owner at the time of Balsillie's NHL pursuits. "The governors have all the cards. You have to appeal to them and make it their idea." The devotee of *The Art of War* had failed to follow one of Sun Tzu's most famous commandments: "The supreme art of war is to subdue the enemy without fighting."

Balsillie's failed quest to acquire a hockey team cost him more than a battered ego. Employees and investors began questioning his dedication at a time when the company faced its greatest competitive challenge. It's not unusual for prominent business leaders to acquire sports franchises, but it is rare to see the boss's personal feuds spattered across front pages for months. Balsillie maintains his hockey quest didn't distract him from his primary job, and many of his RIM colleagues agree. He only spent a call or two a week on NHL business because he had a team of advisers managing his private interests, he says. At the same time, he today concedes the high-profile battles with the NHL created the impression his mind was elsewhere. "I do regret that there was a false public perception that I was not fully engaged in my duties as co-CEO of RIM. I think it gave media and various pundits an easy pass to write negative stories about RIM without ever getting to learn our business," he says.

Both Basillie and Lazaridis had a number of outside distractions by 2009. In addition to hockey, Balsillie was extending himself in government and academic fields. He sponsored and chaired a Toronto-based foreign relations policy institute, the Canadian International Council, which hosts conferences that star political experts from around the world. He endowed a Waterloo think tank, the Centre for International Governance Innovation. By 2009 CIGI had secured C$100 million in federal and provincial funding to research, study, and enhance understanding of global government, economic, and legal issues. The institute also partnered with two Waterloo universities to create the Balsillie School of International Affairs.

While Balsillie pursued the NHL and supported his think tanks, Lazaridis chased his own quixotic dreams. His new ambition was the holy grail of theoretical physics: harnessing microscopic subatomic particles. The engineering student inspired by maverick physicist David Bohm now had the means to promote innovations in quantum mechanics. Silicon Valley owed its origins to Bell Labs, the AT&T ideas factory that led to innovations in transistors, lasers, silicon cells, and communications. Lazaridis envisioned a Canadian equivalent that might one day make Waterloo "Quantum Valley," home to advances in quantum technology. It was theoretical physics that helped lead innovators to transistors and chips, crucial breakthroughs for computing and mobile communications. "I saw how powerful theoretical physics were in the last century. I saw how important it was to everything we did at RIM," says Lazaridis. The United States had science foundations to support physics research, and as early as engineering school Lazaridis dreamed of building one in his backyard. "It was one of those things that I told myself in university that if I could afford it I would start one up." He took his first step in 1999 by donating C$100 million, a contribution he later increased by C$75 million, to found the Perimeter Institute, a center devoted to theoretical physics that today employs over 150 scientists. In 2008, he announced a C$100 million investment in a more ambitious project, a University of Waterloo center devoted to new applications in quantum computing and nanotechnology.

Balsillie and Lazaridis were dreaming big, pursuing a world beyond RIM, because they could. They had hundreds of millions of dollars to spend and a growing appetite for success outside an increasingly stressed RIM. Apple, one of Silicon Valley's most successful companies, was starting to outsmart RIM in the mobile world. A patent war defeat and options scandal had cast a cloud on its management. And the personal relationship between Balsillie and Lazaridis was unraveling. RIM was developing a leadership problem at a time it most needed a strong management team. Where was the company's board of directors? As a confidential report would soon reveal, RIM's board was not in the habit of questioning management.

/ / /

RIM's top officers squirmed under a microscope all through the summer of 2009. As part of its settlement with the Ontario Securities Commission, the company hired the global consulting firm Protiviti to assess its boardroom and management practices. There was no welcome mat for Protiviti's team when it arrived in Waterloo. Balsillie and Lazaridis had a longstanding aversion to consultants; they cost too much, didn't understand the business, and wasted valuable time. Protiviti's consultants quickly understood RIM didn't want them rummaging around in its affairs.

According to a confidential seventy-two-page draft report shared only with RIM's board and the OSC, Protiviti said there were "significant challenges to our review process." RIM officials took months to hand over boardroom minutes, and when documents arrived, substantial passages were redacted. Examiners weren't allowed to copy most documents. Access to managers was limited. They were able to secure interviews with five RIM executives, but all but one were canceled. When Protiviti asked for new meeting times, "we were advised that further requested interviews would not be scheduled," the report said. In RIM's defense, Balsillie says Protiviti reached beyond its mandate, disrupting business and "racking up bills."

Despite being put through an obstacle course, Protiviti collected enough information to paint a disturbing portrait of boardroom and management practices. Two years after the backdating investigation prompted Balsillie to step down as chairman, he hadn't been replaced. Nor did the rapidly growing global business have a chief financial officer, a post left vacant when Kavelman, another OSC backdating target, moved to another job in the company. And despite being excoriated by the OSC for misusing option grants, RIM was still having trouble getting options right. Protiviti found 12 percent of option grants awarded to employees in one quarter exceeded internal company limits. One employee received duplicate option grants within a two-month period in 2009. When Protiviti asked for board minutes relating to the employee's lucky options score, the relevant passage was redacted.

Protiviti's employees were more disturbed by evidence of what they called lax executive accountability. Traditional standards for measuring CEO accomplishments didn't seem to exist at RIM. There were no written job descriptions or performance objectives for Balsillie or Lazaridis—benchmarks used by directors to measure compensation. Also missing was a succession plan. Incredibly, no one was being groomed to grab the reins if something happened to the CEOs. Weak accountability was a problem at other levels. The company set goals for lower-level managers, but Protiviti found employees "were not held accountable for meeting the objectives."

One important duty of public company directors is to oversee strategic planning, but in Waterloo it seemed like an afterthought. RIM's board paid "limited attention" to strategic planning according to Protiviti. In 2009, the year Apple started taking big bites out of BlackBerry's market share and RIM was betting heavily on Storm phones, the board's Strategic Planning Committee met exactly once, for less than two hours, according to Protiviti. As RIM stepped up acquisitions of technology companies to bolster BlackBerry services, directors had little time to assess some deals. According to Protiviti, directors sometimes learned about deals during the same meeting they were asked for approval. Elsewhere, the board's audit committee was asked to review financial press releases after publication. RIM's employee count soared 53 percent to 12,800 in 2009. The surge of new hires was so great that "a number" of new executives were not vetted or approved by the board, Protiviti said. The report attributed the board's inactivity to a lack by some directors of "sufficient understanding of the company's business" and excessive deference to Balsillie and Lazaridis. "For these and other reasons, there has been some hesitancy for directors to question or challenge management," the report concluded.

Protiviti's report landed like a bomb in RIM's executive offices the fall of 2009. In media and investment circles, RIM remained a global success story. Revenues were nearly doubling annually and the company was adding new

BlackBerry subscribers at a remarkable rate of 49,000 daily. RIM's executives believed they deserved accolades, not a scathing report. RIM's response to the report was aggressively defensive. In a filing to the OSC, the company dismissed Protiviti's findings as "unnecessarily judgmental," "inappropriate," and "objectionable." What mattered most to investors, its executives believed, was growth and profits, and few could top RIM's record there. If governance was so bad at RIM, why was the company prosperous?

Balsillie later complained that Protiviti's report "was very harsh on RIM's governance even though we were at the time the fastest-growing company in the world and very profitable too." The consultants' best insight, he says, was a call for directors with industry experience. "Mike and I were basically on our own, navigating unchartered waters," he says today. "Mike and I made mistakes, but they were honest mistakes. We were 100 percent dedicated to RIM's success and would have immediately welcomed any resource that would help us, especially new tech-savvy board members. But these people were in very short supply in Canada, despite the false myth that we sought to 'control the board.'" To other RIM insiders, the weak board was the legacy of two strong-willed founders who favored compliant directors. RIM's global sales chief, Patrick Spence, says Balsillie and Lazaridis assembled a board of directors that would allow them to run RIM "the way they wanted." RIM's co-CEOs, Spence says, would have benefited from more experienced and independent directors when the company struggled with legal and product reversals. "Those two are smart enough to know now that if they picked other people, maybe it would have helped along the way and helped them. That's the way they should have been looking at it, as opposed to something that maybe rubber-stamps."

Protiviti's long list of RIM governance failures, which included 106 recommendations to beef up company leadership, was to be publicly released as part of the OSC settlement agreement. But after a six-month tug-of-war between RIM, Protiviti, and the regulator, a watered-down fifteen-page compromise was quietly posted April 2010 on a remote corner of the OSC's website. RIM didn't issue a press release or file the report at the online library for Canadian public company regulatory filings, the System for Electronic Document Analysis and Retrieval. It would be fifteen months before the media discovered the abbreviated study.[13] The final public report made no mention of RIM's efforts to rein in Protiviti. Nor did it reveal concerns about the board's oversight challenges. The big media reveal was Protiviti's recommendation that RIM appoint an independent chairman of the board to ensure "strong and active independent leadership to exercise effective oversight of the co-CEOs, who are founders of the company and who exercise great influence in all aspects of RIM's affairs."

Eight months later, on December 16, 2010, RIM announced that the chairman's seat, empty for three years, had been filled. Earlier in the day its board voted to give co-CEOs Balsillie and Lazaridis the additional duties of co-chairmen. Ignoring Protiviti's recommendation and standard Canadian boardroom practice of separating the jobs of chair and CEO, RIM handed supervision of its board to two bosses whose personal relationship was in tatters. Lazaridis and Balsillie had dodged the governance police with their new boardroom clout, but the controversy over their leadership was just beginning.

13 / / / DISCONNECT

Jim Balsillie wasn't going to waste a minute of the short flight to New Jersey aboard RIM's Dassault Falcon 900 jet. The RIM chief had been summoned to Verizon Wireless headquarters in Basking Ridge, and as they sat in their boardroom in the sky, Balsillie led a team of RIM sales executives one last time through the possible scenarios that lay ahead. Mike Lazaridis was not along for the ride. The man who had sold Verizon on Storm had turned down his partner's invitation to face the carrier alongside him.

It was spring 2009, and the Storm's initial success was now a distant memory. "It was the best-selling initial product we ever had," says Lazaridis, with 1 million devices sold in the first two months. "We couldn't meet demand." But as Verizon customers—many of them first-time BlackBerry buyers—began using the Storm, something didn't seem right. The browser was painfully slow. The clickable screen didn't respond well in the corners and the device often froze and reset. BlackBerry devotees who tried Storm found it awkward and slow typing with one big button, rather than a physical keyboard. The reviewers had been right. "The thing was a mess," says Jon Rettinger of the consumer gadget review site TechnoBuffalo. Rettinger was one of the first people to get his hands on the device before it was released to the public. "It was fine for phone calls, but unusable for any sort of input at all." Customers flooded back to stores dissatisfied with their touch-screen BlackBerrys.

Balsillie knew returns were high. What he didn't realize was how severe the problem was. As their meeting got under way, Verizon's chief marketing officer, John Stratton, laid out the shocking news to his guests from Waterloo. Virtually every one of the first batch of about 1 million Storms shipped needed replacing. Many of the replacements were being returned as well. The Storm was a complete failure, and he wanted RIM to pay. "You're going to make us whole on the money we've spent fixing your Storm product problems," Stratton told Balsillie, "or we'll revisit our whole supplier relationship with you. This is your responsibility. We expect you to step up because this is your fault, not ours." Verizon wanted close to $500 million from RIM.

The options were dire. If Balsillie gave in, it would set a bad precedent and wipe out that quarter's earnings. RIM would have a public relations fiasco on its hands, forced to reveal how poorly Storm had fared. RIM had worked hard to build its relationship with Verizon, but there was no certainty that caving would win him any favors with an unsatisfied customer.

"I can't write a check like that," Balsillie said. Instead, he and his team walked Stratton through the action plan they had rehearsed on the plane. Balsillie offered Stratton a range of concessions, including a free repair and upgrade program and a cache of complimentary BlackBerrys. The fix would cost RIM more than $100 million, but that would barely dent RIM's income statement compared to the bath it would have to take to make Verizon whole.

Stratton wasn't happy, but he had little choice. Verizon had signed a "take-or-pay" deal, meaning it was stuck with the units it committed to buy. Stratton warned Balsillie this would dramatically change the carrier's relationship with RIM. But Balsillie and sales vice president Craig McLennan, who attended the meeting, believed Verizon would forgive them. "RIM had faced challenging situations in the past and we'd always figured out a way to make it work," says McLennan.

At first, that seemed to be the case. Verizon launched promotions to move more Storms through mid-2009 and committed to sell the sequel, Storm 2, that fall. But McLennan soon sensed something wasn't right. Demand from Verizon for the Curve, another BlackBerry handset, fell significantly below expectations over the summer months and its commitment to Storm 2 was lukewarm. If the carrier was still looking for its Apple killer, McLennan could tell from the size of its order that Storm 2 wasn't it. Whatever Verizon was planning to promote during the upcoming pre-Christmas marketing blitz that year, BlackBerry wouldn't get the starring role. "We knew something was going on; we just didn't know what or with whom," says McLennan.

/ / /

Storm's failure was a rude awakening that resonated deeply within RIM. For the first time since it went public, RIM had delivered a product that widely missed the mark. Given the opportunity to vault past Apple and regain its lead in the smartphone race, RIM had fallen short. RIM was used to winning praise and adulation for its devices; now critics were questioning whether it could still innovate."Everybody was upset. It was demoralizing for the whole organization," says Don Morrison. "You're shattering the very fabric of what BlackBerry stood for." Larry Conlee, who accepts his part of the blame for Storm, says: "We thought it was within our ability to get it done. We were wrong. I think people were embarrassed."

But Lazaridis didn't treat Storm like a failed product. It was RIM's first crack at a new technology. Sometimes, like with the Bullfrog and the Leapfrog a decade earlier, manufacturers needed a second try to get things right. When he looked at Storm, Lazaridis saw its technical achievements: it had a good camera, video streaming capabilities, a great speaker, and a replaceable battery. It was Verizon's first 3G device. Most of all, he loved the clickable screen. Lazaridis hated the sensation of typing on glass, of using a touch-screen keyboard that didn't physically respond to every click. He couldn't fathom that consumers might not love his clickable screen—it had to be the fault of his staff for delivering a poorly built product. "We let Mike down, in his mind, because he made a request and we didn't deliver," says Morrison. "Whether the request is reasonable or not is not part of that sentence." David Yach, Lazaridis's chief technology officer in charge of software, shouldered much of the blame from Lazaridis for Storm's shortcomings. "He would say, 'You must have crappy people,'" Yach says. "He was clearly frustrated. From his perspective he felt that he was let down."

If the smartphone world was shifting to touch, Lazaridis was convinced Storm was the kind of device BlackBerry should continue to make and one that consumers would embrace. RIM would try again with a clickable screen on Storm 2. Lazaridis believed it would succeed now that the bugs on the original Storm were fixed. Despite Storm's dissatisfied customers, there was still huge consumer interest: one year after the Storm launch it ranked third only to the Pearl and iPhone in buyer intentions among prospective U.S. smartphone buyers, according to the market research firm comScore. But the improvements on Storm 2—including new technology that enhanced the click screen's responsiveness—didn't help: sales were tepid. It wasn't until well into development of a third clickable touch-screen device for AT&T in early 2010 that Lazaridis abandoned the click feature altogether. That only happened after the carrier requested RIM drop the mechanical technology and just do a regular touch screen, like its rivals.

Although the market rejected his initial touch-screen approach, Lazaridis believed the four pillars of BlackBerry's success—good battery life, miserly use of carrier spectrum, security, and the ability to type—still applied in the new smartphone world and gave his company its competitive advantage. To him, those elements "made a BlackBerry a BlackBerry," says one former top-level executive. Two years after Apple's launch, it still amazed Lazaridis that iPhone users had to cart around adaptors to power up depleted batteries. His early prediction that Apple would cause AT&T headaches also proved right. By 2009, users of the network-hogging iPhone were squeezing the carrier to its capacity, reducing overall network reliability for all customers. Consumers took to social media to complain about the lousy service and Consumer Reports ranked AT&T worst for dropped calls. The mobile carrier's CEO, Ralph de La Vega, further rankled customers by warning he would have to start jacking up prices or cap data use. AT&T hadn't counted on the flood of data use that was overwhelming its network, and Apple's unwillingness to help worsened relations between the two. While AT&T was activating millions of iPhones per quarter—drawing customers away from other carriers—and charging 1.6 times more than other subscribers, the huge subsidy it paid Apple to offset the cost of the iPhone cut deeply into its earnings.[1]

But there was no going back. Apple may have broken the rules for smartphone makers, but it was setting the agenda for the wireless industry. RIM, like others, were now followers. "We built a perfectly evolved, optimized service and product offering that made the industry take off," says Lazaridis. "There was a point where the carrier, by changing the rules, forced all the other carriers to change the rules eventually. It allowed Apple to reset what the expectations were. Conservation didn't matter. Battery life didn't matter. Cost didn't matter. That's their genius. We had to respond in a way that was completely different than what people expected."

By early 2009, Lazaridis decided the answer was to put a better Internet browser on the BlackBerry. He had long been frustrated that RIM's browser was inferior to the one on his computer. Most websites were not built for mobile devices, so in the early days RIM had custom-built technology that grabbed data from the sites and filtered them into barebones versions of the pages for BlackBerry users—the "baby Internet," as Steve Jobs had called it. Yach's team had built a new browser for Bold and Storm that more closely resembled the iPhone's browser, but it was often slow and awkward; pages didn't fully display and were harder to navigate.

Lazaridis realized that to match Apple, RIM would have to base its next browser on the freely available technology called WebKit. It was commonly used on personal computers and rendered the best handheld surfing experience available, like the iPhone's Safari browser. That summer, Lazaridis bought a Toronto start-up called Torch Mobile for $13.6 million. Torch had built WebKit browsers for Motorola, and Lazaridis was convinced it made the fastest mobile browser in the market. Now it was his.

/ / /

If the failure of Storm sent Lazaridis back to the lab with a sense of purpose, it left Balsillie winded. For a leader who thrived on ambiguity, Balsillie found it hard to grapple with the new competitive dynamic. Speaking to students at the Asper School of Business in Winnipeg in June 2009, he declared: "Strategic ambiguity [is] death to a company. . . . It paralyzes organizations." Unbeknown to the students, he was talking in part about his own company.

To Balsillie, RIM was in an existential crisis, mired in what he describes as "strategic confusion." The company's business had been disrupted on several levels, with no obvious path forward. Was RIM supposed to defend the QWERTY keyboard, or jump all-in and become a touch-screen smartphone maker? Was it supposed to challenge Apple at the high end of the smartphone market or focus on the lower end with devices like its Curve and Gemini models, which were driving heady sales gains in foreign markets where Apple wasn't yet a factor? Should the company stick to its closed, proprietary software technology or open its platform?

One of the biggest puzzles was what to do about apps. For years Balsillie had fought carriers for the right to sell apps to customers, reassuring them RIM was "constructively aligned" with the wireless carriers. Then Apple waltzed in with an app store despite AT&T exclusion from any app revenues. Now RIM was forced to play catchup. Unlike RIM, Apple had an army of outside developers who had already built consumer apps for its computers and iPods and were primed to do the same for the iPhone. By the time BlackBerry launched its app store in spring 2009, iPhone customers had already down-loaded 1 billion apps.[2] But, Balsillie wondered, was RIM taking the right ap-proach or should it stick to its "constructive alignment" narrative and leave the sale of apps to carriers?

Balsillie struggled with each question. "I was strategically confused for a period of time when the game changed," he says. "There was tremendous limbo-esqueness. Where do we dance? Apple had the same strategy clearly in 2007–08 that we had in 1999, and now we had to re-examine" every ele-ment of RIM's approach. "The Storm failure made it clear we were not the dominant smartphone company anymore. We're grappling with who we are because we can't be who we used to be anymore, which sucked. . . . It's not clear what the hell to do."

The duo at the top of RIM had survived several near-death experiences together, but their relationship was still smarting from the options scandal, and neither could rely on the other like they had in order to push the com-pany forward. Lazaridis didn't have a revolutionary device for the Apple era that hungry young evangelists could peddle to dazzled stockbrokers and CEOs. Balsillie didn't have a BlackBerry Connect–type play to rope in the competition and corner corporate customers.

Few outsiders would have described RIM as struggling in 2009. RIM was adding more than 1 million BlackBerry subscribers a month; revenue in its fiscal year ending February 28, 2009, almost doubled to $11 billion, and it grew another 35 percent the next year as Fortune crowned RIM the fastest-growing company in the world. Interbrand named BlackBerry the world's sixty-third most valuable brand, ahead of Avon, Harley-Davidson, and Porsche.[3] That November, the board approved the purchase of another Falcon jet.

But RIM's growth had pulled it in different directions. By 2009, sales to the stalwart corporate and government market had crested. The vast major-ity of sales were coming from consumers, a group RIM knew little about. An increasing number of customers were in markets like South America, the Mid-dle East, South Africa, and Indonesia that were still dominated by old-style Nokia and Motorola cellphones, and where RIM was still the top purveyor of smartphones—for now.

Trying to satisfy two sets of customers—consumers and corporate users—could leave the company pleasing neither. When RIM executives showed off plans to add a camera and game and music programs to some of its products to several hundred Fortune 500 chief information officers at a company event in 2010, they weren't prepared for the backlash that followed. Corporate customers didn't want such personal distractions on their smartphones, said a former RIM executive who attended the session.

Meanwhile, the rush to sell consumer apps exposed one of RIM's glaring shortcomings: it had never adequately invested in software tools or offered much support to outside developers, which frustrated many who tried to write programs for BlackBerry. "We got caught flat-footed as the nature of app development changed," says Yach. It had never been a priority because mobile apps had never been a big moneymaker until Apple changed the game. Balsillie initially thought RIM only needed a handful of consumer apps to be competitive. "I didn't believe in the consumer app game," he says. "I'll own that."

Not only was Apple's development platform easier to write for, its operating system also supported more vivid apps. BlackBerry's operating system was based on Java, a computer code that corporate customers liked because it was secure, dependable, and ideal for thousands of no-nonsense business applications like programs for traveling repair service pros. Where it fell short was on graphics: Java took longer to process and was not well suited for high-performance graphics, like 3-D effects on games. "It was difficult to get the app community to rally around the platform, particularly the consumer guys, because the platform really wasn't built effectively for them," says Tyler Lessard, RIM's vice president of developer relations at the time. "It was difficult to build what we'd refer to as sexy apps that had a really great user experience." As the months went by, the iPhone app store offered tens of thousands and then hundreds of thousands of apps. BlackBerry never managed to attract more than a fraction of that amount.

RIM tried to downplay the lack of apps on its platform, arguing there was a lot of repetition or frivolity out in app world. "We don't need two hundred fart apps," Alan Panezic, RIM's vice president of platform product management, told an interviewer in defense of his company's smaller app offering compared to Apple's.[4] "For us, apps are all about adding real value to the end user's life and creating revenue for developers." But that ignored the fact that some of the most popular apps, including Netflix and Instagram, bypassed RIM altogether.

/ / /

The same problems that bedeviled app developers also thwarted RIM's own software engineers as they began to adapt their new Torch browser onto the existing BlackBerry operating system. It took an agonizingly long time to fix the BlackBerry code to accommodate Torch, and then the browser ran slow— but it wasn't Torch's fault. "The challenge we had was that the Torch browser was written assuming it had a fully featured operating system underneath it," says Yach. It didn't. Ever since RIM had built its first cellular BlackBerry nearly a decade earlier, it had used a variation of Java to run the device. It was a clever decision at the time: the custom-built Java operating system was so self-contained that RIM could power the entire device with a single computer chip, not two, like most other handhelds. That was a big part of the reason it was so efficient with batteries. The Java system was a versatile workhorse. It worked with different chips and different networks, ran the operating system, supported outside applications, protected the radio from interference, and contained security features that made it perfect for the tasks of its business and government users. "We had always kept costs of devices down and had very skinny operating systems," said Yach. "It only had what it needed, nothing more. It was small and efficient, but now we needed something else."

What made the Java system ideal to run a narrowly focused e-mail device left it ill-suited to handle the more complicated functions of a smarter smartphone. The iPhone operating system was based on the powerful software that ran full Macintosh computers. RIM, by contrast, had been patching up the same skinny operating system for years, making it increasingly unwieldy, slow, and long due for an overhaul. The system was so tangled that Lazaridis often referred to Java as "spaghetti code."

To compete, Lazaridis realized RIM needed more than a browser: it needed a new operating system to support that browser and other features. RIM had to move away from writing proprietary custom-built code and instead use open-source language commonly used by software engineers. He had to open up BlackBerry and invite the world in before outside developers turned their back on RIM for good.

"The challenge went to the bones of the company," says Lazaridis. "We said, 'What this really means is we are not positioned for the future.' And that's what we had to get to. The tricky part is, how do you take an organization that had been so successful, had literally changed the world, and get them to embrace a whole new platform, a whole new technology, a whole new operating system—literally, a whole new language?"

For Lazaridis, this meant he would be putting RIM through its biggest transformation ever. He had to reach "a new equilibrium" for the company, and he could see that by the time he was done, he would need a lot fewer people working on software than the roughly five thousand people now reporting to David Yach. "We had no choice," says Lazaridis. "I told Jim when we started, 'You realize that very few companies have ever survived a platform change.'"

/ / /

By 2009 another challenger was gaining ground in the smartphone war. The secret smartphone team deep within Google had immediately known it would have to completely change course the moment Steve Jobs unveiled the iPhone in January 2007. Ten months later, Google announced it wouldn't make a smartphone at all; it would license its operating system, Android, for free to any handset maker that wanted it. There wasn't much interest initially. Google had to pay HTC millions of dollars to make the first Android phone, the G1,[5] which sold poorly after it was released by T-Mobile two months before Storm. Carriers were leery of Google. Like Apple, they viewed the rapidly growing software company with suspicion. Google had entered the bidding for wireless spectrum in 2007, driving up prices for operators that actually needed the capacity. It was a move Verizon CEO Ivan Seidenberg likened in an interview with author Ken Auletta to "wak[ing] up the bears"—that is, wireless carriers. He warned they might "come out of the woods and start beating the shit out of you."[6]

But in March 2008, Lowell McAdam, the chief executive of Verizon's wireless division, left the bear claws at home and visited Eric Schmidt at Google's Silicon Valley campus for a friendly chat. They agreed to set their differences aside and continue talking.[7]

After the disappointment of Storm, Verizon was still looking for its Apple killer. "We needed to get in the game," John Stratton told *Wired* magazine in 2011. "And we realized that if we were going to compete with the iPhone, we couldn't do it ourselves."[8] Verizon decided to make a big bet on Android. Now it needed to find a phone maker. It turned to the manufacturer that had slipped through RIM's fingers just months before: Motorola. Shortly after rebuffing RIM's takeover entreaties in August 2008, Motorola's new handset boss, Sanjay Jha, declared the struggling electronics company would start making Android phones.[9] At the time it seemed like a desperation move by the fading cellphone maker. By early 2009—as the Storm debacle unfolded—Verizon, Google, and Motorola were working together on a new touch-screen phone to come out for the following holiday season. While Balsillie puzzled over the future of apps, Verizon shook off its past fears and encouraged Google to launch a robust and well-stocked app store for Android.[10] Google in return agreed to give its entire 30 percent cut on the sale of apps to the carrier. The walled garden RIM had struggled against for years was opening up.

Motorola's phone had a slide-out keyboard and a full touch screen. It looked cold and unfriendly, so the team gave it a cold, unfriendly name: Droid.[11] After its Storm launch fell short of expectations in fall 2008, Verizon positioned Droid as its anti-iPhone for the 2009 holiday season, backed by a $100 million marketing campaign.

The first time he saw the Droid advertisements in October 2009, McLennan was taken aback. Some commercials portrayed an alien robot invasion. Others boldly declared "iDont," a play on iPhone that highlighted all the shortcomings of the iPhone that Android addressed, including the ability to run multiple apps simultaneously, take five-megapixel pictures, and allow users to customize the device. "It was bold and muscular," McLennan says. "I thought it was polarizing, appealing to males, robotic, and macho."

If the Droid invasion was meant to capture iPhone customers, however, it had a very different effect. Droid did not put a dent in Apple's roughly 25 percent share of the U.S. smartphone market.[12] Instead, Droid immediately muscled away customers from Palm and Microsoft, which saw their collective share collapse over the next year. Before long, Droid was taking a bite out of BlackBerry as well. RIM's North American sales for the third quarter, which included the busy Thanksgiving sales season, fell 5,000 units below its internal forecast of 6.2 million smartphones. It was a slight miss in an otherwise good quarter and was obscured by its mushrooming international growth. But it was a sign of things to come. The next quarter, RIM fell 652,000 units short of its internal goal in North America. Apple had trimmed RIM's share of the U.S. smartphone market from close to 50 percent to the low 40s, but it held there until mid-2010, when RIM's market share started shifting to Android. Google ended 2010 with the top-selling smartphone platform in the United States and worldwide, featured on nearly 80 million smartphones in dozens of countries, up from less than 1 million two years earlier.[13] Much of that could be traced to the opening RIM left when it failed to give Verizon an effective rival to the iPhone two years earlier. "If Storm had worked, Verizon would never have done Droid," says Balsillie. "When we didn't do the job for Verizon, they gave the keys to the kingdom to Google."

If Apple's arrival and Storm's failure had left Balsillie in a state of strategic confusion, the ascent of Android made RIM's situation even more complicated. RIM wasn't just competing with one or two handset makers, but with dozens, even hundreds—all given a new lease on life by Google's smartphone platform, licensed for free to any taker. "The game had changed for RIM," says Balsillie. "We were no longer marching to Pretoria. Now it was about surviving."

/ / /

RIM's sales VP, Craig McLennan, was bracing for another bad meeting with Verizon. Nearly a year had passed since Balsillie had turned down the carrier's half-billion-dollar demand for the Storm debacle. Now, RIM's share of Verizon smartphone sales was in free fall, from 96 percent in the third quarter of 2009 to less than 40 percent by early 2010 as the Droid captured a significant chunk of its business. RIM couldn't afford to make another mistake with Verizon. But as he entered a Barcelona hotel accompanied by his other CEO, Mike Lazaridis, McLennan sensed RIM was indeed about to once again let down the largest wireless carrier in the United States.

It was February 2010 and a delegation of RIM executives was in the Spanish cultural and corporate capital for the wireless industry's big annual convention, which had uprooted from Cannes several years earlier. Verizon had sent out word to the handset manufacturers: it was investing billions of dollars in the latest network technology, known as 4G, to deliver significantly faster wireless Internet speeds than 3G. The carrier expected to roll out its 4G network at the end of the year and wanted to make sure its handset suppliers were ready.

Unlike rival handset makers, Lazaridis didn't come to Barcelona armed with 4G device prototypes, but with a physics lecture. He was never shy about teaching carrier executives how network technology worked—Lazaridis often knew better than they did—or explaining how "new" and "more expensive" rarely translated into better performance. If the science wasn't sound, he'd say so. "One of the things that we've really internalized here at RIM is the belief in the numbers . . . and the general understanding of physics," Lazaridis had told an interviewer two years earlier. "The bottom line is that physics rules. . . . In a high-tech environment, if you don't understand the physics of your particular industry or your particular technology [or] the limitations imposed by those physics or mathematics, it's really at your peril."[14]

He was usually right: the performance of the latest and greatest network technology often fell short of the hype. He'd seen carriers invest tens of billions of dollars to upgrade their networks to 3G, when in his mind 2.5G still sufficed. "BlackBerry worked perfectly on 2.5G. It was all you needed," says Lazaridis. "So any upgrade to the network to some new technology, from a BlackBerry value proposition, provided only cost, complexity, and delay." Lazaridis and his engineering team had studied 4G technology and knew how Verizon's existing system worked. Now he was going to explain to Verizon why they were wrong about 4G.

Verizon Wireless's marketing vice president, Jeff Dietel, ushered Lazaridis, McLennan, RIM handset boss Thorsten Heins, and the CEO's chief technology adviser, radio engineer Mark Pecen, into a hotel meeting room where a half dozen Verizon counterparts awaited them.

Lazaridis had no 4G devices to show them. Instead, he told the Verizon team he didn't think the carrier could pull off its 4G plans. It would be difficult to do the network upgrade based on its existing technology, he said, because that would require its network technology supplier Qualcomm to make a heavy investment of its own. "My message was that I thought that 4G was amazing," says Lazaridis. "I thought 4G was going to happen. I just didn't believe there was a need for us to build 4G devices to work [with Verizon's existing technology] ever. I thought when they go to [4G] they would phase out" their existing technology standard, known as CDMA, in favor of an updated technology better suited to 4G. Lazaridis had long harbored doubts about CDMA and couldn't foresee how RIM could build a device for such a network. RIM had no existing products large enough to fit the chipsets and antennae required for 4G. It would have to make much bigger devices, and they would burn up batteries quickly and cost $100 more each to produce. "It was an ugly solution. It was big. Lot of parts," says Lazaridis. RIM had been testing a 4G phone in its lab, but Lazaridis didn't like its battery performance and had the project stopped.

As Lazaridis and his network specialist Mark Pecen spoke, McLennan could see the Verizon team getting impatient. Lazaridis was not telling the carrier team what they wanted to hear. "You could tell by their body language," McLennan says. It was going to be a long hour. "We went in with the premise that we would educate them on 4G and the shortcomings of the technology," McLennan says. "I don't think we were aware how far down the path they were" to investing in 4G. "We went in and talked network, and our competitors went in and talked the product they were going to build for that network. That was the disconnect."

When Lazaridis finished, Dietel told the RIM team "Respectfully, we've made our decision." Verizon would indeed be launching 4G. The investment would give the carrier the equivalent of a brand-new highway to handle data traffic that was starting to clog its existing network, and which would become further congested once Verizon was able to start selling iPhones in early 2011. It would be heavily promoting 4G phones to move customers over to its upgraded network. With his talk of preserving precious network capacity, Lazaridis was peddling an old story, and it didn't resonate as it once had. Consumers were stampeding to buy Apple and Android devices and carriers needed to give them the bandwidth space to run. Physics no longer ruled; market realities did.

As they left the meeting, McLennan and Heins knew something bad had just happened. RIM had again failed to deliver what Verizon was looking for, and this time didn't even seem the slightest bit interested. It was one thing to try to play catchup in the smartphone race with Apple, but here, RIM was taking itself right out of the running of the industry's next big wave. Ultimately, Lazaridis would realize his mistake. Verizon's chief technology officer, Richard Lynch, who pushed 4G, "was right, I was wrong. He was going to put in 4G in North America come hell or high water," says Lazaridis.

By then it would be too late. On their flight back to North America, the key discussion point for Verizon executives was, "How do we turn off Black-Berry?"[15] RIM's largest customer "put us in a corner that day," says a RIM insider with first-hand knowledge of the carrier's thinking. By 2011, Verizon would shift most marketing support away from RIM phones to 4G products and to the iPhone after AT&T's four-year exclusive ran out. RIM had failed to deliver an Apple killer when its top customer needed it or a 4G phone when Verizon wanted it. The consequences would come to haunt RIM at its darkest hour.

14 / / / GOAT RODEO

For the first time since the options scandal, Lazaridis was feeling invigorated about RIM. He couldn't wait to share the news. "I have seen the future," he wrote in an e-mail to Balsillie in October 2009. Lazaridis had found what he was looking for to secure the future of the company. RIM not only had a chance to leap ahead of Apple and Google, he felt, but could set a course for a decade of groundbreaking leadership in mobile computing.

The reason for his excitement was a brilliant and outspoken programmer named Dan Dodge. Like Lazaridis, Dodge was one of the most celebrated scientist-entrepreneurs to emerge from University of Waterloo in the early 1980s. Dodge's company, Ottawa-based QNX Software Systems, built a program known as a microkernel that acted as the nucleus of some of the most powerful systems in the world. QNX's technology, called Neutrino, powered the Cisco routers that ran the Internet, as well as nuclear power plants, credit card authorization systems, air-traffic control systems, high-precision medical equipment, and digital entertainment systems in luxury cars. The QNX technology was famous among industrial controls experts for its reliability and its "self-healing" ability to recover from software faults on the fly. Machines based on QNX technology had operated continuously without a software glitch for over a decade: a customer once told *Fortune* "the only way to make this software malfunction is to fire a bullet into the computer running it."[1] In 2004 Dodge sold the company to Harman International Industries and stayed on to run it. Now he wanted out from under the control of the cash-strapped stereo maker; he reached out to RIM.

Lazaridis and Yach flew to Ottawa on a company jet and met Dodge at the airport, where he pitched them on QNX. Lazaridis was smitten. Dodge was a kindred spirit—a scientist by trade and hobby who spent evenings and weekends coding and held strong opinions about his field—a "geek's geek," as Yach describes him. "We just got excited thinking about all the possibilities" about working together, says Lazaridis. Dodge, an excitable lanky man with a high, squawky voice and a striking resemblance to Microsoft founder Bill Gates, believed that "without software, life as we know it would grind to a halt," he wrote in a 2006 column for a computing trade publication.[2] Dodge was on a mission to show developers "the true potential" software could unleash and urged them to "ramp up their efforts to ensure the products they unleash upon the world aren't compromised by poor design, bad code or malevolent hackers."

Not only was Dodge a genius and a successful entrepreneur, "he was somebody that was current," says Lazaridis. Dodge had built a system that was as secure as BlackBerry "but far more advanced, far more sophisticated, far more solid," Lazaridis says. It was written in the fast C++ computer language using open-source industry standards, unlike BlackBerry's closed system written in slower Java. Lazaridis was particularly excited that QNX supported Adobe Flash, used to program the sophisticated video and gaming software on the Web, as well as open-source browsers like the one made by Torch, and its software worked with the most cutting-edge computer chips. By combining QNX's technology with the latest processors and other innovations coming to market, Lazaridis believed RIM could put an elegant, sophisticated, full computer experience in the hands of users—and put RIM back into the lead of the smartphone race. "I saw a much bigger opportunity for the future of RIM than just BlackBerry," he says. "I saw that QNX could play a huge role in that."

RIM began negotiating with Harman and bought QNX in April 2010 for $200 million. Lazaridis was eager to get QNX working on RIM's next generation of smartphones—but first he had to make sure Dodge's technology could be scaled down to a palm-sized device. By early 2010, he had a secret assignment for Dodge and the QNX team. If Dodge delivered, it would herald massive changes within RIM.

/ / /

As Lazaridis gazed excitedly into the future, other RIM leaders were growing anxious about the present. With Apple and Android eating into BlackBerry's market share, many RIM executives, impassioned by the belief they worked for one of the most innovative and exciting companies in the world, fell into despair, feeling powerless to do anything about their company's fortunes. Bruised by the Storm experience and confused by the apparent rift between Balsillie and Lazaridis, executives feuded more frequently over turf and for the attention of their CEOs. Some turned to Don Morrison, the company's kindly Father Time, who had long been the de facto friend-in-need for executives. Morrison in turn referred them to Donn Smith, the unorthodox personal life coach who had helped Balsillie pull himself back from the edge during the NTP crisis. Morrison had become a disciple after Balsillie sent his wife and him to see Smith when their marriage almost unraveled in the fall of 2009. After three days in British Columbia with Smith, Morrison says the marriage was saved. He was convinced he had found the antidote for RIM's troubled management in Smith. The company wouldn't be able to fix its problems unless its executives could reclaim their confidence and "internal perfection" through Smith's I Am Energy program, Morrison thought. Over the next two years, Morrison would refer three dozen RIM executives to see his and Balsillie's personal saviour, with costs covered by RIM's leadership training budget.

It would take more than a self-help guru to fix the issues at RIM. As Lazaridis and Balsillie struggled to chart a new course for the company, its future direction became increasingly unclear and many insiders felt they lacked leadership when they most needed it. The two-headed structure exacerbated the problems. It presented challenges at the best of times: Lazaridis was a technologist who had little patience for administration, while Balsillie disdained organizational structure altogether. Many executives had overlapping roles, with multiple people doing the same jobs, some reporting to more than one boss. Both CEOs wanted to keep alive the entrepreneurial spirit that made RIM nimble when it was outsmarting giants, but that was difficult as the company's ranks expanded to fourteen thousand employees globally by early 2010 and it trailed in the smartphone innovation race.

Making matters worse was the departure of Larry Conlee. The chief operating officer reporting to Lazaridis ran a tight operation in product engineering and manufacturing but he always wanted more. Around 2005, he made a play to become president of the company, proposing to have Morrison and his sales and marketing organization report to him instead of Balsillie. "Accountability would have been better than it was" with the two organizations under one leader who reported jointly to the co-CEOs, Conlee says. Lazaridis was in favor but Balsillie preferred the status quo, so nothing changed. "I didn't really worry about it" at the time, says Conlee. "Mike and Jim . . . had to give something up" for Conlee to get what he was asking for.

By 2009, Conlee was in his early sixties, with young grandchildren and a new pair of knees. He was a multimillionaire, thanks to his RIM stock options. He had stayed at RIM longer than expected and plateaued in a role lacking the full responsibilities he felt he should have. With no prospect of advancement, he decided to retire that June. "I had done all I could do," Conlee says.

Conlee left on good terms, but his departure couldn't have come at a worse time. The ex-Motorola veteran and astute corporate politician had done more than keep operations humming. He was a leveling force between the two CEOs, ensuring they were always aligned on vision and priorities. Conlee was one of the few executives who could speak the truth to Lazaridis without fear of being thrown out of his office; and he made time every week for one-on-one meetings with Balsillie. Conlee also possessed a rare gift—what he called a "pocket veto" from both CEOs. "One of [them] once said, 'If something blows up and you can fix it on your own, I don't need to know about it,'" Conlee says. With that power, Conlee had a free hand to get things done and hold people accountable, leaving his direct boss, Lazaridis, to focus on technology. When Conlee left, so did the accountability culture he had established, and nobody replaced him in the unsung role of keeping the now fraught Lazaridis-Balsillie partnership in sync. "Larry is what made the company work," says Aaron Brown. "Things started getting loose and lazy once he left."

Conlee's responsibilities and title were split between handset chief Thorsten Heins and manufacturing head Jim Rowan, both of whom he had groomed, leaving Lazaridis with two chief operating officers; a third, Morrison, still reported to Balsillie. Lazaridis's direct reports, including software head David Yach and chief information officer Robin Bienfait, met regularly with Morrison to ensure they were on the same page, "but nobody could stand up and say 'Okay, all opinions heard, this is the decision'" as Conlee had done, says a former senior executive. "It slowed the company down. It was not that people didn't perform in their roles; it was just purely the structure that was established did not lead to good, sound, and convergent decision making."

With Conlee gone, inertia and frustration set in at the senior levels. "There wasn't the individual accountability that we needed," says Morrison. "It was too splayed because it was across three different organizations. Now, all of a sudden, Mike is trying to manage something, but he doesn't have the genetic code Larry has."

RIM was entering a nightmarish year. By the end of 2010, it would lose its crown as the leading smartphone platform to Google's Android. But as RIM struggled against external forces, some of the greatest battles would be fought within the company. The two organizations reporting up to each CEO became increasingly dysfunctional silos and breeding grounds for distrust, politics, and factionalism, as layers of ambiguity and uncertainty consumed the company's top executives. Initiatives that required cooperation among groups in different units often stalled unless they had the attention of one of the top chiefs. "It turned into a goat rodeo," says Morrison. "We became collectively ineffective at moving from the idea stage to the conversion of an idea into a commercial success for anything other than devices."

/ / /

Paradoxically, as the company's pace of growth dwindled compared to both Apple and Android, it was still struggling with its own success, as ever-increasing sales strained the global manufacturing network. As 2010 unfolded, the greatest source of friction between the two sides of RIM was product quality. It had been a mounting problem since at least 2006, when RIM launched the Pearl. Dirt got trapped under the tiny rollerball used to navigate the screen, gumming up its performance. The USB port on BlackBerrys often detached from the circuit board and the plastic lens covering screens on some models cracked easily, says David Van Tongerloo, who managed an independent BlackBerry repair service for corporate customers in Houston from 2006 to 2009. The BlackBerry operating system was nearly a decade old and laden with so many software patches it ran slowly and was overdue for a coding cleanup.

Product issues worsened with the Storm, and customer returns increased; a 2010 release called Torch—a hybrid touch-screen keyboard device using the Torch browser—drew complaints from customers that buttons fell off within days of purchase.[3] "Storm impacted the quality of everything," says Yach. "All products took a dive because we were spread too thin."

RIM could hardly afford another reason to alienate customers. Balsillie had always left the science and manufacturing to Lazaridis's side of the house, but the persistent quality issues frustrated him. He felt something had to be done, even if it meant an unwelcome incursion onto his partner's turf.

Balsillie's sales leaders came to RIM's all-executive Tuesday noon meetings stocked with product complaints from carriers, saying they couldn't make their numbers because of quality issues, and further badgered their engineering colleagues at separate cross-functional gatherings. These meetings had always been forums for openly hashing out business issues, but now they became tense sessions that turned sales and product people against one another.

Balsillie and Lazaridis never called each other out in the Tuesday meetings as relations between their organizations deteriorated. "They were mindful of how they were being perceived" and kept any disputes behind closed doors, says Patrick Spence, who by now was one of three sales vice presidents and Balsillie's most trusted lieutenant. But tensions between the two CEOs were evident to others. Balsillie encouraged his salespeople to press on quality issues and would chime in, "Did you get that, Mike?" to which his co-CEO would tersely reply, "I got it."

The Tuesday noon grillings rattled Lazaridis. He felt blindsided and thought the salespeople were grandstanding. He would stop meetings when they raised quality issues and ask for more information. "What is it? Can you send me details? I need to understand," he'd say. Lazaridis would leave the meetings steaming, then walk into a meeting with his direct reports and Morrison at 1:00 p.m. where he would let loose and demand answers. By early 2010, Lazaridis's chiefs were telling their assistants to clear their Tuesday afternoon schedules in anticipation of long, difficult meetings with their boss. "I got the worst of it," says Yach, an assessment shared by others. "After hearing about an issue for the first time at the Tuesday noon meeting, I'd immediately e-mail folks to get me background and updates in time for the one o'clock meeting. My most common thought [during the Tuesday meetings] was, 'I miss Larry.'"

Sometimes, Lazaridis says, his direct reports would tell him they were already well aware of an issue raised by Balsillie's side of the house and dealing with it. "It bothered me that I was hearing about stuff [from salespeople] that I should have heard from the team that reports to me every week," says Lazaridis. Morrison says, "It became evident [Lazaridis] was losing control of some of these problems and he wasn't getting straight answers . . . [or] support from people he needed."

Identifying the problems was easy enough. An internal audit in 2010 found "significant challenges" in the company's product development process, including general disarray and lack of consistency from program to program, while a second audit that year noted "the quality of our handheld products does not meet RIM's expectations, or the expectations of our carriers." Accountability for product quality was spread across several functions and executives, complicating decision making and hampering efforts to improve quality. "The functional orientation of the Quality organization structure negatively impacts the communication and collaboration between quality teams and creates situations of competition and even conflict between groups, duplication of effort, and limits information sharing," the second audit read.

Figuring how to fix quality proved more daunting. Part of the problem, says Yach, was that the company had millions of stockpiled units and parts that had been made when quality problems were at their worst. Yach figured the best way to improve customer perceptions was to stop selling the older devices, but "as a management team we didn't make that decision."

When Balsillie raised quality issues in private with Lazaridis, "I don't recall a heated conversation, but I do recall Mike saying, 'This stuff is really, really hard,'" says Balsillie. "Mike refused to acknowledge that we had any material technical issues, to the point that he would miss meetings so that he didn't hear the negative feedback and hoping that we would not discuss it in his absence. That was wishful thinking, and I personally didn't think we had any way around it. If anything, everyone was counting on Mike to see the flaws first and fix them as soon as possible."

Lazaridis says he recognizes the company had challenges but largely dismisses the issue, saying it would be common to any company that was growing as fast as RIM, juggling multiple versions of products for hundreds of carriers. "Yes, we had legitimate business quality execution problems," he says. "Anybody does, with a complex product."

Lazaridis's chiefs, pressured by their boss, Morrison, and, indirectly, Balsillie, realized they had to do something. They struck a task force to root out the causes of quality issues and fix them. But Morrison grew frustrated by the lack of progress. "You could never find someone who would stand up and take accountability," he says.[4] "I wanted to know who was responsible for product introduction. I wanted to see attribution lists [detailing specific reasons for product returns], understand the most egregious problems, who was dealing with them." Where Morrison expected straight answers and action plans, he says the task force instead delivered complex slide presentations without a clear path to fixing the problems. "I don't think the task force was a very effective group," he says.

By mid-2010, Balsillie was losing patience. He decided to bring the quality issue to a head, exposing the board to the extent of the growing rift between the two CEOs. That June, Balsillie, Morrison, and his sales vice presidents—Craig McLennan, Rick Costanzo, and Spence—took over a board meeting, held at Langdon Hall, a luxury resort-spa located in a nineteenth-century estate mansion near Waterloo. The retreat was supposed to be about the company's global operations and led by director and strategy expert Roger Martin. Instead, Morrison and the sales VPs forced their own agenda on the meeting, detailing quality issues they felt weren't being addressed. Balsillie cued them along and pressed Heins to respond. For the most part, Heins sat silently, getting redder, according to observers. Lazaridis walked in late—he claims not to have been invited—and immediately became defensive. When Heins said he was confident the company could turn around its fortunes in the United States, Balsillie shot back: "Would you bet your house on it?" Heins said no.

Balsillie and his team were troubled by the reaction of directors, who were reluctant to take sides or challenge either of the company's builders. "Jim was always complaining about something," says one person close to the board. Other than Antonio Viana-Baptista, a former telecom CEO who Balsillie had recruited to the board, the directors asked no questions, according to Balsillie, Spence, and McLennan. "I was so disappointed by that," says Spence, who Balsillie by then had earmarked to the board as a potential successor. "You expect a higher level of engagement, passion, excitement, and interest" from the board—particularly "if I was identified as a high potential person and somebody that was important to the organization."

Concerned by the apparent disinterest among directors, Balsillie brought the quality issue to a second board meeting that summer. At that encounter, "Mike dismissed the severity of the quality issues" and said everything was "under control," says Balsillie. "The board accepted Mike's representation almost on faith, and I wasn't going to seek a pointless showdown with him then and there, so they just moved on. I don't think the board quite ever accepted" the depth of the problem, Balsillie says. "Everybody is going, 'Our stuff is great,' and I'm going, 'We're going to get killed.' I said to the board, 'We can halve the size of the company as easily as double it. . . . We're deluding ourselves here.'"

To those insiders who witnessed the quality debate but weren't aware of the prior tensions between the CEOs, it was alarmingly clear the relationship between Balsillie and Lazaridis had gone cold. "It was a shock to Mike that [they] would be so vocal about quality in front of the board, and Mike was blindsided," says Yach. "Absolutely" it was an affront to Lazaridis and his team, says another person at the Langdon Hall meeting. "From my perspective, that was as much of an affront as I'd seen at any point. You could see the tension between the two sides of the company."

"You're looking at the company and saying, 'It's dissonant and you guys stopped getting along,'" says Balsillie. "Yeah, well, it had to do with this infestation of cockroaches, okay? We all got irritable when there were eight billion cockroaches in the house. Before there were cockroaches, all was fine. When the structure changes, everybody struggles."

/ / /

As the quality debate raged, Balsillie turned his attention to another dilemma: how to protect and build RIM's nondevice revenues. RIM's supremacy in wireless e-mail had left carriers beholden to paying for access to its complex data traffic system. RIM increasingly relied on those fees; they accounted for $2.2 billion of revenue, or 14 percent of the total, in the year ended February 27, 2010. But because the fees had significantly higher profit margins than handsets, they accounted for most of the company's $2.5 billion net income.

That left RIM in an awkward position against Apple and Google. Apple made money selling songs, movies, e-books, and apps to iPhone customers—content that consumers willingly bought. Google wanted Android on as many smartphones as possible to increase the reach of its powerful and popular advertising-supported search service. RIM's dominant source of extra revenue, by contrast, was fees extracted from reluctant carriers, who despised paying them.

Balsillie and Lazaridis knew these digital revenues were under increasing threat. Carriers for years had pressed RIM to lower the fees. iPhones and Android devices were drawing market share from RIM, and they didn't charge fees, as the carriers constantly reminded the RIM bosses. Furthermore, Google incentivized the carriers to push Android devices by giving them its 30 percent cut from each app sale. Microsoft had also weakened one of RIM's longstanding competitive advantages. RIM built the BlackBerry system around a program that extracted e-mail from Microsoft Exchange servers and "pushed" it to devices through its network. RIM's lead in push e-mail was untouchable until Microsoft changed its e-mail software in 2006, enabling other smartphones, including Apple and Android products, to send and receive messages over the Internet without having to go through RIM's expensive Relay system. The smartphone e-mail service provided by Apple and Google wasn't as secure or instantaneous as RIM and used more data and battery power, but for most consumers it was good enough. Carriers were locked into contracts with RIM to continue paying the service access fees, but that wouldn't last forever—particularly since RIM engineers knew Microsoft would eventually force RIM to use its new program, called ActiveSync, to deliver e-mail the same way as Apple and Android.

To Balsillie, it was vital to grab greater control of RIM's digital platform and install an experienced leader to expand its offerings of apps, games, media, and new digital services such as electronic payments. He thought he found the answer after RIM director Roger Martin reintroduced him in January 2010 to Jim Tobin, a Harvard Business School classmate who worked at a variety of telecommunications and technology companies. Balsillie hired Tobin that month as a senior vice president, thinking he was getting an experienced executive who would add critical content and services to RIM products to keep up with competitors. Instead, Tobin's arrival exacerbated divisions at the top levels of the company. By the time Tobin left eighteen months later, his name would be one of those linked with dysfunction at RIM's highest levels at the time.

Tobin came to RIM with an impressive pedigree. A classmate of Balsillie's at Harvard, Tobin had worked as a consultant at McKinsey before moving to vice president posts at Bell Canada, AOL, and Comcast Cable. He was intelligent and polished, speaking in abstract, big-picture terms "at a higher plane of existence than a lot of people," says Jeff McDowell, a senior vice president who reported to Tobin. But in a company where small-town values still defined the culture, Tobin rubbed many people the wrong way—especially Lazaridis. "RIM had never had anybody like him before," says McDowell. "He was the first guy to come in and talk vision and strategy" other than the co-CEOs. It didn't help that Tobin regularly cited his credentials and the famous CEOs he'd encountered and constantly dropped Balsillie's name, saying he was carrying out some agenda or other on behalf of the CEO. Tobin would liberally invoke their relationship at Harvard, leaving the mistaken impression they were still close. Once he casually mentioned he'd recently had dinner at Balsillie's house, a story that spread rapidly throughout the company and left a bad taste with many people denied such an intimate audience. "It was insecurity coming in at a senior level in a company where most of the guys had worked together for years," says Tobin. "It was amateurish for me" to cite credentials "in a place where nobody really cared about anything other than what you were doing for them, for RIM or for RIM's customers."

If Lazaridis chafed at an executive seen as "Jim's guy," Balsillie also didn't think much of a senior executive that Lazaridis had recruited, his old friend David Neale. The long-time Rogers executive who had helped steer Lazaridis to wireless data in the 1980s joined RIM in April 2010 as a vice president, advising the founder on strategy and marketing. Neale and Balsillie disliked each other. Balsillie viewed Neale as an unquestioning yes man at a time Balsillie believed his partner needed to confront hard truths about the business. Neale in turn didn't think highly of Balsillie's behavior and brusque manner. "He and I did not enjoy an easy relationship," says Neale. To other senior executives, Tobin and Neale seemed like two more wedges distancing the CEOs from each other. "The seeds [of division] I think were sown by the kind of people they were bringing on the team," says Spence. "You see the distance because of the people they're hiring; they're not aligned on who is the right person for the organization."

Personality and style notwithstanding, Tobin was thrust into a difficult situation in his new job. Tobin didn't meet Lazaridis until he started; at their first encounter, the founder grilled Tobin on his high-tech experience and declared that Tobin should really be working for him and not Balsillie if he expected to oversee a software business.[5] "I realized every single meeting I had with Mike I had this awkward position of being a direct report to Jim in a meeting where Jim wasn't there and I didn't really know the status of their relationship at any given moment," says Tobin. "I spent a lot of time with [Lazaridis] going, 'So what exactly are you supposed to do?'"

Complicating matters was the fact that the job Balsillie gave Tobin was occupied by someone else: Alan Brenner, a veteran Silicon Valley software engineer and executive who had run part of the Java business for Sun Microsystems before joining RIM in 2007. Brenner created the BlackBerry app store and was responsible for the business performance of the platform division—until Balsillie convinced Lazaridis to let his side of the business take over that responsibility. Under Balsillie's direction, Tobin was to assume bottom-line accountability and leave Brenner in charge of product development. Brenner continued to report indirectly up to Lazaridis; Tobin reported directly to Balsillie.

It was the kind of split that may have made sense in the past, emulating the division that defined the company from the co-CEOs down. But the state of relations within the company and mix of personalities doomed the arrangement from the start. "These were very challenging competitive moments for RIM," says Brenner, who credits Balsillie for identifying value-added services as the correct strategy to counter Apple and Android. "Regrettably, his [Balsillie's] instructions were somewhat vague and Jim Tobin and I ended up with different interpretations of what was to be done."

Brenner was unwilling to give up part of his responsibilities and didn't get along with Tobin. It took them months to negotiate the transfer of responsibilities and executives; Tobin wanted to control project management and set the road map for what services and apps would be developed, but the two never reached an agreement and that role largely stayed with Brenner. "I think Alan assumed that my job was to market and sell whatever [apps and services] he wanted to build, and my instructions were that he needed to build to what I required," says Tobin. "Because the roles and responsibilities weren't clear, it created some conflict. Alan felt he was capable of handling the business side as well as the technology side." Balsillie didn't agree—he felt Brenner should stick to technology—and Lazaridis didn't care; when Tobin tried to escalate the issue to both Balsillie and Martin, he was redirected to Yach, Brenner's boss, who sent him back to work things out with Brenner.

To many it made no sense to split the responsibilities between two people; it just caused confusion and gridlock. "Those two jobs aren't really separate," said McDowell. "Tobin wasn't looking for Brenner to tell him what to do, and Brenner wasn't looking for Tobin to tell him what to do. . . . The net result is a stalemate."

/ / /

As Lazaridis began speaking to a conference hall full of customers, developers, and carriers in Orlando on April 27, 2010, he betrayed none of the turmoil and conflict that was opening fault lines throughout RIM. "At BlackBerry, we love what we do, and what we do comes down to one thing: making the BlackBerry experience more useful and accessible to as many people as possible for both work and play," Lazaridis said in his keynote address to the company's annual Wireless Enterprise Symposium. He ended his presentation by inviting will.i.am of the pop group Black Eyed Peas, BlackBerry ambassadors who had several other corporate sponsorship deals, onstage to extol the virtues of the company's devices.

It was a departure for a leader who was more comfortable at a chalkboard talking network physics to be reciting marketing-speak from a teleprompter. But by early 2010, RIM was in the midst of an effort to establish itself as one of the world's leading brands—with Lazaridis leading the charge. The RIM chief, who had recently starred in an American Express commercial, had long seen himself as the company's leading brand aficionado—a role Balsillie, who had little interest and no training in marketing, was more than happy to leave to his partner. Lazaridis diligently tracked the company's standing in global brand rankings and was elated when BlackBerry rose nine spots in Interbrand's annual ranking of best global brands to reach fifty-fourth in 2010, with an implied brand value of $6.8 billion, ahead of MTV, Nestlé, and Adidas.[6]

In the early years, BlackBerry was marketed virally: the company relied on the efforts of evangelists and CEOs who showed off the device to colleagues and sent messages with the tagline "Sent from My BlackBerry Handheld." For years Lazaridis led a collective of executives known as the "chief marketing office," which oversaw the company's marketing efforts, largely centered on leveraging the rich marketing budgets of wireless carriers and ensuring BlackBerrys were well represented and promoted in retail stores.

But now that consumers made up the majority of BlackBerry buyers, Lazaridis and other top executives felt the company needed something more: a high-concept brand campaign that captured and promoted the abstract elements of what made BlackBerry distinctive. Efforts started in earnest with the Pearl launch in late 2006. In 2009 RIM hired Keith Pardy, a veteran marketing executive who had spent most of his career at Coca-Cola, to head the BlackBerry maker's marketing efforts. "I was looking at it, saying, we need to become a lifestyle brand," says Lazaridis.

Pardy defined the essence of BlackBerry as a product people loved and one that made people love their work more because the device made them more efficient. Lazaridis fell in love with the ensuing campaign, defined by its slogan, Love What You Do. But something was strangely wrong about the campaign, and several of the company's marketing executives knew it. Selling

soft drinks that were little different from the competition required a different marketing approach than pushing technology: it wasn't enough to speak
in abstract terms about the brand; the advertising also needed to speak about
product features and capabilities. There was none of that in the Love What
You Do campaign that ran through 2009 and 2010. As portrayed in the global
campaign created by the agency Leo Burnett, BlackBerry was no longer a tool
for making buttoned-down businesspeople more efficient, but a lifestyle
accessory used by texting teenagers, fashion designers, and musicians—
accompanied by the Beatles' "All You Need Is Love." The ads said little about
the features or "value proposition" of the device, and some barely even showed
the devices at all, instead presenting a montage of people break dancing,
kissing, rock climbing, and playing soccer.

As part of the campaign, BlackBerry snagged one of the biggest names in
rock and roll, U2, by sponsoring its world tour. Like the Black Eyed Peas, U2
was no stranger to corporate sponsorships: it had loaned its name, music, and
images to Apple to sell iPods and would in 2014 return to Apple to endorse
its newest iPhone. Lazaridis flew to Dublin and spent a day hanging out with
frontman Bono. They talked about quantum physics at a pub and walked
along the beach, trying to hash out ideas for BlackBerry commercials featuring U2. As they strolled side by side, Lazaridis said, "This is all about love,
and love what you do. . . ." The RIM chief was struck by an idea. "Why don't
we turn it on its head?" he told the Irish superstar. "We love you guys, and a
lot of people do. Why can't we say, 'BlackBerry Loves U2'? It was a nice pun
too." Lazaridis says Bono "loved it right away." The ensuing ad featured nothing more than shots of the band in concert, followed by the tagline "Black-
Berry loves U2."

Many, including carriers and RIM's own marketing executives, saw the
brand campaign as puzzling, vague, ineffectual, and out of touch and questioned why RIM wasn't using its marketing dollars to offer a rundown of the
features that set the devices apart. In trying to strike a balance between advertising to its core enterprise users and to consumers, it did not effectively
reach either. Instead, the campaign presumed the world's smartphone users
were in love with BlackBerry—at the very moment Apple and Android were
establishing themselves as the new standard-bearers of telecommunications.
The target audience for the campaign was the smartphone user who saw no
need to use anything else for any of life's mobile communications needs than
BlackBerry, whether at work or play. "We were marketing to ourselves. And

more importantly, we were marketing to Mike Lazaridis," says Brian Wallace, then VP of global digital marketing and media with RIM. "Mike liked our advertising because our advertising was made for him."

A company that was at war with itself and, in some quarters, overly en-amored with an aging product line, was about to address the critics with one of its biggest product gambles ever.

15 / / / FAULT LINES

Mike Lazaridis was getting exasperated. As he outlined plans for RIM's latest top-secret device to a dozen executives at a meeting in Ottawa in April 2010, one person pushed back. Ian Simpson, RIM's vice president of platform and product software, said there was no way the company could meet Lazaridis's deadline and have product ready to ship by September. The RIM boss had imposed tight deadlines before; this was different. RIM wasn't building another smartphone, but a handheld tablet computer. It was a new type of product for RIM. It would run on a new operating system made by newly acquired QNX with features that had never appeared on any BlackBerry. Simpson was adamant: a project of this scope couldn't be done in five months.

Lazaridis didn't appreciate being openly challenged. QNX, he was sure, could get the system done quickly. He became visibly upset as Simpson held firm. "Mike was definitely at the boiling point," says David Yach, who wasn't at the meeting but heard about it soon after. After the meeting, a British firm that had signed on to develop the user interface on the device quit the assignment. Lazaridis blamed Simpson and had him removed from the project—he didn't need a "Dr. No" standing in the way, he told Yach. "I don't mind being called Dr. No," Simpson said upon learning of Lazaridis's rebuke, "as long as it's spelled K-N-O-W."

In spring 2010, Lazaridis was swept up with a sense of urgency to produce a tablet—a handheld computer larger than a PDA but smaller than a laptop—as soon as possible. A mass market tablet had been the holy grail of the computing industry for decades, but previous attempts had been unreliable, clunky, or difficult to operate. Goaded by its enterprise customers to develop a large-screen BlackBerry, RIM had tinkered with spin-off projects, including a digital book reader, a digital picture viewer, and a program to project the contents of smartphones onto computer screens. None had made it to market. But as millions of people adjusted to browsing the Internet and reading books on handheld screens and as the cost of LCD screens dropped, the tablet's time seemed at hand. By early 2010, RIM had a plan to produce a tablet with a seven-inch-long screen—small enough to fit in a coat pocket or purse—with a high-quality, high-definition screen, a fast browser, a sharp camera, and great sound. The device would be called PlayBook.

But Apple once again set the agenda when Steve Jobs unveiled its tablet in late January 2010. With its ten-inch multitouch screen, familiar features including iTunes, a full browser, and lots of apps, plus an electronic reader, all wrapped in an elegant and accessible design, the Apple iPad would become one of the fastest-selling electronic devices ever when it hit the market that April. One of the iPad's strengths was that it looked like a larger iPod or iPhone, complete with the all-glass screen and a single home button, but it was better suited to applications that called for a larger screen, including games, watching movies, and reading. By offering an instantly accessible and familiar user experience, Apple broke the computing industry's decades-old tablet curse.

Lazaridis and Balsillie immediately recognized the threat posed by the iPad. Apple was making inroads into its "enterprise" base of business and government users with the iPhone. Recession-racked companies let employees use their own smartphones for work rather than issuing them with expensive BlackBerrys. The iPad was a bigger worry: it was the first handheld device that could threaten RIM's dominance of the enterprise wireless handheld market: the iPad was perfectly sized for reading work documents and easier to use in meetings than a laptop. Within ninety days of its release, half of the top one hundred corporations in the United States were testing iPads, and executives weren't giving them back.[1] "This terrified me the most," says Balsillie. The two CEOs agreed RIM had no choice: it had to get its tablet to market as soon as possible.

As Lazaridis examined the iPad for weaknesses, he found several. It didn't have a camera or a connection port to link to high-definition media devices. It didn't run Adobe Flash, a software and multimedia platform that supported sophisticated graphics, videos, games, and online magazines; Steve Jobs hated

Adobe for slighting Apple a decade earlier.[2] Most of all, it didn't have RIM's secret weapon: QNX and its elegant operating system. Lazaridis was convinced RIM could build a better machine that delivered what Apple didn't—in less than half a year. Simpson wasn't alone in his skepticism. Software head Yach had his doubts as well. He was one of the first to realize that if RIM was going to get PlayBook out by fall, the company would have to make compromises.

RIM was in a tough position. It was essentially a one-product company whose one product was starting to look vulnerable. It had never made a personal computer and was in the early stages of figuring out how to make a smarter smartphone. It could ill afford to make any mistakes after Storm and turning down Verizon on 4G. Not only was RIM developing a new type of product; it was once again being forced to react rapidly and defensively to a powerful competitor that had defined the market. As Lazaridis's engineers scrambled to keep up, their boss was about to spark further turmoil among their ranks.

/   /   /

With the purchase of QNX, Lazaridis had a grand scheme in mind. Over the past decade, RIM had upended the wireless market and changed the way people communicated. The arrival of Apple and Google to mobile data meant RIM had to up its game.

His plan was to first see what QNX could do with a tablet. He likened it to giving QNX "training wheels" before taking on the task of overhauling his beloved BlackBerry from the inside—as well as the entire software organization that provided its digital core—to build RIM's smartphone of the future. "I was basically putting the company through the biggest transformation they had ever experienced," he says.

Lazaridis had a blueprint inspired by Clayton Christensen's acclaimed 1997 management book, *The Innovator's Dilemma*.[3] The Harvard professor argued that for established companies to succeed against disruptive competitors, they had to empower small, cloistered teams. These autonomous groups, unsullied by the parent company's set ways, would develop disruptive technologies of their own and could eventually subsume other parts of the organization. It was tumultuous but necessary to stay at the forefront of innovation.

Lazaridis became convinced RIM's software organization needed to be upended from within after Dodge and Torch Mobile founder George Staikos convinced him BlackBerry's Java system was unsuitable for future RIM products. Java "was great for what it was back in the day, but the world moved on," says Staikos. "BlackBerry should have moved on a lot earlier. Mike is not particularly a software guy, so he doesn't understand the design and architecture of the software as well, and wasn't fully aware what had evolved over time."[4] Staikos says Lazaridis became alarmed in early 2010 when a group of legacy engineers unfolded a huge, complicated diagram showing how the Java system would handle the touch-screen capabilities of the Torch browser. "When he saw that, he said, 'Wow, we have a real problem,'" says Staikos. "Things were going up and down through the Java [system], back and forth," resulting in longer processing times that slowed the device's responsiveness. "What it really showed me," Lazaridis recalls, "was that we had to downsize the company to the new reality."

Lazaridis came to see the Java-based BlackBerry operating system, Yach, and much of his software organization as the main obstacles holding the company back. When Yach's software group complained about deadlines, Lazaridis saw an organization that was always demanding more time and resources to work on a complex legacy system that required too much of both. With its use of C++ code and efficient design, QNX could build the next generation of BlackBerry software with a fraction of the people that Yach oversaw. As Lazaridis increasingly turned to Dodge for technology advice, "you could see [the credibility] of David and his team plummet," says an engineer who was close to the key players.

Lazaridis charged Dodge and his team, sequestered in their Ottawa offices, with developing the PlayBook operating system and reporting directly to him. "We embraced [*The Innovator's Dilemma*] and did our best to reinvent the company," says Lazaridis. "Everything would have to change." As for Yach's staff, "A lot of those people weren't going to be there by the time we got to the next equilibrium."

Lazaridis's special treatment of QNX deepened fault lines in a company that was already descending into dysfunctionality. "Interdepartmental politics became really bad," says RIM's former architecture systems vice president, Allan Lewis. "The old guard was reluctant to leave behind all their previous work and didn't feel it was appropriate for Dan and the QNX team, who didn't understand the BlackBerry history, to make decisions." Old-guard engineers were upset as the company turned away from its collaborative culture, and frustrated that they weren't invited to help build a core part of the future. Instead, they were asked to clean up the code on RIM's legacy operating system to power one more round of Java-based BlackBerry smartphones.

The concerns extended beyond bruised egos. Many senior engineers, including Yach, worried about QNX's ability to hit the September deadline. QNX's speciality was creating microkernels—building blocks—not full operating systems. It hadn't built a self-contained consumer device system. The QNX technology also wasn't efficient at using battery power—given the size of systems QNX ran, that had never been a concern. RIM engineers joked that the only battery-powered systems that used QNX technology were systems inside cars, running on the vehicles' massive batteries under the hood.

Lazaridis's deadline presented a challenge: there wasn't enough time to get BlackBerry e-mail on PlayBook. Not only would the e-mail application have to be rewritten—an enormous undertaking—but if RIM wanted to provide access to one corporate e-mail account from two devices, it would also have to update its BlackBerry enterprise server software deployed with 250,000 large customers, since the software only supported one device per account. That would take a year. If the device was to be out by fall, it couldn't have its own native BlackBerry e-mail.

Lazaridis had another idea. Using technology RIM had previously developed, it could wirelessly tether, or "bridge," BlackBerry customers between their smartphones and PlayBooks so the tablet could emulate the smartphone's e-mail box on its screen. "Bridge was the plan from the beginning," says Lazaridis. It allowed RIM to offer BlackBerry e-mail on the PlayBook without the time-consuming work needed to make it native to the device. And since it only had to communicate wirelessly with a local BlackBerry device, and not a cellular network, it wouldn't have to be submitted for lengthy testing and approval by wireless carriers. It also meant PlayBook users wouldn't need a second account to get Internet service. But PlayBook customers would have to own BlackBerrys if they wanted to access e-mail, making the device an accessory to RIM's flagship rather than a stand-alone device. "We opted to just go for Bridge because it was one less thing on a long list of things to be done," says Yach. "Part of it was expediency. I think I would have pushed a different decision" without such an aggressive deadline.

The solution was clever but flawed. By adopting Bridge, Lazaridis was solving a RIM problem, not a customer problem. The iPad came with e-mail native on the device. If iPad users opened their e-mail box, their messages were there. To get BlackBerry e-mail on the PlayBook required a series of steps. First, users would have to download the Bridge app to their devices, then set it up to "pair" the smartphone with the PlayBook. Finally, users would have to wait several minutes for the bridged e-mail box on their PlayBook to fill up with e-mail from their BlackBerry. They would have to repeat the final step each time they used it, since the e-mail box vanished from the PlayBook once the connection was cut. If they kept the two devices bridged for long, the wireless activity would drain both batteries quickly.

As a user experience, it was at odds with Lazaridis's original guiding principle for the BlackBerry: that RIM should "remove think points" and make the device easy and intuitive to use. "This was pretty much the exact opposite," says Jeff McDowell, senior vice president of enterprise marketing. "You were *adding* think points"—and immediately disadvantaging PlayBook compared to the iPad. Even more perplexing, RIM could have easily provided access to consumer e-mail services on PlayBook such as Hotmail and Yahoo Mail, but Lazaridis was so enamored of Bridge that RIM didn't bother to develop that capability in time for launch.

Throughout RIM, the decision to launch PlayBook without native e-mail was greeted with disbelief. How could the company that popularized wireless e-mail do such a thing? Balsillie says he was "hugely disappointed" the PlayBook didn't have native e-mail, but backed his partner; Bridge "had my full support," Balsillie says. The idea of bridging also made some RIM executives nervous: how would carriers react to a device hitched onto a BlackBerry's wireless Internet access? This was a service carriers provided for $10 a month. Lazaridis instead spoke openly about how PlayBook users could avoid paying extra, which their big customers did not appreciate. RIM no longer seemed "constructively aligned" with them. "Mike was persuasive and thought PlayBook paired with a BlackBerry was a valid market proposition," says Yach.

Lazaridis's desire to break from the past led to another difficult choice. Because the iPad shared an operating system with the iPhone and iPod, the new platform quickly had tens of thousands of apps available for customers. BlackBerry Java apps were dowdier, but there were thousands of them used by millions of enterprise customers. None would work on the new operating system for PlayBook. Lazaridis was effectively turning his back on developers and enterprise customers who built and used the programs, negating the "ecosystem" effect RIM could benefit from if it had adapted its Java operating system to the tablet. Lazaridis felt he had no choice—RIM couldn't survive by prolonging the life of an outdated operating system, and he needed QNX to start building RIM's future.

That meant RIM had to select other platforms for developers to build apps for PlayBook. Lazaridis chose to lead with Adobe AIR, which QNX used on its in-car systems. Adobe AIR was a software platform based on Flash, a hugely popular platform used by developers to create slick graphics and run video over the Internet on personal computers. However, because Apple's mobile devices didn't support Flash, few developers bothered to write mobile apps using Adobe AIR. PlayBook's support of Flash would differentiate the company; Lazaridis thought scores of Flash developers would embrace the PlayBook and write apps for it. "We expected them to take the step with us," he says.

In reality, "Adobe had a limited developer base and very few people using it for mobile—almost none, in fact, as PlayBook was to be the first mobile device with full support for AIR," says Tyler Lessard, RIM's vice president of developer relations. "The big bet was that the big community of Flash developers would hop on board. Unfortunately, it didn't really happen."

While the PlayBook would eventually support five development platforms, RIM only released Adobe programming tools to developers before launch. Few developers took up the call. "AIR never made any sense to me at all," says Trevor Nimegeers, a Calgary-based software entrepreneur whose firm, Wmode, had built BlackBerry apps for corporate and government users for years. He felt disappointed and betrayed that PlayBook wouldn't support Java apps. "Essentially RIM was asking us to retool our people, fight with unproven nonmainstream tools, and rewrite our existing applications at huge cost only to be rewarded with a completely uncertain marketplace. I found it comical, actually." In the end, Nimegeers' firm, like other developers, passed on building apps for PlayBook. Soon after PlayBook launched, Adobe would drop support for AIR on mobile altogether.[5]

What RIM needed was someone in a senior role to ask tough questions about PlayBook. Were the lack of e-mail and the app gap critical shortcomings in the emerging tablet space? Did RIM have a clear sense of what PlayBook was supposed to be? Was it for consumers or business and government users? Did it contain the right features and technology to appeal to either? What was its unique selling proposition? "It wasn't clear why we were doing PlayBook, how it fit into everything else," says Patrick Spence.

Instead, any such concerns were swept away. Lazaridis had pushed Dr.

No out of the way and wasn't heeding concerns raised by Yach. Lazaridis and Dodge were enamored of their machine: its dual-core processor allowed users to perform multiple tasks at once; the browser ran well; the operating system was highly responsive; the video and sound quality were superior to the iPad. "There was no question people in the company loved PlayBook," says Lazaridis. "I loved my PlayBook." Balsillie stayed out of technology discussions. As for the company's board, it lacked anyone qualified to even know what questions to ask, let alone the right answers. "Nobody on the board was able to say, 'That's a good thing or a bad thing, or this and that,'" says one person close to the board. The directors "just didn't have enough technical knowledge." Other directors were frustrated with RIM's last minute planning and market research for new product launches. "As was sadly the custom," director Roger Martin said, marketing plans for new devices such as PlayBook were "constrained by the fact that there was already a finished product." When the board was presented with a tablet that lacked basic features such as e-mail, Martin said he told the board "the most plausible pitch" for the incomplete PlayBook was that "iPad was for fun" and PlayBook was for productivity. "It wasn't a compelling pitch. But we needed to have some positioning for it and it was the best I could come up with," he said.

/ / /

If few people were asking the right questions internally about PlayBook, the company suffered from the opposite problem as software engineers considered what to do with the BlackBerry smartphone. For close to a year, through early 2011, Lazaridis and his developers debated how to proceed on the Black-Berry's next smartphone operating system, delaying its development as Android stole its market share.

Lazaridis always wanted QNX to build the operating system and for another newly acquired software company called The Astonishing Tribe to build the user interface. Yach figured it would take longer for QNX to build the new BlackBerry system than Lazaridis expected: BlackBerry's existing operating system had about 25 million lines of code, and it would take three thousand people more than a year to build the new system. Yach thought it would be best for RIM to keep releasing updated Java-based BlackBerrys to protect market share in the meantime, even if they did not deliver the next-generation experience that QNX promised.

Yach charged his software teams to work on alternative plans. Two possible solutions emerged, neither of them ideal: Yach favored running the existing Java BlackBerry platform on top of QNX's core technology in order to support existing apps. But many developers, including Alan Brenner, championed a different approach: tacking the BlackBerry interface on top of an Android operating system with QNX at its core. Android offered ready-made technology that would enable RIM to push out a new device to market quickly, with a running start in consumer apps, where Android was a significant player. But it would also mean apps developed for BlackBerry wouldn't work anymore. By late 2010, Yach embraced a third option: combining RIM's Java operating system with Android's.

Lazaridis wanted no Java on future BlackBerrys and was troubled by Android: he felt an Android BlackBerry would be less distinguishable from countless other smartphones and would be far less secure than the QNX or existing BlackBerry operating systems because Android was written using publicly available open-source code. Businesses were sure to reject it.

Nevertheless, Lazaridis allowed the debate to play out for months. "There was no right answer," says one engineer involved in the discussions. "You just needed to pick an option and run with it. There was more and more discussion about looking at options than making a decision. And making the decision wasn't easy because ownership wasn't there. I think the decision was clear in Mike's mind: there was going to be a rewrite, done by brand-new people. It was probably the right decision. But the execution of that decision," in the engineer's view, "was done poorly."

After months of debate, in early 2011 Lazaridis decided to stick with his original plan—have QNX build the BlackBerry operating system, called BlackBerry 10. He believed Dodge could have the work done in time for an early 2012 launch. "If I wasn't able to implement the dynamic smoothly and seamlessly and it took a year . . . okay, maybe I could have done better," says Lazaridis. "If you want to blame somebody, blame me."

Yach understood what this meant for him. "Mike wanted Java eliminated from the device; while he didn't say it explicitly, his comments made it clear he felt our Java base was the reason BlackBerry was losing market share. He was a firm believer that having Java on the BlackBerry 10 device would be its downfall. In hindsight, that was the beginning of the end for me. Mike decided I was 'stuck in the past' and started shutting me out." The man who had built one of the world's first successful smartphone operating systems realized his days at RIM were numbered.

/ / /

As conflicts raged throughout RIM in 2010 the first trouble signs appeared in its U.S. results. Apple's arrival in 2007 had dented RIM's U.S. market share but had not slowed its growth. But once Android appeared, RIM's U.S. hand-set sales growth ground to a halt: for seven straight quarters, from late 2008 until late summer 2010, revenues in the United States hovered around $2 bil-lion for each period. Sales then fell precipitously over the next year, to $1.1 billion in the quarter ended August 27, 2011, as Android siphoned away mar-ket share and became the world's leading smartphone platform. RIM's share of Verizon smartphone sales dropped to 14 percent in the last three months of 2010, from 60 percent a year earlier, according to internal RIM data; the drop was pronounced at Sprint (from 63 percent to 22 percent) and T-Mobile (from 60 percent to 18 percent) as well.[6]

There was another winner besides Google: Samsung. The Korean con-glomerate that had so badly wanted a BlackBerry Connect deal shed its mantle as a perennial also-ran cellphone maker to emerge as a major force in smartphones in 2010, going all-in with Android. Samsung's size and scale meant it could outspend other Android makers like LG, Motorola, and HTC on marketing and carrier promotions while still making low-cost phones. Samsung had another advantage: it was one of the world's largest electronic component manufacturers, supplying rivals, including RIM. If Samsung lost a smartphone sale, it still made money supplying components to the winner. As a critical supplier, Samsung had first access to the newest technology, pri-ority on supply, and the ability to peek inside its competitors. When Balsillie saw Samsung's huge marketing splash at the same 2010 conference where Lazaridis lectured Verizon on 4G, "it gave me chills," Balsillie says, leaving him worried by what RIM was up against. By fall 2011, Samsung was the larg-est smartphone vendor in the world.[7]

Overall, RIM's numbers told a different story. Total revenues in the twelve months ended February 26, 2011, were up 33 percent year-over-year, reaching $19.9 billion, as sales outside the United States, Canada, and Great Britain more than doubled to $8.5 billion from the prior year. Globally, BlackBerry was still hot. Much of the world's wireless telecommunications infrastructure was at least a decade behind North America, western Europe, and advanced Asian countries. Carriers in countries like Indonesia, Brazil, and South Af-rica weren't investing in 4G—most didn't even have 3G. With its stingy use of precious bandwidth, BlackBerry was ideal for these networks, just as it had once been for North American and European carriers. RIM developed a cut-rate BlackBerry phone called Gemini, which worked well on pre-3G networks and sold for under $200. In those markets, the iPhone was too expensive, and its better browser and abundance of apps weren't as much of a draw. "The Gemini singly drove all of RIM's global growth in 2009 and 2010 and was by far the best-selling BlackBerry of all time," says Balsillie.

From Jakarta to Johannesburg, Riyadh to Rio de Janiero, BlackBerry became a sensation, embraced as a powerful status symbol—"the device of strivers and celebrities alike," according to a report from Nigeria and Indonesia by the *Globe and Mail's Report on Business Magazine*.[8] In Haiti, the band Fresh Up sang of a woman who threatened to dump her boyfriend if he didn't buy her a BlackBerry.[9] A character in the Nigerian film *BlackBerry Babes* made good on a similar threat.[10]

The most compelling feature driving BlackBerry sales in the developing world wasn't wireless e-mail but another application that had been included with devices since the mid-2000s: BlackBerry Messenger. While BlackBerry was losing the app race in North America, BBM was establishing itself as BlackBerry's first "killer app" since wireless e-mail, and the first globally successful app of the smartphone era. In late 2008, 4 million people used BBM. Two years later the number reached 28 million, and by September 2011, it was 60 million.

BBM's runaway success was almost as unimaginable as its unlikely birth. BBM was the brainchild of a trio of young RIM employees who were looking for something to do following a rare slowdown in 2003 when the company had to lay off 10% of staff. Strategic alliances manager Chris Wormald and programmers Gary Klassen and Craig Dunk, along with two co-op students, explored how to adapt popular instant messaging services such as Yahoo Messenger for BlackBerry. These services enabled users to have real-time text "chats" at their desktop computers over the Internet, typed into a small box in the corner of their browsers.

As they delved into instant messaging, the group realized those deskbound chat services had a critical shortcoming: there was no way to know if the person at the other end had received the message, or was even there. At the same time, the three men, who all had infant children at home, were contending with a different challenge: how to reach their wives during the day. Calling was disruptive, particularly if they were trying to put their babies to sleep.

What if there was a better way to communicate without making the phone ring?

The three struck upon the idea of creating a "data call": simulating a phone call through a series of instant messages between BlackBerrys. Creating the data equivalent of an interactive voice call would require the "speaker," or sender, to know his message was both delivered and received. The recipient would have to know that once she opened the message, the sender was informed it had been read. People would no longer send data messages into the void, unsure if they arrived or were read.

Building on an existing program that enabled BlackBerry users to swap simple text messages known as PINs, the group created QuickMessenger, later renamed BBM. When a sender dispatched a BBM message to another BlackBerry user, a D, for delivered, would appear next to the message on the sender's BlackBerry when it arrived. Once the recipient opened the message that D turned into an R, for received, notifying the sender the message had been opened. "We were stunned at how well the Ds and Rs provided a real-time mobile-aware sense of presence," Klassen says.

Those two letters transformed instant messaging into intimate and interactive data conversations between BlackBerry users, particularly since devices were always on, connected, and usually close by. "It's a phone conversation with the time-boundedness taken away," says Wormald. "The pain of phone calls is they're forced to be synchronous—I talk, you listen, you talk, I listen. This was still linear, but it provided the cues necessary to know we were having a conversation. Once you read my message, you realized the important psychological impact: I knew you'd read it, and you knew that *I* knew that you'd read it."

Wormald realized the power of BBM, which was still being tested internally, when he gave his wife and mother BlackBerrys during a trip to Disney World with his three children in early 2005. As Wormald sat on a ride, a man in the vehicle ahead pulled out his cellphone and negotiated loudly with his wife about where they would meet next. "The magical moment was interrupted," Wormald says. A minute later, Wormald felt his pocket buzz. He pulled out his BlackBerry. It was his mother: Meet me at the ice cream stand. He discreetly replied he'd be over soon, put the device away, and turned his attention back to the ride. After five days of BBM messaging in Florida, his mother wanted a BlackBerry. "She didn't even own a cellphone," says Wormald. "She was hooked. If you had asked me then, 'Are you going to kill phone calls with this,' I would have said yes."

Back at RIM, not everyone was enamored of the BBM trio spending so much time on a self-directed pursuit outside of their duties, known in industry parlance as a "skunkworks" project. Klassen's boss would shoo Wormald away if he saw him in the building, scolding him for distracting Klassen from his duties; and he gave Klassen a bad performance review—for spending time creating BBM. "Getting something to happen often takes a certain amount of self-initiative," says Klassen. "There was a lot of work done during evenings and weekends."

Finally, the BBM group was ready for the big test: winning Lazaridis's approval. Wormald's boss had BBM secretly loaded onto the BlackBerrys used by the CEO and his family. Once they came upon the app, they tried it and were hooked. Lazaridis's assistant, Abbey Gilhula, was one of the first heavy BBM users; to see Lazaridis, one had to go through Gilhula, "and the way you got to Abby was on BBM," says Wormald. BBM was quickly adopted throughout RIM.

BBM was ready to take to market by 2005. At first the carriers didn't want BBM on BlackBerrys: they were suspicious of any service that enabled users to communicate without paying them anything. For a while RIM hid the free BBM download in the BlackBerry help menu, but by 2006, as RIM prepared its big push into the consumer market, it convinced carriers to preload the app onto devices.

BBM became popular in North America and Britain when RIM cranked up consumer sales, but its reach was transformative as RIM expanded globally. Its popularity spread quickly: BBM messages used little data and arrived instantaneously, making the service a welcome alternative to costly voice calling and text messaging services, especially in poorer countries.

BBM was also private and discreet. Messages were encrypted and passed only through RIM's Relay system, not through servers controlled by corporations or governments. Each user was identified by the unique but anonymous PIN number associated with his or her device, a randomly generated collection of eight alphanumeric characters. If users chose not to reveal their identity, it would be impossible to know who they were. It was an irresistible tool for teenagers in conservative countries to communicate with friends and romantic interests away from the prying eyes of parents. In Dubai, young women embroidered their PIN numbers on flaps inside their burqas, turning them out discreetly to encourage men they fancied to BBM them, according to a senior RIM executive.

Not everyone was so coy. Pizzerias and politicians in developing countries advertised their PINs on the sides of delivery trucks, on posters and bumper stickers. Venezuelan president Hugo Chavez called his BBM and Twitter account "my secret weapon.[11] In the United Arab Emirates, sheiks paid upward of $10,000 for a phone with a "golden PIN," a device that carried an auspicious series of numbers and letters, such as 777.[12] BBM users ran businesses and news services through BBM; in Bahrain, journalist Muhannad Sulaiman Al Noaimi sent daily summaries of breaking news and press releases to about 40 percent of the country's seventy-eight thousand BlackBerry customers.[13] BBM was a powerful communications tool, even revolutionary, for millions of people. For some repressive and security-minded governments, it would prove too revolutionary.

/ / /

BBM's success was bound to spark competition, and in 2009 and 2010, a rash of rival mobile instant messaging services began appearing around the world, including WhatsApp, Line, WeChat, and KakaoTalk. Unlike BBM, they worked across multiple platforms other than BlackBerrys and drew millions of new users each month. The one that irked RIM the most was Kik Messenger. Kik was hatched by a University of Waterloo engineering and mechatronics student named Ted Livingston who had completed three co-op work terms at RIM, including time on BBM. In 2009 Livingston decided to forego his fourth year to develop his fledgling start-up. His initial plan was to develop a music-sharing service that worked with BBM, but after several months he decided to instead create a BBM-like chat application that worked on all smartphones. Livingston approached his former superiors in early 2010 and encouraged RIM to broaden BBM to work on non-BlackBerry devices. With its head start in mobile instant messaging, he believed RIM could crush any rivals if BBM was available on all platforms. He even told RIM in March 2010 he would stop developing Kik if BBM went "cross-platform." But the company wasn't interested.[14] "They absolutely refused and they said, 'No, we won't do that,'" Livingston said in a 2013 interview.[15] "To be fair, from their perspective, it was hard. They said, 'People are buying BlackBerrys for BBM.' That was a real risk."

Livingston launched Kik Messenger in April 2010 and claimed in court documents he told RIM of his plans. He was even invited to speak at a BlackBerry developer conference that September. But relations changed after he relaunched Kik in October. After fifteen days, Kik had signed up 1 million users. At that point, Kik alleged in court documents, senior RIM executives "embark[ed] on a campaign to destroy or seriously harm Kik." RIM terminated its agreements with Kik, removed Kik from its app store, and sued Kik for infringing on its intellectual property.[16]

Livingston asked one of his investors to intervene: Jim Estill, RIM's longest-standing outside director. Estill responded by pressing Don Morrison to meet Livingston. According to a December 2010 memo from RIM's law firm Bennett Jones to the board's audit and risk management committee, Estill did not disclose his personal interest in RIM's newest rival to Morrison or the board. The relationship raised a potential conflict of interest, the legal memo warned. Estill resigned shortly after the conflict issue was raised. He concedes his involvement with Kik put him in potential conflict with his position as a RIM director. "I thought I disclosed it from the start, but I could be mistaken," he says. "That's why you resign, you do the right thing."

The spat with Kik was a warning shot in a larger battle that would play out within RIM over the next year, opening the greatest rift within the wounded company. As it lost its lead in the smartphone race, some RIM executives realized that if they did nothing, BBM would be surpassed by more open mobile chat services. Within months, it would become the personal mission of Jim Balsillie to make sure that didn't happen.

/   /   /

Lazaridis watched in horror as the cabin of RIM's Falcon became a blood-soaked mess. As the jet touched down in San Francisco on December, 7, 2010, a RIM developer on board reached into his bag. The plane hit a bump on the runway, causing him to slice open his hand on a carpet knife inside. "I've never seen so much blood—it was everywhere," says Lazaridis. The engineer tried to compress the wound "but it was just spurting out," says Lazaridis. "We had to call an ambulance to come right to the plane. He was ready to pass out."

It was an ominous start to the day. Lazaridis had flown in for an onstage interview at a conference with the tech industry's best-known journalists: Walt Mossberg and Kara Swisher. Lazaridis brought a working prototype of the PlayBook and was keen to show it off, but after the bloody landing, he was rattled.

It had been a tough fall for the PlayBook. Dr. No had been right: the September deadline was impossible. Yach could see that QNX was overwhelmed by the task of delivering the PlayBook operating system. He loaned about twenty engineers to help QNX develop PlayBook, but behind the scenes he asked hundreds more of his reports to help with an array of tasks so Dodge's team could finish the project. Many had to be trained in C++ or Adobe AIR, adding further delays. Lazaridis's plan for following *The Innovator's Dilemma* strayed from the script: it was evident QNX couldn't do the job on its own and needed the help of the very engineers Lazaridis was trying to separate them from. Accommodating the new reserves delayed work on the update of the legacy BlackBerry operating system and ratcheted up ill-will among Yach's legacy developers. By September, Lazaridis was only ready to announce the PlayBook's impending arrival. It would be seven more months before Play-Book launched. By then, the iPad 2 was out, and it had a camera.

As RIM executives discussed how to take the device to market, they realized that with no native e-mail, no accessibility to virtual private networks, and no ability to hook up to printers, they couldn't market PlayBook as an "enterprise" device to their core business and government customers; it lacked too many features to be a must-have work tool. Instead, they settled on describing it benignly as "professional." "It's all we had," says Jeff McDowell.

The company wasn't faring better developing PlayBook's consumer appeal. Jim Tobin was supposed to strike content deals to provide multimedia offerings on the PlayBook and kept confidently telling colleagues that Rupert Murdoch's News Corp., Condé Nast, and online magazine provider *Next Issue* would be on board. But in the end they weren't. Tobin says he was "bluntly blindsided by the lack of certain features in the final product" and that media companies were scared off when their own research suggested PlayBook wouldn't do well. But Lazaridis felt misled and pressed Balsillie to let Tobin go. Meanwhile, with few mobile developers working on Adobe AIR, the PlayBook's app deficiency was glaring.[17] Steve Jobs added insult to injury in mid-October when he said during an Apple earnings call that he couldn't foresee RIM catching up to Apple because it had to venture into the "unfamiliar territory of trying to become a software platform company. I think it's going to be a challenge for them to create a competitive platform and to convince developers to create apps for yet a third software platform."[18]

Balsillie was starting to worry that PlayBook was "half-baked," but he did what he had always done: talked up the product like it was the best device ever made. In public, Balsillie went on about how great Flash was and dismissed the "appification" of the Web, suggesting Apple relied so heavily on mobile apps because its browser wasn't able to deliver an adequate Internet experience without Adobe.[19] Some observers thought Balsillie was losing it, but he was just making the best of a bad hand, says Patrick Spence. "His way of dealing with those situations was to go even more extreme the other way. . . . I think he was trying to overcompensate for not being in that strong a position. If Mike said Adobe's the thing and we're betting on AIR, Jim's like, 'I'm going to sell the shit out of it.' "

Lazaridis appeared nervous and halting as he walked out to meet Mossberg and Swisher.[20] He fumbled as he set up the PlayBook for a demonstration. Lazaridis had expected friendly questions, but the conversation took a sharp turn. After letting Lazaridis wax on about PlayBook's technology, Mossberg cut in: "Look, I'll just be blunt about it. There's a growing consensus that your BlackBerry platform . . . [is] looking old."

Lazaridis's answer confounded them. "By focusing on the tablet market, we see an opportunity to free where the smartphone can go," Lazaridis said, breaking into a visible sweat. "We free it to become . . . a much more focused communications tool."

Swisher was perplexed. "So what you're saying is the tablet is the phone?" she asked. Lazaridis tried to explain RIM was now able to "optimize both of those worlds," but he made little sense, going on about multicore processing and pulling in random details about the company's global success. A blog covering the event on Gizmodo was titled "Can You Figure Out WTF RIM's CEO Is Talking About?"[21] As Lazaridis talked about the BlackBerry of the future, he seemed to be dismissing the company's current smartphones. His interviewers looked as uncomfortable as their guest. "It wasn't my best day," says Lazaridis.

Perhaps the most telling remark was when Lazaridis declared that the three "defining characteristics of the tablet market" would be security, reliability, and multitasking. Lazaridis had it wrong. What Apple was teaching the mobile market was that consumers cared about three different things: style, content, and easy use. Four months away from the launch of PlayBook, RIM was still struggling to define the market for its new product.

16 / / / WATERLOO SPRING

"Depart! Depart!" chanted thousands of protesters pushing past police barricades in Cairo's Tahrir Square. The demonstration on January 25, 2011, was not violent. Instead of rocks and Molotov cocktails, these dissidents carried BlackBerrys and iPhones to post images on Facebook trumpeting President Hosni Mubarak's faltering hold on Egypt. The country's eighty-two-year-old leader would be safe that night once police reinforcements chased protestors from the square. But the fight was far from over. Arab Spring was gaining momentum and Mubarak's thirty-year-old regime wouldn't survive unless it found a way to quell the uprising.

Balsillie was in a Swiss mountain town when he learned what kind of retaliation Mubarak had in mind. RIM's chief had flown to Davos to join his friend, Wall Street legend George Soros, for the annual gathering of business and political royalty at the World Economic Forum. Other visitors included Microsoft's Bill Gates, China's prime minister Wen Jiabao, and former U.S. president Bill Clinton. Balsillie and Soros had come to announce a $50 million joint investment in a new global economic think tank, the Institute for New Economic Thinking. Balsillie had been looking forward to the trip for weeks, a welcome breather from anxious days and sleepless nights worrying about BlackBerry's precarious U.S. sales. He and Soros had finished announcing their pact and Balsillie was driving to a celebratory dinner at a downtown restaurant when his BlackBerry buzzed with a call pulling him back to Waterloo.

It was RIM's Vancouver-based chief legal counsel, Karima Bawa. A senior official from Egypt's telecommunications regulator had just called to deliver an ultimatum, she said. State-owned Telecom Egypt had yanked the plug on BlackBerry service in the country, and it would stay off-line until RIM handed over encryption keys for coded e-mails and messages traveling through Egypt over RIM's secure network. As his car moved through the snow-quilted streets of Davos, RIM's boss struggled to make sense of what was happening. What did a phone maker from Waterloo know about tyrants and revolutions? "I'm shitting my pants," Balsillie says, shaking his head, remembering the stress that night. "I didn't take this course in business school."

Balsillie did, however, understand that by allowing Egypt to decode encrypted BlackBerry messages he could be giving up protestors who relied on BBM messages to coordinate covert activities. "I didn't start a tech company to help totalitarian governments kill protestors," Balsillie told Bawa. Government prying was old ground for RIM's chief and his legal counsel. BlackBerry's protected network had been a magnet for prosecutors and governments for years. If police wanted access to e-mails, they needed a warrant. The same went for foreign governments; they had to demonstrate a legal right before RIM granted any access. By 2011 this last legal boundary was becoming tenuous, as India, Russia, and Arab governments pushed carriers and network operators such as RIM for access to encrypted wireless messages. In reality, RIM had no ability to help these regimes crack business e-mails, the bulk of its traffic, because corporate customers own a unique set of encryption keys inaccessible even to RIM. The company could, however, decode consumer messages relayed over its BBM service and BlackBerry Internet Service, a situation that left subscribers in the crosshairs of angry security agencies. The Egyptian ultimatum capped off weeks of difficult and still unresolved discussions with Indian security agencies demanding access to BlackBerry messages.

Balsillie would spend little of his long anticipated celebration dinner with Soros and friends. For most of the night he was outside the restaurant, working his BlackBerry, talking to Bawa and other RIM officials, weighing a response to Egypt's ultimatum. Saying no to the Arab nation meant kissing good-bye to one of RIM's fastest-growing markets, a loss it could ill afford as American customers retreated from BlackBerrys. But the financial hit and shareholder anger couldn't be as bad as aiding and abetting execution squads. After several back-and-forth calls, Balsillie arrived at a decision. "We're out of Egypt now; we're not doing it," he instructed Bawa. As it turned out, Balsillie would never have to explain his decision publicly. The next afternoon, the desperate Mubarak government ordered Egyptian carriers to shut down, blocking everyone except the country's stock exchange from Internet access. "We dodged a bullet. BlackBerry was no longer singled out," Balsillie remembers. The Egyptian outage only bought Mubarak some time. Two weeks later, on February 11, the Egyptian leader resigned. By then Balsillie was back at RIM with Lazaridis confronting their own insurgency.

Waterloo Spring began early 2011, weeks after RIM's directors appointed Balsillie and Lazaridis cochairs of the board. The decision to promote CEOs who had been sanctioned by regulators became a lightning rod for shareholder frustration. The two had paid huge regulatory penalties for an improper scheme that directors had missed for years. Now the same men were going to oversee the board? Frustrated with RIM's deteriorating competitive position, shareholders pushed back. Privately, some urged company directors to reverse the controversial appointments and instead appoint an independent chair. The dissent put Balsillie and Lazaridis, RIM's eternally confident leaders, on the defensive. The pair had been driven for years by the conviction that aggressive tactics would prevail in the ferocious smartphone race. Anyone who questioned them didn't understand the rough-and-tumble wireless industry. Faced with rebellious investors, RIM's bosses did not respond with grace or introspection. Their standard defense was to fix bayonets and charge.

Balsillie learned about shareholder complaints upon returning from Davos. An early challenger was the Ontario Teachers' Pension Plan Board, one of Canada's largest retirement savings reservoirs and a vocal enemy of poor corporate governance. Although the pension fund held a modest amount of stock, one portfolio manager was so alarmed by what he saw at RIM that he contacted a company director about his concerns. Upon learning that a shareholder had gone over his head to a director, Balsillie was furious. "Don't your people realize how I'm working for shareholders?" Balsillie complained to Teachers' CEO, Jim Leech, over the phone. Leech heard Balsillie out and then offered him a chance to tell his side of the story in a meeting with Teachers' portfolio analysts and governance experts.

The meeting, which took place in Teachers' offices in Toronto's north end, did not go well. Basillie angrily chastised the portfolio manager who had approached Martin. While a half dozen Teachers' representatives looked on, horrified, Leech cut him off. "Stop! If you're coming in to berate Teachers' employees, this meeting is over now," Leech said. Recalling the incident, Balsillie argues that *he* was the one who was under attack. "It was an intense exchange where they were trying to intimidate me," he says. The temperature of the meeting room dropped when Balsillie, recovering his upbeat bluster, predicted a rosy future for PlayBook and forthcoming new BlackBerry phones. When Balsillie left, the fund managers turned to Leech, mouths agape. Balsillie's optimism was stunning. As part of standard market research they'd recently called a variety of market experts about distressing signs about RIM's core U.S. market. Demand for BlackBerrys was withering, they learned. Didn't Balsillie understand how serious the company's troubles were?

The answer to that question came a week later, March 24, 2011, in the form of a purposely understated press release that would be received by investors as a flare from a sinking ship. At the close of stock market trading that Thursday afternoon, RIM announced a much weaker outlook for fiscal first quarter profits than financial analysts were expecting. The shortfall was not huge, no more than 11 percent. Publicly traded companies often issue profit guidance that disappoints investors. But it was a rarity for RIM; its sales and profits had grown steadily for a decade. That was part of its mystique: Lazaridis's and Balsillie's company was the arrow shot straight up in the air that never came down. Any bad news was extraordinary. Making matters worse, RIM tried to soft-pedal the unhappy report. Investors never like unpleasant surprises. Weak excuses, though, they really hate. On a conference call that day with analysts, RIM trotted out the oldest business excuse in the book: bad weather. In RIM's case the adverse climactic event was a devastating tsunami in Japan. While the Asian country was indeed home to some of RIM's parts suppliers, investors didn't buy what sounded like a schoolboy's dog-ate-my-homework excuse.

During the call, Balsillie explained the company was undergoing a transition as it waited for the imminent PlayBook launch. The coming tablet, Balsillie enthused, "may well be the most significant development for RIM" since BlackBerry launched in 1999. The promise was not reassuring. PlayBook was late and it would take more than a tablet to reverse RIM's sinking stock price, which had started to slide in recent weeks. The extent of the company's U.S. troubles had been masked for months because BlackBerry sales were rocketing in emerging markets such as Indonesia and the Middle East. The latest quarterly results confirmed what smart investors already suspected: RIM was in trouble. A day after the somber quarterly report, RIM's stock fell 11 percent, to $57.

RIM rattled its investors a month later by lowering its already weak outlook for the first quarter, forecasting it would earn no more than $1.37 per share, 11 percent below the previous target. It's rare for companies to reduce expectations twice for the same quarter, and this time out RIM's vague explanation—lower shipments and weaker selling prices—was the last straw for increasingly skeptical investors. RBC Dominion Securities financial analyst and long-time RIM cheerleader Mike Abramsky advised investors that the company had "little or no credibility" after the unexpected reversal.[1] The business media were harsher. "A corporate tragedy is under way at the proud Canadian firm Research In Motion," reported the *Wall Street Journal*.[2] The next day, RIM's stock fell below $49 a share, a sickening tumble that was far from over.

Investors had to wait until mid-June for a fuller explanation in RIM's quarterly report. It made public what company executives had known for months: in the U.S., carriers were staging a headlong retreat from BlackBerrys, shifting their support to iPhones and a new generation of Android phones. Revenue from the U.S. market was down 36 percent to $1.3 billion from the same period a year earlier. The full extent of the reversal was not revealed in the quarterly statement but rather explained in internal documents for the board. RIM's biggest U.S. customer, Verizon, had slammed the brakes on BlackBerry. In the last three months of 2010, Verizon sold 800,000 BlackBerrys, a jarring 60 percent decline from the final quarter of 2009. The number would drop to 400,000 during the next quarter. In the space of less than two years Verizon went from buying more than 95 percent of its smartphones from RIM to 5 percent. The news was no better at Sprint, T-Mobile, or AT&T. Sales to the three carriers were down more than 50 percent in less than two years. In total, the company shed 1.3 million U.S. subscribers in the quarter, more than double the number lost one quarter earlier. RIM, the first-place innovator of the North American smartphone market, was on the verge of becoming a distant third in a market dominated by Apple and Google.

One of the key explanations for the implosion was that RIM didn't have a fourth-generation phone. Samsung had already launched a 4G phone and iPhone was months away from the upgrade. Lazaridis's prophecy that 4G phones would quickly drain batteries was technically correct. But nobody seemed to care. Carriers and consumers weren't put off by the inconvenience.

Carriers had invested in new network technology to build more bandwidth capacity and stoke more traffic and fees from customers clamoring to download movies, sports broadcasts, and online games onto phones. Marketing budgets previously allocated by carriers for BlackBerry promotions were redirected to their competitors' new 4G phones. RIM had once again misjudged the consumer market. This time, however, there was little air cover to regroup and fight. When the ill-fated Storm arrived in 2008, RIM was rolling out its new line of BlackBerry Bolds, one of the company's most technically and commercially successful phone series. In 2011, the only RIM product slated for release was an updated version of the Bold.

Without a 4G phone to compete against a new generation of Android phones, RIM's management had to confront a stark truth: for ten years RIM had prospered as a smartphone maker by constantly innovating and rolling out enhanced devices, software, and network upgrades. As long as it held the lead with pioneering smartphone technology, RIM prevailed against bigger competitors with deeper pockets and more diversified product portfolios. If Apple or Google stumbled with a product, they could recover with sales from other divisions. In Apple's case it was computers, iPods, iPads, and online app and music sales; Google had search engine advertising revenues. That wasn't the case in Waterloo. RIM was a one-product company struggling with a damaged brand image and an outdated product. Years of strategic confusion and poor product execution had caught up to the BlackBerry maker.

In a way, Lazaridis was right about drained batteries being a problem—only it was he and Balsillie who were running out of power. Battered by the patent wars, the product failures, and their bitter falling out over the securities scandal, RIM's bosses had lost their mastery of a smartphone market that had exploded after the 2006 launch of its first full consumer smartphone, the Pearl, into a global market with sales that would top 1 billion handsets annually in 2013. Product mistakes in this environment of hypergrowth and constant innovation could be fatal, leaving once dominant players so far behind industry leaders they could never catch up. RIM had thrived in the high-stakes wireless market in its early days because it was more innovative and nimbler than industry leaders such as Motorola, Nokia, and Palm. Now two of Silicon Valley's most visionary powerhouses, Apple and Google, had moved onto the field. They had shifted the smartphone market away from Lazaridis's vision of a simple mobile e-mail device to a handheld mini-computer that was loaded like a modern Swiss Army knife with practical and whimsical add-ons. For years Lazaridis and Balsillie had bravely battled everyone from the Topper to Steve Jobs. Now, it seemed, all they had left to fight was each other.

RIM's internal challenges were the talk of Silicon Valley. "They've been caught flat-footed," Jean-Louis Gassée, a Palo Alto venture capitalist and former Apple executive told the *New York Times* in April 2011. "They've built a tremendous company; they are people with distinguished backgrounds. They are not idiots, but they've behaved like idiots."[3] Internally, the company had become so dysfunctional that once loyal employees turned to blogs to vent their frustrations. A favored outlet was the tech blog *Boy Genius Report*, which had leaked many RIM product details in the past. In an open letter to RIM's senior management team in June, a writer identified as an unnamed high-level RIM employee began: "I have lost confidence."[4] The writer anguished over internal chaos and delays, lack of discipline and accountability, and called on the CEOs to make drastic changes, including finding "a new, fresh thinking experienced CEO" to replace them. When RIM responded with an upbeat, everything-is-under-control message later that day, the blog was flooded with e-mails from past and present RIM employees about the company's travails. One complained of "smart, talented and capable people handcuffed" by internal processes that were "destroying the company" and its people. The discontent prompted one online poster to nickname the company "Research in Mutiny."

All Lazaridis and Balsillie had left to hang their hopes on were PlayBook and, hopefully sooner than later, BlackBerry 10, the phone that would finally deliver 4G and better browsing capabilities. PlayBook was a trial run for the powerful new QNX operating system that would power the BlackBerry 10 phone, then slated for launch in early 2012. If RIM triumphed with PlayBook it would get a second act and a springboard to operate everything from phones to home entertainment systems. Underlining PlayBook's importance, Lazaridis agreed to leave RIM's hectic BlackBerry 10 project in early April to promote the tablet on a media tour. BlackBerry's eternal champion, accustomed to adulatory press, was in for a shock. In Canada Lazaridis had always been able to play to local pride. No more. When *Globe and Mail* reporter Omar El Akkad traveled to Waterloo to visit Lazaridis, he got an unexpected reply after wondering aloud what might happen if PlayBook failed. "Are you Canadian?" Lazaridis asked El Akkad, a Canadian citizen of Egyptian descent. Sweeping his arm toward RIM's sprawling campus of buildings and nearby research institutes he and Balsillie founded, Lazaridis waved the flag, "Jim and I have invested a whole bunch in this country and community . . . gosh look at the success."

He became even more defensive with U.S. media. When *New York Times* reporter Ian Austen questioned Lazaridis about the company's negative outlook and shrinking stock price, RIM's co-CEO seemed breathtakingly indifferent to his shareholders' tribulations. "Why is it that people don't appreciate our profits?" he asked Austen. "Why is it that people don't appreciate our growth? Why is it that people don't appreciate the fact that we spent the last four years going global? Why is it that people don't appreciate that we have 500 carriers in 170 countries with products in almost 30 languages?"[5] Driven by his confidence in BlackBerry's destiny, Lazaridis seemed incapable of accepting that RIM was largely the author of its own misfortunes. To him, critics were misguided nonbelievers. "I don't fully understand why there's this negative sentiment, and I just don't have the time to battle it. Because in the end, what I've learned is you've just got to prove it over and over and over," he told Austen.

What little capacity Lazaridis had for tough media questioning evaporated by the time he sat down to discuss PlayBook with BBC's Rory Cellan-Jones in London.[6] Fatigued from days of cross-Atlantic travel and frustrated with a faulty BBC camera that required Cellan-Jones to retape the interview, Lazaridis became irritable when the technology reporter shifted from PlayBook questions to a more sensitive subject. Was Lazaridis worried RIM security would be compromised by pressure from India and other nations to pry into BlackBerry messages? "That's just not fair. . . . We don't have a security problem," RIM's chief grumbled. "We've just been singled out, right, because we're so successful around the world." When the reporter pressed again about government interference, Lazaridis grew petulant, offering a rare public acknowledgment of the strain he was under. "We're dealing with a lot of issues," he told the BBC. "I think that we're doing our best to deal with the kind of expectations that we're under."

At that point, he'd had enough. "Turn that off," he said, gesturing to the unwelcome camera. Walking away, Lazaridis gave little thought to the aborted interview. He'd assumed security questions were off the record. Besides, with BBC's technical screwups he was running late for a plane he had to catch to New York, where RIM would be throwing a launch party the next day for PlayBook. By the time Lazaridis woke up in his Manhattan hotel room the next morning his botched BBC interview had gone viral. "It all went crazy,"

Lazaridis would later say, blaming the network for a conversation he believed was private. "It was quite a blow to his esteem," says David Neale, Lazaridis's friend who had been recently recruited to help promote RIM's products. Neale had breakfast with Lazaridis that morning in New York. "This was a 180-degree swing from a celebrated can't-possibly-do-anything-wrong visionary to a flawed, failed leader. It was a shocking experience," he says. For RIM's directors and executives, the debacle was further evidence that the co-CEOs were losing their grip. Balsillie was butting heads with shareholders and Lazaridis was systematically turning off the media.

"The two of them were so fragile," says Neale with a sigh.

/ / /

It was every marketing team's worst nightmare: weeks before PlayBook's mid-April launch, RIM's advertising agencies and marketing staff were staring at empty whiteboards. There was a reason for the blank expanse before them: RIM's top two marketing executives had bailed and the company had sent its ad agency packing. Balsillie and Lazaridis didn't like any of the marketing ideas they saw. One campaign was built around the dubious slogan "Amateur hour is over." Another promotion concept featured Tom Cruise's profane, horseshoe-bald movie mogul, Les Grossman, from the film *Tropic Thunder.* Grossman, the idea went, would run his sleazy movie empire from a Play-Book. Yet another concept featured a young girl wielding a PlayBook to sell . . . painted rocks. No, no, no, RIM's bosses complained. Why couldn't anyone identify PlayBook's unique appeal?

The admen didn't have the courage to answer that question. The problem was simple: Balsillie and Lazaridis couldn't themselves agree on who their new product was for and what made it special. "Jim was thinking enterprise and Mike knew we had to be consumer," remembers Neale, who was parachuted in weeks before launch to throw together a marketing campaign. Like everyone before him, he struggled to find a winning idea. No surprise there, according to another RIM official, Patrick Spence, who says no one could identify PlayBook's unique appeal because it didn't exist. "There was nothing distinctive about it," he says today, "[no reason for] people to get excited about it."

RIM's biggest marketing challenge was that PlayBook was going after the iPad market with few of the applications found on Apple's breakthrough tablet, which controlled three-quarters of the U.S. tablet market. Even more perplexing, PlayBook lacked the very thing that made RIM a global success: e-mail. RIM devotees who prized instant messaging would have to deploy a wireless bridge from their PlayBook to a BlackBerry and wait minutes for e-mails to migrate to the tablet. Yet another problem that you would never expect from a RIM product: the wireless bridge sucked batteries dry within hours. With PlayBook, Lazaridis had broken his own golden rule: waste not, want not. There was none of the specialized media content Tobin had promised to deliver. A final consumer turnoff: the tablet launched with only 3,000 apps, a fraction of the iPad's 65,000 app arsenal.[7] When it came to content and critical functions, PlayBook was a poor alternative to the iPad.

The half-baked tablet presented RIM's promotions staff with a challenge. Without e-mail, contacts, and calendars, PlayBook was a poor sell for business enterprise customers. That left professional consumers, or "prosumers," as the target audience—buyers who might be convinced PlayBook was more practical than an iPad toy. "This was the strategy we ended up with given the way the product ended up. It's all we had," says senior vice president Jeff McDowell. By the time Neale was called to the rescue, his team had about four weeks to come up with a concept and deliver three television spots. The results were as hazy as the product itself. Bland ads showcased the few technology advantages PlayBook had over iPad: a Flash player and multitasking operating system. The pitch line was appropriately open-ended: "Why can't every tablet do this?"

Few would remember RIM's PlayBook campaign and tech critics could barely muster the enthusiasm to review the flawed tablet. Warning readers against buying PlayBook, the *Wall Street Journal*'s Walt Mossberg summed up the frustrations of BlackBerry fans everywhere: "I got the strong impression RIM is scrambling to get the product to market." *New York Times* critic David Pogue was less generous: "You read that right. RIM has just shipped a BlackBerry product that cannot do e-mail. It must be skating season in hell."

Making matters worse, some of RIM's long-standing carrier partners hated the tablet. By bridging PlayBook to BlackBerry phones for Internet access, RIM aimed to save consumers the cost of a separate wireless data plan. Customer savings, however, meant lost revenue for RIM carriers, none of whom were eager to see PlayBook succeed without the extra data plan. AT&T refused for months to certify PlayBook for sale to customers. Behind the scenes, the carrier made a number of demands, including compensation for lost data revenue. "AT&T was mighty harsh," remembers Balsillie. "It was a messy time." Messier still because RIM's only other sales channel, consumer electronics stores, were ill-prepared to sell the devices. RIM shipped PlayBooks to major retail clients, such as Best Buy, which had preserved premium display space for the new product. Unfortunately, RIM had neglected to create a demo program to showcase and explain its latest product. With no helpful presentation on the screen of the device, shoppers were left to rummage around PlayBook programs on their own. Countless PlayBooks were immobilized after customers armed the devices with passwords, which the sales staff couldn't unlock. "This happened hundreds of times," says McDowell. Batteries were another headache. They drained so quickly that display tablets conked out, a problem some stores remedied by plugging what were supposed to be mobile PlayBooks into electrical outlets.

As PlayBook troubles piled high, the public veneer of RIM's unified leadership began to crack. During his ill-fated media tour, Lazaridis insisted, as he does to this day, that PlayBook's awkward e-mail bridge was a practical, money-saving solution for customers. Balsillie, however, realized the company's new product had none of the features valued by BlackBerry's loyal customers. In the middle of the first week of the product launch, Balsillie made an astonishing pronouncement to the *Wall Street Journal*. Addressing consumer concerns about PlayBook, he said, "We will have if you want [direct e-mail access] within . . . sixty days." In addition to undermining his partner, Balsillie threw RIM engineers for a loop. They'd have to scramble to get native e-mail up and running on the PlayBook.

From conception to delivery, the PlayBook launch was an unqualified corporate fiasco: production teams were out of sync; the product itself was rushed; its marketing strategy, one of the company's biggest, was a disaster. RIM's CEOs weren't even reading from the same script during public appearances. "I saw a lot of confusion," said Larry Conlee, who returned briefly to RIM in mid-2011 after PlayBook's launch to relieve Don Morrison, then undergoing treatment for prostate cancer. "It seemed all parts of the company had problems. I was shocked by the degree of it." PlayBook was the manifestation of RIM's internal problems—"a crippled product" that should never have shipped, Conlee says. Had he been at the company earlier, he says, "I probably would have laughed first and yelled second. 'What do you mean you want to take e-mail off?'" When he read through internal records and met with team leaders, Conlee was dismayed to see how RIM had devolved from a hardworking army of team players into splintered squads of finger pointers. No one took ownership for PlayBook's failures. "It was just . . ." Conlee pauses, thinking back to the grim summer of 2011. "Chaos is a good word."

/ / /

Lazaridis and Balsillie believed they had time to set their floundering company on a more profitable course. Overseas sales were strong and it seemed no one could touch its core market, with BlackBerrys outselling iPhones ten to one among business and government users.[8] The other advantage was that RIM had no debt. By 2011 it was sitting on nearly $3 billion in cash and investments, enough money, the CEOs agreed, to buy RIM time for a turnaround. Their visions of saving RIM, however, were so diametrically opposed that they further polarized a company that was becoming incapacitated by internal strife.

Lazaridis believed the solution lay in the new BlackBerry 10 smartphones. His focus was on overhauling RIM's operating system to be more competitive with Apple and Android smartphones. Despite the market failure of PlayBook, the "flawless" performance of its QNX operating system promised to sweep in "a renaissance for the company," with a powerful new platform for BlackBerry 10 devices, Lazaridis says. The new QNX-based smartphone, originally expected for 2011, would be ready for release by early 2012, he told the board.

Balsillie emerged from his strategic fog with another plan. His vision of a new software-and-services business had evolved to the point where he now believed it represented a more prosperous future for RIM than turning around its flailing handset business. Lazaridis had asked Balsillie in early 2010 to find global partners for pending BlackBerry 10 software. Balsillie embraced the idea. Dreaming big as always, Balsillie and director Barbara Stymiest approached Felix Chee, the Canadian representative of China Investment Corp., at a dinner for U.S. president Barack Obama during the G20 summit in Toronto in June 2010. Chee had made a fortune for the Beijing-based fund by placing contrarian bets on Canadian resource companies caught out by the financial crisis. He saw the potential for another score when Balsillie and Stymiest asked if CIC would back a licensing venture offering Chinese phone makers rights to BlackBerry 10 software. Chee thought they would seize the chance to leap past foreign firms such as Nokia, which dominated domestic handset sales.

By mid-2011, RIM's China strategy was taking shape. RIM allocated $30 million to build data centers in Beijing and Shanghai; CIC tentatively agreed to buy a controlling stake in a Chinese firm that would license BlackBerry 10 software to local phone makers. RIM would get $5 for the sale of each handset using its software—generous terms that Balsillie says would have generated $1 billion in annual profit. "RIM was being handed a lottery ticket," he says. If the China plan succeeded, RIM could offer the same deal in India.

Some RIM colleagues were uneasy with the strategy and worried that copycats would cannibalize RIM's handset sales, a fear Balsillie rejected. Under his plan, licenses would be limited to countries where BlackBerry was a marginal player. Others feared alienating the U.S. government. Would military and security forces continue to use BlackBerry if China was plugged into the same system? According to one senior RIM executive at the time, "Jim didn't see the optical risks China posed for our U.S. market."

The China strategy was one-half of a two-part licensing strategy that Balsillie was convinced could save RIM by making the company's proprietary software and services available on rival handsets. After meeting with several carrier CEOs in February 2011, he came away with a view that the company had to undergo a brutal transformation to save itself—"strategic chemotherapy," he called it. Daniel Hajj Aboumrad, CEO of the Mexico-based carrier América Móvil, delivered the grim prognosis that RIM would succumb if it didn't pursue a radical course of attack. With cheap Androids flooding the market, he warned that his company, controlled by Aboumrad's father-in-law, billionaire Carlos Slim Helú, would shift much of its business to the Google platform unless RIM slashed its prices.

Balsillie concluded that RIM's hardware business would never recover. "When the game changes, if you're not able to become what the game is now, you must pivot to another game," he says. "I saw a tsunami of Androids coming and didn't want to bet everything" on BlackBerry 10 smartphones. RIM, he says, had to offset the vulnerability of the hardware business with "a big, big shift."

Balsillie's pivot strategy originated with Aaron Brown, the RIM midlevel executive charged with collecting the monthly service access fees from carriers. By 2010, RIM was earning $800 million per quarter in revenue from these fees. Carriers were always pushing RIM to lower the fees, and Brown could see it would be hard for RIM to hold them off much longer as its market position weakened. To protect those revenues, RIM had to find a new reason for carriers to keep paying. The answer, Brown thought, was to capitalize on one of RIM's few remaining successes: BlackBerry Messenger. The mobile instant messaging service and upstart rivals, including WhatsApp and Kik, were starting to threaten a lucrative source of revenues for carriers: text messaging. In 2010, carriers globally earned over $100 billion in revenues annually from short message service, or SMS, sent between mobile phones. The service cost so little to run that the vast majority of sales flowed to the bottom line as profit. Carriers typically charged $10 to $20 per month for SMS plans in developed markets. BBM and its rivals, by contrast, did not require a separate monthly fee, so customers could send hundreds, even thousands, of messages per month at no cost provided they stayed within the limits of their data plans. The popularity of these and other messaging platforms such as Skype skyrocketed. In 2011, users sent 4.4 billion of these so-called over-the-top messages per day, just over a quarter the number of SMS texts sent. It was just a matter of time before instant messaging surpassed SMS text volumes.

Carriers were just starting to grasp the emerging challenge: their profitable SMS revenues would gradually erode as customers turned to BBM and its peers. If one of these instant messaging apps became the global standard for smartphones, SMS revenues could plummet. Worried carriers banded together to build their own instant messaging platform, called Joyn, but, as with past carrier-led initiatives, it gained little traction with consumers and few carriers adopted it. One commentator labeled Joyn "zombie technology."[9]

The prospect for instant messaging becoming the defining killer app of mobile was exciting, but Brown was deeply troubled about how BBM fit into that evolving landscape. Competition among instant messaging apps was inevitable, but BBM was handicapped because the service only worked on BlackBerrys. If it stayed within the RIM ecosystem, BBM would lose its appeal in a world where consumers wanted the freedom to send instant messages to any friend, regardless of whether they were using Android, Apple, or BlackBerry phones.

If RIM lost a BBM subscriber, it would also likely lose a handset sale and the associated service access fees. No other instant messaging service had that problem—they were software start-ups with a handful of employees, not hardware manufacturers. It was important to maintain and build BBM's popularity. The best way to do that, Brown felt, was to make it available on Apple and Android smartphones as a cross-platform application. This strategy presented a paradox: opening BBM to rival smartphones would eliminate one of RIM's few distinctions and potentially prompt scores of customers to abandon BlackBerry. But they were already leaving. By opening up BBM to other platforms, RIM might still lose handset sales—but at least it would create new opportunities in a booming mobile service. While the idea sounded risky, Brown believed it was a better choice than the status quo, and just might save RIM.

Brown introduced his idea during a phone call with Balsillie on a Sunday in early 2011. RIM, Brown explained, could position BBM as a solution for carriers. They could preserve their SMS revenues by offering the instant messaging service as part of their basic monthly talk-and-text plans, no matter what brand of smartphone customers used. Brown called the plan "SMS 2.0." With BBM's enhanced features, SMS users would flock to using BBM instead and the user base of RIM's instant messaging application would balloon. In exchange for embedding BBM in their basic plan to customers, RIM could agree to slash its service access fees to $1 from an average of about $4 per user.

It was a daring trade: if RIM was willing to sacrifice most of the service fee revenue and profit derived from its existing base of BlackBerry users, it could potentially more than make that up by expanding its BBM user base many times over among Apple and Android users. "This would have added $1 billion in service margin to the company annually and 100 million subscribers within a year, and built a new story for the BlackBerry brand, a new type of relationship with carriers," says Brown.

Balsillie was intrigued but not immediately sold. The next day he floated the idea during a meeting with AT&T executives. They loved the concept of protecting their SMS business by harnessing the popularity of BBM. At that moment, Balsillie bit hard on SMS 2.0. It was as revolutionary as the first BlackBerry. "I thought, 'Oh baby, it's 1999 for us all over again if we pull this off,'" says Balsillie. He believed RIM could become bigger than Facebook by offering carriers a new offering built around BBM. But "we had to go fast," he says. "If this didn't happen, I had nothing else."

Balsillie became so attached to the SMS 2.0 plan that he had RIM commit more than $125 million to buy a pair of companies to bring the strategy to life. New York–based Live Profile was a start-up instant messaging firm that gained 15 million active users within months of its April 2011 launch. Its messaging software worked on Apple and Android platforms and its technology shared enough similarities to BBM that the two services could be easily stitched together, turning BBM into a cross-platform offering. Balsillie believed RIM had to offer other features as part of SMS 2.0, so his company also bought NewBay Software, a content storage firm that was already selling its services to carriers. With NewBay, RIM could sweeten the SMS 2.0 pitch by adding the ability for customers to store songs, pictures, and other digital content through their phones in an online "digital locker."

Balsillie and Brown fleshed out several options. Carriers could offer an expensive plan that included BBM plus one gigabyte of cloud storage. Or, if carriers in developing nations committed to selling cheap BlackBerrys instead of Androids, RIM would waive the service access fee but still throw in BBM. That way, Balsillie figured, RIM could protect against declining handset sales while continuing to build the BBM network.

Lazaridis gave Balsillie his okay to pursue the strategy, but he had reservations: if BBM was available on rival smartphones, would people stop buying BlackBerrys? "I was making sure that whenever we figured out how to launch this thing it wouldn't kill our [handset] business," says Lazaridis. "It was up to Jim to convince the board that there was a strategy to actually get this into the market."

Some carriers responded positively and by mid-2011, Balsillie was calling SMS 2.0 RIM's top strategic priority. Balsillie thought he only needed a few carriers to sign on: a major player in the United States, one in Europe, and a global player such as Telefónica. If they joined, others would follow. But Balsillie didn't have to just win over carriers. He faced a tougher challenge convincing RIM colleagues his plan wouldn't kill the company.

RIM's directors were running out of time. They had faithfully backed Balsillie and Lazaridis through so many storms: regulatory sanctions, product disappointments, and growing evidence, as one person close to the board puts it, that the CEOs were no longer "acting like a partnership." The board's loyalty endured because they believed the founders, fathers of an improbable global technology success, had the talent to pull RIM out of its tailspin. "We were reluctant to get tough with them; they were successful executives," one director explained. Another factor was the absence of successors. Directors had to be careful about alienating Balsillie and Lazaridis because there were no experienced understudies. Thorsten Heins, a Lazaridis lieutenant, and Patrick Spence, Balsillie's candidate, were identified internally as potential CEO material, but the board had limited contact with them and neither had the kind of broad executive training needed to run a struggling global company. With no stand-ins in the wings the CEOs had the upper hand. "If we were to say to Jim and Mike, 'Well we're the board and you should go away now,' they would have laughed at us," RIM director Roger Martin later told the *Globe and Mail*.[1] By mid-2011 there was no more time for excuses. The board was under too much pressure from shareholders to shake up the executive suite.

What started as quiet objections by a handful of shareholders was shaping into a full-blown revolt. Northwest & Ethical Investments, a small Toronto fund manager, pushed RIM's directors into a corner by threatening to call a shareholder vote if the company did not appoint an independent chair. It's not uncommon for shareholders to push for a nonexecutive chairman to strengthen board independence. But few motions succeed because investors are loath to destabilize companies with boardroom coups. Initially a committee of independent RIM directors urged Northwest in private discussions to back away from its request. The directors lost their pull, however, when the company released first-quarter results.

On June 16, 2011, RIM announced that its financial condition was much worse than feared. For the fiscal first quarter ended May 28, RIM reported a 12 percent drop in sales from the previous quarter, to $4.9 billion, while profits plunged 26 percent to $695 million as its U.S. subscriber base deteriorated. In response, RIM began layoffs, the first in nearly a decade, trimming its workforce by 10 percent, including, for the first time, senior executives such as David Neale and Jim Tobin. Others, including some old-timers who had grown weary of the infighting and product failures, put up their hands and asked for buyout packages. RIM could no longer deny its condition. The small technology company that had sidelined so many larger players as it established the global smartphone market was now succumbing to its savvier rivals Apple and Google. By the end of the week its stock price dropped below $28, erasing more than 50 percent, or $20 billion, from its peak 2011 market value. The nosedive prompted some major shareholders to publicly call for Lazaridis and Balsillie to step down as board chairs. Rather than listen to their shareholders, the embattled chiefs dug in.

In a conference call with financial analysts on the day of the grim earnings report, Balsillie and Lazaridis presented a resolute and united public front to their fractured partnership. To their critics and disappointed shareholders they had a simple message: Trust us and us *alone*.

Appointing an outsider to run the board, Balsillie warned, would damage a company that he and Lazaridis were repositioning. "Taking the company to the next level of success and growth is also something neither of us can do alone. It's something that would be incredibly challenging for someone from outside the company to manage successfully at this critical time in RIM's development," he said. Lazaridis reinforced the happy marriage narrative. "Jim and I recognize each other's strengths and regularly discuss and work together to determine the best way to execute on the incredible market opportunity ahead of us," he said. "While I can't promise that there won't be bumps in the road ahead, I can assure you that Jim and I have never been more committed to the business and that our interests remain closely aligned with those of our shareholders." With no new product details or delivery schedule to reassure investors, Lazaridis resorted to a moth-eaten mantra: "The BlackBerry platform provides the best balance in terms of cost, battery life, performance, and network efficiency."

Some shareholders responded by unloading tens of millions of shares within days of the news. Others talked of insurrection. In June, Northwest went public with its call for a vote on an independent chair at RIM's July annual meeting. The stand attracted immediate support. A few days prior to the annual meeting, a confidential report prepared by RIM's proxy adviser suggested that 47 percent of votes cast would back the Northwest rebellion. Not a majority, not yet, but too close for comfort. To avoid a possible humiliation, RIM's independent directors made peace with Northwest. The fund manager agreed to withdraw its motion in exchange for a commitment from an independent committee of RIM directors to decide within seven months whether to appoint an independent chair. The deal bought time for RIM's board, while sending a strong signal to Balsillie and Lazaridis that they were under scrutiny. But two months later a small Toronto merchant bank, Jaguar Financial Corp., urged the board in a public statement "to seize the reins . . . before more market value is lost." The message from investors was clear. Unless the CEOs delivered a huge win with BlackBerry 10, their tenure was in jeopardy.

Adding more stress, Lazaridis and Balsillie had to make room for some backseat drivers. In early October, RIM's board pushed for an outside consulting agency, Monitor Group, to help reverse sagging U.S. sales. Boards seldom second-guess executives by calling for outside consultants. It's even rarer to recommend a consulting firm with ties to company directors. RIM director Claudia Kotchka, a former Procter & Gamble executive who had previously tapped Monitor for consulting projects, proposed hiring the consulting firm. Director Roger Martin said he "heartily endorsed and supported" Kotcha's recommendation. Martin founded Monitor's Canadian branch and spent thirteen years with the firm as a consultant until 1998. Lazaridis and Balsillie, still bruised by Protiviti's damning board report, viewed consultants as overpaid nuisances. They would have to tolerate them now.

While the board asserted itself, Lazaridis and Balsillie moved into higher gear. They had overcome so many daunting challenges before; they could do it again. The CEOs had been so young and inexperienced when they defied the limits of wireless technology, outsmarted much larger adversaries, and danced around domineering carriers. Their triumphs changed how the world communicated and levitated a technology baby into a $20 billion global titan in just over a decade. It had all happened so fast. A torrent of demand meant RIM had to grow almost overnight from a young business into a global force with the kind of leadership and expertise to confront bigger and more ruthless Silicon Valley adversaries. For most of its history RIM had prevailed because its two CEOs acted as one: different men united by a vision of how to develop their business. As the company began to break apart under the pressure of legal, regulatory, and competitive pressures, so too did their partnership. At the very moment a unified executive front was most needed, Lazaridis and Balsillie pulled the company in different directions with opposing strategic ambitions.

Lazaridis staked the company's future on hardware. Working with QNX's Dan Dodge he oversaw teams of engineers designing new hardware and software for BlackBerry 10 phones. The team worked around the clock. "We had to change," says Lazaridis. "We retrenched. We studied. We worked hard. It's almost like everything else took a backseat. Our families took a backseat, our personal lives took a backseat . . . to make sure that we were making the right decisions." Still, setbacks were frequent, supplier issues delayed chipsets designed for BlackBerry 10, and Ottawa-based QNX once again needed help from RIM's veteran BlackBerry engineers in Waterloo.

Balsillie, meanwhile, saw a brighter future in software. He spent much of 2011 in company jets, visiting carriers and other potential partners with his SMS 2.0 plan for a new BBM instant messaging–based offering. The concept was radical and required face time with prospective partners. RIM's lead salesman knew he would need big-name partners to impress a board he felt had grown "twitchy" from shareholder pressure. There were also challenges at home. His marriage with Heidi had ended and he had moved to a converted mill east of Waterloo to start a new life with Neve Peric, an executive at the Waterloo governance think tank Balsillie founded. Alone and restless on overnight flights, he took to writing a novel, pouring a version of his life into a manuscript in hopes of making some sense of his complex personal narrative. He describes the novel's protagonist as a "neurotic WASP with a Métis background" who challenged boundaries. Writing was a small escape from the pounding RIM and its leaders were taking. "I was scared sleepless," is how Balsillie remembers the long fall months of 2011.

/ / /

When a business declines it begins gradually, almost imperceptibly, until so many failures pile up that the unraveling arrives with unnerving speed.

RIM had been in a slow descent ever since the Storm debacle in 2008. It waited too long to recognize the need for a new operating system to compete with Apple and Google, and when it finally jumped by acquiring QNX, internal disarray slowed its delivery. RIM's decline gathered speed in the early hours of October 10, 2011, when Lazaridis was woken by a phone call. The company's data center in the British city of Slough was knocked out. When he arrived several minutes later at RIM's Waterloo campus, the scale of the crisis was projected on large digital screens in the control room of the network operating center. Many of the screens, once alive with blinking lights signifying traffic volumes, were now blank. All of Slough's servers were down, and the onslaught of rerouted overseas BlackBerry messages had overwhelmed RIM's mother ship. The Waterloo network operating center was lifeless within hours of Slough's collapse. The only place messages were still moving was South America. BlackBerry messages circulated for another day until a flood of BBM messages hailing a key goal at a Buenos Aires soccer match toppled RIM's last standing data center.

Hours turned into days, and still no BlackBerry service. RIM offered few explanations and no reassurances to more than 70 million customers stuck with dead BlackBerrys. "People across Dubai will start committing suicide soon if BBM doesn't come back on. The whole city is addicted," wrote one online commentator in a story about BlackBerry's troubles in the *Guardian*. So addicted that police in the United Arab Emirates attributed a steep decline in traffic accidents to the outage.[2] Finally, early on October 13, RIM released a short video statement from Lazaridis that was more alarming than reassuring. Dressed in a black BlackBerry polo shirt, appearing exhausted and puffy after seventy-two mostly sleepless hours of work, Lazaridis read stiffly from a teleprompter. "I'd like to give you an estimated time of full recovery around the world, but I cannot do this with certainty at this time," he almost sighed. "We're working tirelessly to restore your trust in us." Media critics were unforgiving. "It is time to hang up on the stock," railed the *Wall Street Journal*'s influential Heard on the Street column.[3] "It doesn't rain, it pours. Or in RIM's case, it Hurricane Katrinas," said the *Sunday Times* of London.[4] "BlackBerry sorry, but is it too late?" asked the *Chicago Tribune*.[5]

After three days, the backlog of BlackBerry messages began slowly coursing through RIM's network. It would take much longer to restore the company's reputation with customers. RIM quietly paid more than $50 million to compensate carriers for lost wireless data income. Once RIM learned that the root cause of the server breakdown in Slough was a defective Cisco router, Balsillie demanded compensation from the California network equipment maker. After weeks of discussions with senior Cisco officials, the California firm agreed to provide about $30 million in cash and other compensation to RIM.

The outage, the largest in RIM's history, was a damaging blow to the company's vulnerable CEOs. Their handling of the crisis set off a fresh round of questions about management practices. When he was marooned in Dubai, Balsillie's once seemingly endless reservoir of energy began to evaporate. He was the company's front man with carriers, which, after the network failure and his unfulfilled promises of a quick recovery, made him an industry punching bag. "It knocked the wind out of my sails," he says. So much so, that in phone calls home to Peric he began to question his future at RIM. For Lazaridis, the failure of a network he had conceived and developed shook his faith in BlackBerry's infallibility. "It was brutal on Mike—it was part of his anatomy" says RIM's Don Morrison.

There would be no relief for RIM's embattled CEOs. RIM again grabbed international headlines a month later, on November 25, as Jakarta shoppers suffered broken bones and other injuries when they were knocked down as hoards of customers flocked to a one-day half-price BlackBerry sale. RIM's local manager was threatened with criminal negligence charges for failing to properly control crowds. Three days later, more police trouble: an Air Canada flight from Toronto to Beijing was forced to make an unscheduled landing in Vancouver after two RIM managers became rowdy. The men were on their way to China to inspect a PlayBook manufacturing facility, when, according to a lawsuit filed by Air Canada, they became so drunk and abusive they had to be restrained. Agitated and angry, the men chewed through plastic restraints, requiring attendants and nearby passengers to physically subdue them until the plane made an emergency stop in Vancouver. Days later, the managers pled guilty to charges of mischief, resulting in more bad press.

Inside RIM, the catastrophe continued. PlayBook had been such a dismal failure the company was forced to announce on December 2 that it was taking a $485 million write-down on unsold inventory. Worse news was on the way. The company's third quarter results, to be announced in mid-December, would show its profits had plunged more than 70 percent from a year earlier. Help wasn't coming anytime soon because the launch of the game-changing BlackBerry 10 was delayed until late 2012. Once the news hit the street it was a safe bet that investors would be calling for a palace coup. "There was this piling on of woes," remembers Larry Conlee. Bad news, he says, "kept loading the wagon, making it harder and harder to pull RIM up the mountain."

/ / /

Lazaridis and Balsillie knew their support was evaporating. Negative attacks from media, investors, and financial analysts were unrelenting. RIM's many complex problems were condensed to one simple narrative: the dual CEO leadership structure was the source of the company's woes. A single, more effective leader was needed. The intense scrutiny meant the two chiefs had to tread cautiously with rattled directors. Instead, on the afternoon of November 11, at a meeting few would forget, Balsillie alienated directors when he most needed their support.

The showdown took place on Cherry Blossom Road on the outskirts of Cambridge, Ontario, where RIM owned an office building. RIM's directors had gathered for a board meeting that included a discussion with the Monitor consultants. Six weeks into an assignment, code-named Project Switchblade, three Monitor consultants had called in via conference call to update the board on their marketing strategy for rescuing RIM's eroding U.S. base. Balsillie was an initial fan of Monitor's plans to step up advertising and product promotions. It would buy RIM more time for Lazaridis to develop its next generation of phones and for him to put the SMS 2.0 plan into play. The consultants, however, would surprise him with a very different message for the board. Time was running out, the advisers warned, because RIM's U.S. customer base was shrinking much faster than expected. In the coming months they calculated as many as 30 percent of the company's remaining customers would likely walk. Monitor recommended the company immediately focus on new product promotions, high-end customer marketing, and improved support of carrier salespeople to stem the losses. The future of the company, they said, depended on a successful launch of new-generation BlackBerry 10 phones. As for the SMS 2.0 messaging plan, the lifeline strategy Balsillie had frantically chased all year, it would only marginally improve the company's fortunes, the consultants concluded.

Balsillie couldn't believe what he was hearing. Instead of discussing marketing plans, the consultants had veered into strategy. The wrong strategy! Didn't they understand how urgently RIM had to seize on his BBM plan if it was to survive? Months of pent-up frustration and anger came tumbling out as Balsillie furiously lectured the advisers. They were amateurs, he said. They didn't understand the shifting smartphone market. The future was software and licenses, not hardware. As Balsillie raised his voice, yelling at times at the consultants, RIM's directors watched in shocked silence. One person who attended the meeting shook his head grimly when recalling the outburst: "He was very emotional." Balsillie would later explain his outburst as the kind of "irritable" reaction that occurs when companies are grappling with "a lot of tension." He became aggressive, he says, to warn directors away from a path he was convinced would lead to ruin. "Did I respond with aggression?" he says. "Yes. But you know what? It is better than folding."

Balsillie had dominated RIM's board of directors for most of the past two decades, winning a receptive audience for his sharp views and strategic acumen. The board seldom questioned him, and Lazaridis had little appetite for the governance and regulatory matters that consumed most meetings. When Lazaridis spoke at board meetings it was usually to give directors samples or prototypes of the newest devices coming down the pipeline. Directors loved the show-and-tell sessions, and, after Balsillie's tirade, a consensus began to take hold at the board that Lazaridis's handset innovations offered the brightest future for the struggling company. Lazaridis offered tangible innovation; Balsillie brought volatility and potentially risky software and service strategies. After Balsillie's tirade, the board had more questions about his leadership than Monitor's proposed course of action. One director described the confrontation as "irrational antagonism." Monitor had been hired at the board's recommendation to help mollify shareholders pushing for new captains. "You co-opt the board," he says. "You work with the board. You don't antagonize the board." Former Monitor executive and RIM director Martin was outraged. Days later he unleashed his own fury, this time on Balsillie, accusing him in an e-mail of "completely unfair (among many other adjectives I could use) assassination of my friends at Monitor in front of the board." Rather than winning directors over, Balsillie had pushed them further away. "I was losing the board. I knew it," Balsillie says.

RIM's board could no longer avoid addressing the spreading rift between the two CEOs. They were driving down such different paths that tensions and disagreements were creating a toxic environment, even at board meetings. It was time to end a damaged partnership. How the divorce proceedings began is a subject of debate. Some RIM directors believe the seeds of a management change were planted when they dispatched two directors, John Wetmore and John Richardson, to visit Lazaridis and Balsillie separately in their offices on December 9. The two directors prepared a nuanced script for each CEO in the hopes they would arrive at the right conclusion. The board, Wetmore and Richardson explained to the CEOs, was under enormous pressure from shareholders to appoint an independent chair and bolster the company's leadership. They favored replacing Lazaridis and Balsillie as chairmen and they encouraged the men to focus on a CEO succession plan. Wetmore and Richardson got little pushback that day and left Waterloo with the hope the duo were ready to groom a new leader.

What they didn't know was that Lazaridis and Balsillie had been having exit discussions for weeks. About the only thing the two men can agree about when it comes to their late fall meetings is that they happened. It is instructive and telling that partners who have different recollections of how they came together in 1992 are also at odds over how they fell apart nineteen years later. The conflicting versions could be a reflection of the opposing personalities of independent, strong-willed CEOs. Just as the professorial Lazaridis and hard-charging Balsillie pursued different tactics to conquer the smartphone market, it is inevitable perhaps that they have constructed clashing narratives about their roles in RIM's rise and fall. It's also possible that by December 2011 their relationship had become so dysfunctional they were no longer listening to each other. It is entirely possible that they are both right.

As Lazaridis tells it, he paid a visit in mid-December to Balsillie at his office in the new RIM B building, a ten-minute drive from the engineering facilities. After the Monitor boardroom showdown and Balsillie's insistent push for a new software and licensing future, Lazaridis, according to associates, was concerned the company was being torn apart by opposing software and hardware visions. The strategies were so starkly different that the CEOs briefly considered breaking the company in two, with Balsillie rolling services such as BBM messaging into a new company and Lazaridis staying with the traditional handset and network business. The wrenching plan, they agreed, wouldn't work because the businesses were simply too intertwined to separate.

Lazaridis remained convinced RIM's future hinged on the pending Black-Berry 10, so much so that he was prepared to resign on the condition that

Balsillie, the vocal handset critic, would follow him. During his meeting with Balsillie, Lazaridis says, "I walked him through the negative press we were getting. I used the words 'We were lightning rods.' . . . Both of us were under huge scrutiny and negative [press] at the time. It just seemed like the right time." The way forward, Lazaridis told his partner, was to promote Thorsten Heins, the six-foot-six-inch executive who ran RIM's hardware division and shared Lazaridis's passion for handsets and the conviction that RIM could reclaim its smartphone title with BlackBerry 10. At the end of his discussion with Balsillie, "I was actually very surprised," Lazaridis says. "He agreed."

Balsillie remembers their falling apart differently, as a less amicable process. After withstanding the blowback from the outage, product failures, market losses, and shareholder activists, he says he "became sick of it" when in December Lazaridis told him the delivery of BlackBerry 10 phones would be delayed until at least mid-2012. At that point something snapped. "As the front guy with the big personality that not everyone likes . . . I am like the easiest prey in the entire country and now I got to [delay BlackBerry 10] another few months?" he says. It was time to throw in the towel. "That was when I decided I was done. I'd had enough." Days later he says he paid Lazaridis a visit in his office in RIM 10. Balsillie says he did not pull any punches when he sat down. "I said, 'You let us all down," with another delay of the BlackBerry 10 lifeline. "I was just mad. I'd had enough."

Balsillie recalls it was his suggestion that the two step down as CEOs and board chairs. Lazaridis, he says, agreed on two conditions: Heins would replace them as RIM's sole CEO and the transition would take place in seven months at the annual meeting. Balsillie says he had concerns about Heins because he had little experience with BlackBerry's global sales, manufacturing, and finance operations. He countered that Patrick Spence, senior vice president overseeing global sales, and Jim Rowan, head of operations, should get senior executive positions to supplement Heins. Lazaridis agreed, he says. They would approach the board together with their plan. Later that night at dinner, Balsillie broke the news to Peric that he and Lazaridis had agreed to step down at the annual meeting. Peric, an experienced marketing manager who had been alarmed by a torrent of negative RIM stories, told Balsillie he could not afford to delay their resignations. Investors wanted immediate change. Agreeing, Balsillie called Lazaridis at home.

"We either do this on our terms or someone else will," Balsillie told his partner of nearly twenty years. "I knew it was time, we had to go."

/ / /

Heins flew from his Florida vacation home to New York with his wife and two children to attend one of the few entertainment perks left to RIM executives. As a sponsor of the 2011 New Year's Eve Times Square celebration, RIM could invite executives to a VIPs-only party at ABC's television studio. Heins, fifty-four, was a long way from his ancestral home. Decades earlier, his father, then a sixteen-year-old high school student, had been dragooned into the German army during the final months of World War II. He was soon captured and imprisoned by Allies until after the war. Released at the age of twenty-four, his father started a new life as a civil servant in Gifhorn, a town near Hanover. Heins senior and his wife, a cleaning woman, were determined survivors who instilled in their four children a tenacious drive. Heins was an ambitious student. He earned a degree as a physicist at the University of Hanover and worked his way up the ranks in the mobile handset division of the German conglomerate Siemens AG. Upon joining RIM in 2007 he impressed Lazaridis and Larry Conlee as an effective and likable manager with chief executive potential. Earlier that year, he'd been promoted to chief operating officer of the company's product engineering group. Tonight he would learn his ascent was not over.

Towering above ABC studio guests, Heins was quickly spied by Balsillie. Tanned and relaxed after a Christmas holiday with Peric in the Middle East, Balsillie gestured for his colleague to join him outside in a small courtyard overlooking Times Square. Staring up at his colleague, Balsillie confided that he and Lazaridis were retiring.

"Wow" is all Heins could manage.

"We'd like you to be CEO."

"Wow."

"There is a process under way," Balsillie continued, "Nothing is certain and done, but this is what Mike and I are supporting. We're definitely retiring."

Balsillie explained that he and Lazaridis informed RIM's board of their retirement plans before Christmas. At that time, they also proposed that Heins become CEO. Balsillie now urged Heins to move quickly to update his résumé and get it to the board. He further suggested he meet with a Toronto investor who would soon be an important RIM player.

Prem Watsa made his name as a contrarian value investor who bet heavily on corporate discards. The sixty-one-year-old Indian immigrant had built

Fairfax Financial Holdings into a C$9 billion conglomerate by success-fully repairing broken insurance companies, restaurant chains, and, after the financial crisis, a near-dead Irish bank. Fairfax had acquired a small 2 percent toehold in RIM's stock in September 2011. Watsa remained convinced the humbled company was a classic value play: the BlackBerry maker had no debt and its core corporate and government business had few rivals. Fairfax's founder, sometimes called "Canada's Warren Buffet," had forged a friendship with Lazaridis years earlier when he replaced the engineer as chancellor of the University of Waterloo. He shared Lazaridis's vision that the company could stage a comeback with a new line of BlackBerrys. The prospect of Watsa's investment support was a lifeline for RIM's struggling board. His thoughts on a new CEO would carry a lot of weight.

The only person more astounded than Heins by Balsillie's New Year's rev-elation was Lazaridis. He'd planned to meet with his partner after the Christmas holidays to tell his handpicked successor the news. Communica-tions had broken down so badly between the two CEOs that they were un-able to even coordinate passing the torch. "It was surprising," says Lazaridis, remembering Heins grateful thank-you call after New Year's. "I felt that was something that Jim and I should have told Thorsten together. It wasn't even one hundred percent approved yet at the time. So he kind of jumped the gun a little bit. That was not the right avenue and time." Balsillie says he broke the news so that Heins would have an updated résumé ready for the board. Another possible explanation is that Balsillie, relieved to be heading for the exit, wanted to hurry the transition along. Now that Heins knew, it would be hard for Lazaridis or the board to change course.

The final weeks of the Lazaridis and Balsillie era were surreal. While the board negotiated a contract with Heins, Balsillie and Lazaridis went about their jobs, telling no one, not even their closest colleagues, of the coming changes. They made their last pilgrimage to Las Vegas in early January for the Consumer Electronics Show, the industry's annual showcase for the lat-est mass market technology breakthroughs. They met in private with Leno-vo's executive team, led by chairman and CEO Yang Yuanqing, to explore licensing RIM's phone software to the Chinese handset maker. They sat down with Microsoft's Steve Ballmer, a longtime BlackBerry admirer. Side by side they glided through the convention, stopping to stare in wonder at Samsung's arena-sized marketing display for its high-end, Android-powered Galaxy Note smartphone. BlackBerry, Balsillie mused, was still late with its 4G phone and had only a fraction of the marketing muscle needed to compete with the sprawling Korean manufacturer. Glad I'm almost out of here, Balsillie told himself.

RIM's board and Watsa blessed Heins as RIM's new CEO later in January. They shared Lazaridis's conviction that BlackBerry 10 was the key to the company's turnaround, and that Heins was the guy to get the product over the finish line. Watsa was so enthusiastic he more than doubled Fairfax's stake in RIM to about 5 percent, while accepting a seat on RIM's board. The departing CEOs agreed to remain as directors, with Lazaridis assuming a new role as board vice chairman and leader of a new internal innovation committee. Before he stepped down as CEO he would help Heins with some final housecleaning. Balsillie learned of one of the changes when he says Lazaridis invited him to a mid-January meeting. In a session Lazaridis does not recall, Balsillie says he was surprised when he walked into his partner's office to find Heins joining the meeting. Why was he here? He was unprepared for the answer. A decision about the China joint venture had been reached, Balsillie recalls Lazaridis saying. After nearly two years of negotiations and more than $30 million of expenses on two China data centers, RIM was pulling out. A nimble tactician who had always been able to spot a roadblock or enemy a mile away, Balsillie was stunned. The parties had already drafted a preliminary agreement and eager partners, including the Beijing fund CIC, were ready to go. Why bail now? Heins, according to Balsillie, warned that the licensing deal would give low-cost Asian manufacturers the upper hand and destroy RIM's future as a handset maker.

"Hardware is already dead," Balsillie remembers protesting. Giant manufacturers such as Samsung were the new kings of the smartphone market, and RIM didn't have the scale to compete in a price war. "All BlackBerry 10 will do is make Samsung rich," Balsillie said.

Balsillie's cynicism was blasphemous to Lazaridis, who remained at his core the science wizard from W. F. Herman High School. To his mind, the best technology would win the smartphone battle. Lazaridis responded to his partner's outburst, according to Balsillie, by turning on him. "Jim, you are killing our hardware."

Tensions continued to escalate in the days leading up to January 22, when the company was set to announce its founders' departure. Watsa encouraged the CEOs to show their support for the company by each buying some RIM stock as they exited their management roles. The pair initially agreed to each buy $50 million worth, but Balsillie, increasingly frustrated with the company's direction, pulled out days before the announcement. It was left to Lazaridis to be the stock angel by writing a $50 million check. Protective of his legacy, Lazaridis hired prominent Los Angeles public relations adviser Michael Sitrick. It was a surprise choice for a retirement announcement. Sitrick was a bulldog crisis manager who straight-armed media on behalf of troubled celebrities like Paris Hilton and Michael Vick, the NFL quarterback sent to prison for fostering a dog-fighting ring. The veteran spinmaster, who had advised Watsa's firm in the past, joined a crowded team of public relations advisers trying to put the best gloss on the management shakeup. RIM's board had already hired New York heavy hitter Joele Frank for public relations advice, and Lazaridis and Balsillie had assigned internal communications staff, lawyers, and directors to oversee the wording of the retirement communique. For all the high-powered help, the message was hopelessly muddled.

A final draft of the handout circulated by e-mail to directors and advisers on January 19, 2012, began with the statement that RIM's board, "acting on the recommendation" of Lazaridis and Balsillie, had unanimously approved Heins as the new CEO. Much of the remaining announcement praised the leadership and devotion of the departing chiefs and their courage in sacrificing short-term gains for long-term growth by acquiring QNX and its operating system. This was hardly a reassuring message to rebellious shareholders. A board faulted for deferring to CEOs would be seen to have bowed again, this time to their proposed successor, Heins, an insider who shared responsibility for PlayBook and BlackBerry 10 delays. Instead of reassuring shell-shocked shareholders that a new beginning was under way, the company chose to honor the status quo, hailing years of strategic confusion and product failures as courageous long-term vision. The approach did not sit well with at least one director.

"Jesus Christ. What are we doing?" director Roger Martin fumed in a blistering e-mail reply to the company's directors, CEOs, and advisers. The press release was doomed, he believed, by leading with Balsillie's and Lazaridis's recommendation for Heins, as their successor. To his mind, the proposed press release failed to send a clear message that meaningful change was occurring at the embattled company. "We have to remember shareholders are pissed," Martin continued. "If Thorsten was so fantastic time and time again, why the huge problems at RIM, people will ask? . . . Let's stop. Let's think. Yes, there are persistent storm clouds and threats. Yes, this company is learning to be a $20 billion company. I get all that. But it doesn't give us license to stop thinking."

Martin's blunt response was not heeded. After a few minor tweaks the press release went out. RIM invited select Canadian and U.S. journalists to Waterloo to interview RIM's CEOs on Sunday, January 22. Reporters were granted access to Lazaridis and Balsillie on condition they not publish stories until later that evening when RIM announced their resignations. The weekend media embargo is a public relations tactic to limit reporters' ability to add other voices to controversial news. Critical shareholders and financial analysts aren't usually available, so reporters have to lean on enthusiastic executives for quotes. In Waterloo that afternoon, business journalists found two remarkably upbeat CEOs. Lazaridis and Balsillie denied rumors of a falling out. They portrayed their resignations as a mutual decision that would give them more time with their families. Both spoke glowingly of RIM's future with Black-Berry 10. "This marks the beginning of a new era for RIM," Lazaridis told his hometown newspaper, the *Waterloo Region Record*.[6]

The careful media management did not sway investors. Seeing little of the fresh leadership they wanted in RIM's executive offices and boardroom, shareholders registered their disappointment on Monday by driving the stock down by more than 8 percent, to $15.56 on the NASDAQ. The new era looked too much like the old era.

/ / /

Balsillie didn't last very long in his diminished role. One month after stepping down as CEO, he dialed into a board conference call to listen to a strategy update by the new CEO. Heins and his team had prepared a PowerPoint presentation on Balsillie's hard-fought quest for the new BBM-based service offering. It had been three months since the ugly confrontation with Monitor's consultants, and Balsillie had convinced himself he had enough momentum to push his plan over the finish line. His pitches to carriers had yielded some support: senior officials from AT&T and Spain's Telefónica agreed to support the concept. As soon as Heins began talking, Balsillie realized with spreading alarm that he had badly misread support for his project.

It took only three PowerPoint slides to bury Balsillie's baby. The messaging strategy, Heins explained, without a hint of regret, would drain too many resources at a time the company was racing to launch BlackBerry 10 phones.

Worst of all, opening BlackBerry's messaging service to other handset makers would undermine the distinctiveness of RIM's phones, posing "significant short-term risk" to the company's handset and service fee revenues. The answer was not diversification, but rather a "double-down" on BlackBerry 10 phones by enhancing BBM services only for BlackBerry customers. Hardware, not software, was the new boss's mantra.

While Heins spoke, Balsillie, sitting in his home office, angrily scratched his pen across a paper copy of Heins' presentation that had been couriered to him. He didn't get it! One of the reasons customers were abandoning RIM was because its BBM messaging service only worked on BlackBerry phones, Balsillie thought. In a world of iPhones and Androids, it made no sense to keep the service closed. Listening to directors' reactions, Balsillie realized his hard-fought plans were dead. Everyone, even Lazaridis, who initially encouraged the project's team, was agreeing. "I never got the feeling any of this stuff was baked," says Lazaridis of the SMS 2.0 strategy. "I was head down into getting BlackBerry 10 out and dealing with those elements of the company that were making money and this other plan was about spending a lot of money." Like Heins, he was worried it would lead to a huge drop in handset sales. "Any plan that supported the core business made sense and we were in favor of. Any plan that pulled away from that, we had to think twice. If we had decided to adopt that kind of slash-and-burn strategy to gain market share we would have been then faced with a shareholder reaction. It would have been hard for us to say, 'Look, we're going to go after this strategy and we believe in the future these large groups of users on an instant messaging service are going to be worth a lot of money.' Who could have said that back then? Nobody."

Balsillie was caught off guard. Heins had been quietly undermining his strategy for months by pushing other executives to reject the plan because it would hurt handset sales. To Balsillie's horror, the board bought the "flawed logic . . . hook, line, and sinker," Balsillie says. He hung up the phone and walked out of his office to find Peric. "I'm resigning from the board," he blurted. That night he decided to sell all his RIM shares after the company released its quarterly results in March. That same month RIM disbanded Balsillie's BBM messaging team, prompting most to leave the company.

Lazaridis hung on for another fifteen months. If he thought life would be easier with his mercurial partner gone and a trusted lieutenant in the CEO seat, he was wrong. Like Balsillie, Lazaridis bristled at being an observer in a company he founded nearly three decades earlier. In his new role as chairman of the innovation committee, he had imagined a new life at RIM as a thinker-in-chief who oversaw handset innovations. It was his turn to be Mr. Micsinszki, his beloved shop teacher at W. F. Herman High School, turning the younger generation on to the wonders of wireless technology. But it didn't turn out that way.

The first tradition to go was Lazaridis's habit of dropping in on engineering labs to offer his thoughts on BlackBerry designs. Comments he made about BlackBerry 10 features and designs weren't always welcome and Lazaridis found himself barred from the labs. Heins, he later learned, had complained to RIM's chair, Barbara Stymiest. There could only be one CEO and Lazaridis had to stop undercutting Heins' authority. Without a specific invitation from Heins, RIM's founder was no longer free to wander through the labs, and many of the suggestions on his long list of improvements to the phone weren't adopted.

Another shock was Heins' decision to change the name of the company Lazaridis had founded three decades earlier to BlackBerry. Research in Motion would be no more as of the July 2013 annual meeting—a move that rankled many old-timers. The biggest humiliation came just before a board meeting in the latter half of 2012. Lazaridis caught up with two of Heins' key outside recruits, new chief marketing officer Frank Boulben and chief operating officer Kristian Tear. When he pressed them on their views about the smartphone business, he was shocked to hear them say the market for BlackBerry's signature keyboard device was dead. RIM would be proceeding to market first with an all-touch smartphone. Lazaridis's strategy had been to introduce two BlackBerry 10 devices, one with a keyboard and touch screen and one with only a touch screen. The new management team seemed poised to abandon the one thing that distinguished RIM from its competitors.

Shortly after the board meeting started, Lazaridis addressed the room. "I get this," he said, pointing to a BlackBerry with a keyboard, "It's clearly differentiated." Then pointing to a touch-screen phone, he said, "I don't get this." To turn away from a product that had been so prized by long-term corporate customers, and instead focus exclusively on selling another all-touch smartphone in a market crowded with them, was a huge mistake, Lazaridis warned fellow directors. "This is our bread and butter, our iconic device," he said. "The keyboard is one of the reasons they buy BlackBerrys."

Some directors agreed, but Heins' new management team held firm, sources close to the board said. "They believed everything was going to full touch" and that the QNX-designed system was clearly superior to what was available on other mobile operating systems, says one source close to the board. To Lazaridis, betting everything on yet another touch screen was too risky. Heins and his team relented slightly. The all-touch-screen Z10 would be issued first, followed months later by a BlackBerry 10 phone with the traditional keyboard and touch screen.

/ / /

Not long after the meeting, RIM's founder decided that a BlackBerry without keyboards meant a RIM without Lazaridis. He explained his decision to RIM's board at a March 28, 2013, meeting by reading a pointed letter. In front of a hushed room, Lazaridis, emotional at many points during the reading, recalled in blunt language the high and low points of RIM's three-decade journey. He reminded directors of RIM's astonishing rise from a penniless start-up to Canada's largest technology company, "a pioneer, innovator, and global leader in the telecommunications market." He conceded "missteps" had been made in recent years but, seemingly unable to dwell on RIM's leadership failings, blamed much of the company's woes on "negative and inaccurate media" stories that he believed were "fueled by short-sellers."

He chastised Heins, whom "I have not always agreed with," for abandoning the physical keyboard in the first phase of its planned launch of BlackBerry 10. The company's future, he insisted, depended on BlackBerry keyboards. The most difficult subject he addressed that day was leaving RIM, "a profoundly emotional time for me," he told the directors. "As you can imagine, for the founder of this company and CEO for twenty-eight years and for someone that ate, drank, breathed, and was on call to RIM for most of my life, it was profoundly difficult for me to let go of the day-to-day operations and leadership of the company by stepping down."

Shortly after Lazaridis decided to cut his ties to RIM, he drove to a Waterloo electronics store. Preparing for what he regarded as an unthinkable future without keyboard BlackBerrys, Lazaridis emptied the store's shelves of BlackBerrys, filling a large box with his purchases. "The most frightening thought," he says, "was that I wouldn't have a BlackBerry."

/ / / EPILOGUE

Jim Balsillie and Mike Lazaridis have had one conversation since parting ways at RIM. The encounter took place in September 2012 at a Toronto fund-raising gala at the Fairmont Royal York Hotel for Ontario's Stratford Shakespeare Festival. After exchanging pleasantries the two men moved on. While the twenty-year partnership is a casualty of the smartphone wars, they both in their own ways remain devoted to the kind of reinvention and gamesmanship that once made them a powerful business combo. Their shared ambition today is to boost technology research and business acumen, ensuring a productive future for Canada in the race for global innovation.

Lazaridis has invested much of his personal fortune in a venture fund and two science institutes devoted to exploring boundaries in physics. The university student inspired by the radical theories of David Bohm now backs an audacious plan to transform Waterloo into a leading center for quantum physics. Balsillie is just as ambitious, though his makeover project is more personal. Scarred and battle-weary after leaving RIM, Balsillie regenerates himself by exploring his native roots and amassing an enormous collection of native art. In quiet Ottawa back rooms, he consults regularly with federal officials about government innovation policy and intellectual property reforms to nurture Canada's thriving technology hubs. Aspiring technology entrepreneurs from the Waterloo area call on him for guidance.

The blueprint for Lazaridis's quantum physics quest is a November 1944 letter written by President Franklin Delano Roosevelt to the Office of Scientific Research and Development. The agency received an unlimited budget during World War II to coordinate innovation with scientists and businesses on secret military projects—atomic weaponry, guided missiles, and radar enhancements. Roosevelt wrote to the agency's head, Vannevar Bush, asking to continue the successful private and public sector alliance. The goal, the president wrote, was "for the improvement of the national health, the creation of new enterprises, bringing new jobs and the betterment of the national standard of living." Roosevelt's vision became the National Science Foundation, which, since the 1950s, has channeled billions of dollars of federal grants into scientific, medical, and computing research at U.S. universities. The funding helped give birth to computing and Internet advances commercialized by Silicon Valley, including a Web search engine project at Stanford University overseen by graduate students Larry Page and Sergey Brin, Google's founders.

Canada has no such foundation, but Lazaridis says Roosevelt's foresight inspired him to push his own version of a private-public partnership. Since 1999 he and his childhood friend, Doug Fregin, have donated more than C$300 million to the Perimeter Institute and the Institute for Quantum Computing at the University of Waterloo. Federal and Ontario governments have matched his philanthropy with close to C$300 million in additional funding. The quantum computing institute is a monument to Lazaridis's conviction that his hometown and former university will be a significant force in the next wave of computing advances.

On one side of the 285,000-square-foot Mike and Ophelia Lazaridis Quantum-Nano Centre sits one of the world's largest quantum computers. The closet-sized machine uses properties of subatomic particles to compute at speeds scientists hope will one day outpace conventional computers. On the other side is a nano-technology department where experiments with microscopic particles are influencing the creation of muscular new materials and instruments for, among other things, construction and medical applications. When Lazaridis welcomed hundreds of academics, politicians, and scientists, including theoretical physicist Stephen Hawking, to the opening of the center in September 2012 he made the same kind of bold promises that RIM's competitors once doubted at their peril. "I believe that the work that will be done here will help transform the way we work, live, and play," he said, "[by] decoding the rules and laws of the universe."[1]

Away from the limelight, Lazaridis's private interests are equally ambitious.

As of September 2014, a private fund he owns with Fregin, Quantum Valley Investments, has invested about $50 million in ventures seeking to commercialize breakthroughs in quantum physics. Since he left the RIM board in 2013, Lazaridis has operated the fund out of a bland, four-story office building near the University of Waterloo. In its first year, most rooms were empty. By the fall of 2014 the building was filled with students, academics, and entrepreneurs huddling around whiteboards or meeting in starkly furnished rooms.

Lazaridis plans to move Quantum Valley to a building he once hoped would be a retreat for RIM engineers. In 2010, after Storm failed and the company struggled with PlayBook, RIM agreed at Lazaridis's request to build a lavish state-of-the-art research center, with an atrium, designer furniture, and high-tech labs, where he could sequester the company's best and brightest. Two years and more than $50 million later, the company completed a contemporary three-story gray brick and glass building north of the University of Waterloo, overlooking a ravine and creek. The 90,000-square-foot building is U-shaped, with glass-covered walkways connecting each floor of two parallel brick structures. The engineering utopia has been virtually unoccupied since it was built. Lazaridis bought the center in 2014 during a massive real estate sell-off by RIM's new management. Lazaridis got a steal, paying only $19 million for the building and more than five acres of land.

Lazaridis's other big project is a two-story, crescent-shaped building that seems to float above a cliff overlooking Lake Huron, west of Waterloo. The 126-acre property at first housed a small cottage that Lazaridis, his wife, and two children retreated to in the summer. A busy schedule prevented RIM's founder from joining his family most weekends. After leaving the company, Lazaridis hired Toronto architect Siamak Hariri to build a residence that could properly show off Canada to visiting academics and politicians. From inside the 26,000-square-foot building, guests can view one of the Great Lakes from a 50-foot-wide window, which Hariri says is one of the largest laminated glass window panels ever made. The inspiration for the building, which the family calls Solaris, is a marble statue of the triumphant Greek goddess Nike that stands in the Louvre. Just as the statue represents victory, Lazaridis views his country home as a symbol of the ingenuity that made BlackBerry great. When he took *Globe and Mail* reporter Renata D'Aliesio on a tour of the home in 2012 he paused to reflect on BlackBerry. Thinking big and acting bold, he said, was "something that has worked for me for decades and I can't see it stopping. I'm not done yet. I'm not finished."

Balsillie says he is finished with business, but like Lazaridis has not stopped thinking big. In the first two weeks after he left RIM in 2012 he slept through most days, waking only for intensive massage therapy to release muscles clenched by years of stress. Since then, he and his partner, Neve Peric have built a life he says is focused on "nourishing." Adding to a collection he started in the early 2000s, Balsillie now owns what he says is one of the world's biggest private portfolios of primitive masks and artifacts, most originating from the Pacific Islands, Africa, Europe, and Middle East. Many masks were made for history's earliest warriors and young men undergoing initiation rites. The life-long Sun Tzu disciple has left the battlefield. He now appreciates war as an art form.

One mythological creature that resonates with Balsillie is the twin-headed serpent. The divided creature is a symbol of the eternal struggle between good and evil, order and chaos, or creation and destruction. Collecting artistic interpretations of the moral contest on primitive masks and sculptures is Balsillie's "inward" and "meditative" way of dealing with his own past. "You have to make sense of these things or they bite you; they bite you bad," he says. Balsillie's inner voyage is not entirely private. As part of an exploration of his family's Métis roots he has met with native Canadian groups to study their art and histories. After emotional sessions with survivors from Canada's infamous residential schools, boarding institutions where many native children were physically and sexually abused, Balsillie has commissioned a survivor to carve a totem pole featuring a twin-headed serpent. The pole will be joined to a hand-carved longhouse to be built near the converted mill where he and Peric live. The longhouse, which will house a gallery displaying much of his mask collection, will be connected to a garden by a low stone wall that Balsillie designed to replicate the snaking form of a two-headed serpent. The wall will stop in the middle of a garden near a full-sized bronze cast Balsillie recently purchased of Rodin's sculpture "The Thinker."

On a brilliant fall day in 2014, Balsillie has as many thoughts as there are colors in the autumn trees surrounding his country hideaway. Like many who have exited businesses with a fortune, he talks with gratitude about the privileges of wealth. He and Peric are active philanthropists, supporting Canadian artists, writers, and musicians. He busies himself with conferences at the Waterloo governance think tank he supports and the economic institute he cofounded with George Soros. He stepped into the limelight briefly in September 2014 as one of the voyagers and sponsors of a successful quest by a

Parks Canada team in the Arctic to locate one of the sunken ships of the doomed expedition led by Sir John Franklin to travel the Northwest Passage in the 1840s. On a less public stage he meets a few times a month with Canadian technology entrepreneurs. He grants each visitor about an hour in a session that is part speed dating, part talent show. In these encounters, he plays the tough judge, brusquely challenging their technology, strategies, and financing as a way of preparing them for the kinds of predators that once threatened RIM.

As he speaks about the risky nature of technology ventures, he turns the conversation to his last, tumultuous year at RIM. For the next few hours he talks with increasing frustration about how RIM might have rewritten its future had the company followed his strategy to shift from its legacy handset business to a new future in software and services built around RIM's BBM instant messaging service. RIM's board and new CEO, Thorsten Heins, dismissed the strategy as risky and marginal, but today instant messaging is the talk of Silicon Valley after Facebook paid $17 billion in 2014 for the money-losing messaging application WhatsApp, with more than 600 million monthly active users. BlackBerry's BBM service had less than a sixth of that amount as of November, 2014. Growing heated as he talks about the lost opportunity, Balsillie stops and bows his head. Rubbing a clenched fist back and forth across his forehead, as if trying to remove some hidden stain, he ends the conversation. "I must not go back to the life of commerce," he says.

/   /   /

Critics called it the best BlackBerry smartphone in years. Navigating the Internet, messages, and phone calls was such a pleasure that *Fast Company* enthused "BlackBerry finally has a little of its swagger back."[1] The phone was not the touch screen BlackBerry 10 that RIM gambled would put the company back on the smartphone map. This new phone was Passport, an oversized phone with a newly designed keyboard unveiled in September 2014 by John Chen, a turnaround expert parachuted in to save a dying company.

RIM's promised new beginning under Thorsten Heins lasted less than two years. His strategy for reviving a failing and divided organization was to wager everything on the company's legacy handset business instead of shifting, as Balsillie urged, to the emerging mobile software services. The BlackBerry 10, finally released in early 2013, was not the iPhone slayer Heins promised.

Not even close. It lacked many of the popular mobile apps on iPhone and Android phones and was hampered by software bugs and a complex user experience confounding to longtime BlackBerry users. BlackBerry was stuck with so many unsold phones that it was forced to put itself up for sale. Several potential suitors, including Lazaridis and his friend Doug Fregin, considered a bid. But it was the company's largest shareholder, Prem Watsa's Fairfax Financial, that prevailed with an offer in late 2013 to lead a sweeping refinancing deal that kept BlackBerry going as a public company and to install Chen as Heins' replacement. In his first year, Chen dramatically shrunk the company into a smaller more unified version of the RIM that had lost its way. Where once RIM had nearly twenty thousand employees and $20 billion in annual revenues, by 2015 those numbers were 6,225 and $3.3 billion. It sold most of its Waterloo real estate and its handsets are now made by a large Taiwan manufacturer called Foxconn Technology Group that has assumed much of the associated financial risks. A company that sold more than 50 million smartphones in its 2011 fiscal year was down to less than 20 percent of that amount four years later. Its global market share was so small, less than 1 percent, that researchers seldom mentioned it in industry studies.[2]

Many observers have already written BlackBerry's obituary. That's fine with Chen. He wants outsiders to underestimate the company as he tries to reinvent it. Chen is producing phones in limited quantities to feed a niche market of loyal customers craving BlackBerry's reliable keyboard and business applications. Chen shares Balsillie's once heretical view that a big part of RIM's future lies with software and global licensing deals—including one with rival Samsung. The new CEO does not have a lot of time to complete his firm's reinvention. The lush service access fees that once generated more than $4 billion in annual revenue have withered to less than half that amount. Innovation in handsets may not help much either. Smartphones can't get much more intelligent, it seems. And while it's true that rising cyber crime has burnished the appeal of BlackBerry's encryption technology, it's too early to say whether security fears will win back customers. Chen is seeking to stretch BlackBerry's QNX operating system beyond phones to manage applications in medicine, automotive, home, entertainment, and other fields.

If Chen's strategy prevails, BlackBerry has a shot at a comeback. Some who stumble suffer the fate of BlackBerry's old adversaries: Nokia, Palm, and Motorola Mobility—shuffled off to new owners, broken up, or sold for parts and patents. BlackBerry's fate remains uncertain, but it is doubtful the company would still be in business were it not for the foresight of Mike Lazaridis and Jim Balsillie. The co-CEOs made multiple mistakes, especially in their final years, but there was enough innovation and cash left to shelter the company through the storms. The Passport and Classic phones launched in 2014 are variations on handsets designed years ago by Lazaridis's engineering team. BlackBerry was able to survive the worst of 2011 and 2012 because Balsillie kept the company debt-free and cash-rich. It would be nice to think that past is prologue and BlackBerry might endure, and that two entirely fallible, very different men who somehow joined together to build an improbable empire would see their legacy carry on in the hands of customers around the globe who will continue to tap away on a product that changed the world. In the technology sector failure is often a precondition to future successes, while prosperity can be the beginning of the end. If the rise and fall of Black-Berry teaches us anything it is that the race for innovation has no finish line, and that winners and losers can change places in an instant.

/ / / ACKNOWLEDGMENTS

This book arose from an investigation into BlackBerry's collapse by the authors for *The Globe and Mail*, which was published in September 2013. That investigation became the foundation of a much more ambitious research effort to document the full story of a small Waterloo company's improbable ascent and decline in the vicious smartphone war that it spawned.

The stories recounted in this book are drawn from interviews with more than 120 people, including BlackBerry's founders, officers, employees, customers, advisors, rivals, and investors. We travelled to Waterloo, Calgary, Ottawa, Toronto, New York, Chicago, Santa Barbara, and Silicon Valley to meet with the book's core characters, each of whom generously shared hours and days of their time. Phone interviews took us to key sources in Finland, Qatar, Great Britain, the United States, and Canada. Detailed recollections, correspondence, and other documents shared with us during interviews were invaluable. Unless otherwise identified, all quoted remarks expressed in the present tense are drawn from those interviews. In addition, dialogue and scenes depicted in the book are based on the recollections of people directly involved. Only a few of the individuals named in this book declined to be interviewed.

At the core of our research is a series of separate interviews with Mike Lazaridis and Jim Balsillie, who graciously welcomed the authors for marathon taped interview sessions lasting, all told, dozens of hours. There were no restrictions or conditions attached to these interviews and we are grateful for their willingness to respond in painstaking detail to all manner of questions, no matter how difficult.

Others were equally generous with their time, insights and patient explanations of RIM's history, culture, technology, and management. The vast majority agreed to speak on the record. In particular, we would like to thank Aaron Brown, Dave Castell, Larry Conlee, Margaret Micsinszki, Don Morrison, Don McMurtry, David Neale, Patrick Spence, Matthias Wandel, Chris Wormald and David Yach. Equally helpful were our colleagues at *The Globe and Mail,* in particular Omar El Akkad and Iain Marlow, who generously shared their insights, notes, and research from their years as RIM beat reporters. Other assists came from Globe colleagues Tara Perkins, Renata D'Aliesio, Steve Ladurantaye, and Rick Cash. We also want to thank the *Globe and Mail*'s publisher, Phillip Crawley, and editor in chief, David Walmsley; our editors, Mark Heinzl and Paul Waldie; as well as past editors, Derek DeCloet, Elena Cherney, and John Stackhouse, for enthusiastically supporting a book that kept us away from the newsroom longer than they would have wished.

This book owes much of its existence to our Washington-based agent Howard Yoon, who cold-called us with a proposal to turn our BlackBerry reporting into a book. Howard led us to our U.S. publisher Flatiron Books, helped shape the book, and was an unflinching midwife during its often difficult birth. We are in his debt. Thanks also to Flatiron's Bob Miller, Colin Dickerman, and James Melia for their unflagging support for this project. Our Canadian agent, Dean Cooke, stickhandled many of the complex issues involved in publishing an international book with grace and finesse. Jim Gifford, our editor at Harper-Collins Canada, was a constant and intelligent editor and friend.

Anyone who has ever written a book understands that the final chapter would never have been written without the love and support of family and friends. Jacquie would like to thank her husband, author Stephen Cole, this book's first reader and editor, for shouldering with unflagging good humor the extra domestic and parental duties that fall to an author's partner. She thanks her sons, Harry and Lewis, for their daily climbs to the attic office in search of a mother. As always, she thanks her parents, Jim and Diana McNish, and sisters Michelle, Rachael, and Cathie. Lindsay Abelarde diligently helped with book research and transcribing interviews and Anabel Silva kept the bar high.

Sean would like to thank his wife, Erin, who took on the thankless role of "book widow" and de facto single parent for long stretches with patience, kindness, and unflagging support. Daughter Clara and sons Ben and Jack were a welcome cheering squad for the "book-ie rookie" in their midst, and were very understanding as he spent long periods burrowed in his basement office while they were scoring goals, performing in concerts, enjoying summer holidays, and trick-or-treating. Erin also provided invaluable constructive feedback on the manuscript. Sean thanks his parents, Carol Silcoff and Brian Silcoff, his step-parents, Gene Swimmer and Janette Hamilton-Silcoff, mother-in-law, Jane Downey, and sister, Marjorie, for their love, support, good humor, and childcare help. Sean is grateful to his aunt Linda Cantlie, uncle Bob Downey, friends David Berman and Nicole Butler, and the McNish-Cole family for kindly providing accommodations, food, drink, and great company during his many trips to Toronto/Waterloo. Finally, Sean thanks old friends who introduced him to key sources, including Ken Murray, Byron Sproule, and George Scriban.

/ / / NOTES

2 / ENCHANTED FOREST

1   Tom Standage, *The Victorian Internet: The Remarkable Story of the Telegraph and the Nineteenth Century's On-Line Pioneers*, New York, Walker & Company, 1998.

2   Lore has it Ericsson's founder, Lars Magnus Ericsson, created the hooked stick so that his wife could stay in touch when she drove country roads. This myth was debunked in 2013 by an Ericsson spokesman, who said the device was created at a later date for Boström. Daniela Hernandez, "The Curious Case of the 103-Year-Old Car Phone," *Wired,* September 20, 2013.

3   Paul Galvin, quoted in "Calling All Cars," Motorola Solutions Inc., www .motorolasolutions.com/US-EN/About/Company+Overview/History/Explore +Motorola+Heritage/Calling+All+Cars.

4   Details about the origins of ALOHAnet were obtained from Norman Abramson's testimony in the civil lawsuit filed by NTP Inc. against Research In Motion, U.S. District Court for the Eastern District of Virginia Richmond Division, Nov. 11, 2002, pp. 859–950.

5   J. M Miles, "Voice/Data Convoy," *InformationWeek,* May 14, 1990.

6   Richard Wise, *Multimedia: A Critical Introduction*, New York, Routledge, 2000, p. 62.

3 / STAYING ALIVE

1   "Mobile Data Will Be a Brave New World," *Kitchener-Waterloo Record*, April 4, 1992.

2   "Prices Cut to $495 or Less for PC Cards, Radio Modules for Motorola Networks," *Mobile Data Report*, December 4, 1995, Vol. 7, No. 23.

3   Ira Sager, "Before iPhone and Android Came Simon, the First Smartphone," *Bloomberg Businessweek*, June 29, 2012.

4   Mike Strathdee, "Waterloo Firm Succeeds in U.S., Ignored at Home," *Kitchener-Waterloo Record,* August 26, 1993.

5   "Dull Year Marked by Improving Hardware, Testing Strategies," *Mobile Data Report*, January 1, 1996, vol. 8, no. 1.

6   Scott McCartney, "U.S. Robotics Dials Up Dollars in Market for Modems," *Wall Street Journal*, July 27, 1995.

7   Cowell did not recall the details of the contract dispute with RIM during a 2014 author interview.

8   Kurt Eichenwald, "Microsoft's Lost Decade," *Vanity Fair*, August 2012.

9   Cheryl Krivda, "Mobile Data Networks: Do They Deliver?" *LAN Magazine*, December 1, 1994.

10 Research In Motion new issue prospectus, October 17, 1997, p. 13. Filed online at the *System for Electronic Document Analysis and Retrieval*, www.sedar.com.

11 Graham Tubbs and Terry Gillett, *Harvesting the BlackBerry: An Insider's Perspective*, Wheatmark, 2011, p. 35.

12 All references to the contents of "Success Lies in Paradox" are drawn from Rod McQueen, *BlackBerry: The Inside Story of Research in Motion,* Toronto, Key Porter, 2010, pp. 115–19.

4 / LEAP

1   Geoffrey A. Moore, *Inside the Tornado,* New York, HarperCollins, 1995.

2   John Colapinto, "Famous Names," *New Yorker,* October 3, 2011.

5 / SPREADING THE GOSPEL

1   The term "evangelist" was commonly used by U.S. computing companies in the 1990s. Mike Boich is believed to have originated the title at Apple in the 1980s,

when he set out to convince developers to create software applications for Macintosh computers.

2   Joann Muller, "Cambridge, Mass. Software Firm Fends Off Microsoft at Conference," *Boston Globe,* September 10, 1998.

3   One of Fabian's best scores happened on another trip to Boston in 1999, when he attended a negotiating seminar at Harvard University. During a break, Fabian pulled out his BlackBerry to show fellow participants. He returned with dozens of leads.

4   Mark Evans, "Stock Sale Ends Dispute Between Com Dev," *Globe and Mail,* February 4, 1999.

5   Douglas Gibson, *Stories About Story Tellers,* Toronto, McClelland and Stewart, 2011, p. 25. Robertson Davies frequently told the story of attending a Vancouver cocktail party in 1957 when news was announced that Canadian diplomat and future prime minister Lester Pearson had been awarded the Nobel Peace Prize for his work during the Suez Canal crisis. An elderly woman attending the party greeted the news by barking, "Well! Who does he think he is?"

6   Michael Gartenberg, "BlackBerry Back in the Game with BB10 OS and Z10 Smartphone," *Computerworld,* January 30, 2013.

7   "Making It Big," *Forbes,* April 16, 2001.

8   Kevin Maney, "BlackBerry: The 'Heroin' of Mobile Computing," *USA Today,* May 7, 2001.

9   Michael Smith, "All Thumbs," *Report on Business Magazine,* March 31, 2000.

6 / TOP THIS

1   After buying Palm in 1995, U.S. Robotics was subsequently taken over by 3Com in 1997.

2   Beth Piskora, "$1.07B in His Palm; CEO Is a Big Winner as IPO Rockets to $53B," *New York Post,* March 3, 2000.

3   The 1994 Simon is widely regarded as the world's first smartphone, but the term didn't appear until 1997 when Sweden's Ericsson promoted the term in its marketing campaign for the GS 88 Penelope, a device that combined mobile computing, text, and voice applications.

4   European Commission, "Microsoft: A History of Anticompetitive Behaviour and Consumer Harm," March 31, 2009, p. 4. www.ecis.eu/documents/Finalversion_Consumerchoicepaper.pdf.

5   Adrian Ryans, "Research In Motion Ltd.," Richard Ivey School of Business case study, University of Western Ontario, published February 9, 2000, www.iveycases.com.

6   Horace Dediu, "In Memoriam: Microsoft's Previous Strategic Mobile Partners," Asymco.com, February 11, 2011, www.asymco.com/2011/02/11/in-memoriam -microsofts-previous-strategic-mobile-partners/.

7   Walter S. Mossberg, "Palm's New Hand-Held Goes Mano a Mano with a Black-Berry," *Wall Street Journal,* January 31, 2002.

8   Douglas McIntyre, "The 10 Biggest Tech Failures of the Last Decade," *Time*, May 14, 2009.

9   "The Emergence of the CIO," IBM corporate report, www-03.ibm.com/ibm /history/ibm100/us/en/icons/emergenceofcio/.

7 / EL CAMINO

1   Quentin Hardy and Joan Indiana Rigdon, "Motorola Overhauls Staff Structure, Slashes Management Pay," *Wall Street Journal*, March 24, 1997.

2   Paul Desmarais died in 2013 at the age of eighty-six.

3   In 2003 the Library of Congress acquired 911 Digital Archive, a large collection of digital e-mails, notes, recordings, and photographs from the September 11, 2001, terrorist attacks in New York, Washington, and Pennsylvania. The New York Graduate Center and George Mason University jointly assembled the collection. Many e-mails in the collection were written by people using BlackBerrys.

4   The worker identified as Craig submitted an account of his experience on September 11 to the 911 Digital Archive. His story included copies of e-mails exchanged on his BlackBerry with his wife and many coworkers in search of missing colleagues. "I am very grateful to have a BlackBerry and to have been able to keep in touch so instantly that day," Craig wrote in his story. See http://911digital archive.org/items/show/17220.

5   Bill Kelley's sisters described his last e-mails during an interview with CNN on September 14, 2002, during a special program called *9/11: What Really Happened*.

6   Michael Martin and Denise Pappalardo, "Carriers Stay Course with NYC Networks," *Network World,* March 11, 2002.

7   Simon Romero, "The Simple BlackBerry Allowed Contact When Phones Failed," *New York Times,* September 20, 2001.

8   Ibid.

9   Lauren W. Wittington et al., "Sorrow and Defiance Security Review Planned," *Roll Call*, September 13, 2001.

10   Ibid.

11 National Journal Staff, "Voices of 9/11," *National Journal*, May 3, 2011.

12 Dawn S. Onley, "Smart-Card Rollout Might Need More Time," *Government Computer News*, July 21, 2003.

8 / GAME OF PHONES

1   Nokia press release, February 23, 2000.

2   Walt Mossberg, "Wireless Carriers' Veto over How Phones Work Hampers Innovation," *Wall Street Journal*, June 2, 2005.

3   LinkedIn page for Matthias Wandel, retrieved October 30, 2014.

4   Kevin Maney, "BlackBerry: The Heroin of Mobile Computing," *USA Today*, May 7, 2001.

5   Brad Stone, "BlackBerry: Bring It On!" *Newsweek*, September 26, 2005.

6   Richard Kay, "How Much Money Does Linley Need?" *Daily Mail*, August 10, 2006.

7   "Transition," *The West Wing*, season 7, episode 19, aired on NBC, April 23, 2006.

8   Marshall Loeb, "Don't Let Your BlackBerry Be Your Boss," *Dow Jones Business News*, June 21, 2007.

9   "You're So Busted!! DDB Canada Battles PDA Misconduct with 'Colourful' Penalty Card System," press release from *DDB Canada*, February 12, 2008, http://www.ddb.com/japan/press/02-12-08_YellowRedCards.pdf.

10 Richard Schmelzer, "Sheraton Provides Guests Vacation from Hand-Helds," *PRWeek*, Octpber 23, 2006.

11 Mike Elgan, "Why the BlackBerry Pearl is the Smart Phone of the Future," *Computerworld*, December 14, 2006.

9 / ROCKET DOCKET

1   Barrie McKenna, Paul Waldie, and Simon Avery, "Patently Absurd: The Inside Story of RIM's Wireless War," *Globe and Mail*, February 21, 2006.

2   Ibid.

3   Ibid.

4   Robin Feldman, Tom Ewing, and Sara Jeruss, "The AIA 500 Expanded: The Effects of Patent Monetization Entities," UC Hastings Research Paper No. 45, http://papers.ssrn.com/sol3/papers.cfm?abstract_id=2247195.

5   "Pager Maker Gets Patent for E-Mail Delivery," *Wall Street Journal*, May 18, 2001.

6   Kevin Restivo, "The Firm That May Run RIM Off the Court," *National Post,* December 8, 2005.

7   *Federal Judicial Caseload Statistics, Table C-5: U.S. District Courts Median Time Intervals from Filing to Disposition of Civil Cases Terminated, by District and Method of Disposition, During the 12-Month Period Ending March 31, 2001,* Administrative Office of the United States Courts, Washington, D.C., www.uscourts.gov /uscourts/Statistics/FederalJudicialCaseloadStatistics/FederalJudicialCaseload Statistics2001.aspx.

8   Mosahid Khan, "The Surge in Worldwide Patent Applications," World Intellectual Property Organization, June 6–10, 2011, p. 5.

9   Chetan Sharma Consulting, *Mobile Patents Landscape: An In-Depth Quantitative Analysis,* 3rd ed., 2014, www.chetansharma.com/MobilePatentsLandscape_2014 .htm.

10   All references to the proceedings in original NTP-RIM case are drawn from court transcript, *NTP Inc. v Research in Motion Ltd.,* U.S. District Court for the Eastern District of Virginia, Richmond Division, November 4–21, 2002, Civil Action 3:01CV767.

11   Author interview with Rose Ann Janis.

12   Theodore Schleifer, "In Virginia Trial of McDonnell and Wife, an Imposing Judge Sets the Pace," *New York Times,* August 10, 2014.

13   District Judge James Spencer, Memorandum of opinion, filed in *NTP Inc. v. Research in Motion Ltd.* May 23, 2003.

14   Donn Smith, *Internal Perfection: The New Frontier for Performance, Well-Being and Health, 2013,* available at www.iamenergy.ca/internalperfection.php.

15   "Patent Office Rejects NTP Claim Ahead of BlackBerry Injunction Hearing," *RCR Wireless* News, February 23, 2006.

16   Brian Baxter, "Hitting the Jackpot," *American Lawyer,* May 1, 2007.

10 / THE JESUS PHONE

1   Walter S. Mossberg, "Wireless Carriers' Veto over How Phones Work Hampers Innovation," *Wall Street Journal,* June 2, 2005.

2   Fred Vogelstein, *Dogfight: How Apple and Google Went to War and Started a Revolution,* New York, Penguin Group, 2013, p. 45.

3   "U.S. Wireless Data Market Update 2006," Chetan Sharma Consulting, Chetan-sharma.com, 2006.

4   Vogelstein, *Dogfight,* p. 47.

5   Ibid., p. 45.

6   Ibid.

7   David Pogue, "iPhone Soars (Even with AT&T in Tow)," *New York Times*, July 2, 2007.

8   Walter Isaacson, *Steve Jobs,* New York, Simon & Schuster, 2011, p. 395.

9   Ibid., pp. 417–8.

11 / STORM

1   Chris Sorensen, "CEO Balsillie Shrugs off 'BlackBerry Killer,'" *Toronto Star,* July 7, 2007.

2   Brad Stone, "BlackBerry's Quest: Fend Off the iPhone," *New York Times,* April 27, 2008.

3   Vogelstein, *Dogfight*, p. 120.

4   Andrew Bary, "World's Best CEOs," *Barron's,* March 24, 2008, p. 33.

5   Jim Balsillie made these remarks during a June 2, 2009, talk to students at the Asper School of Business in Winnipeg, Manitoba.

6   Stone, "BlackBerry's Quest."

7   Transcript from interview with Mike Lazaridis conducted by Ron Milton in "The Laureate: Journal of the Computerworld Information Technology Awards Foundation," June 2008, pp. 8–17.

8   Nick Wingfield, "iPhone Software Sales Take Off: Apple's Jobs," *Wall Street Journal,* August 11, 2008.

9   Isaacson, *Steve Jobs,* p. 502.

10   Ted C. Fishman, "What Happened to Motorola," *Chicago Magazine*, August 25, 2014.

11   David Pogue, "No Keyboard? And You Call This a BlackBerry?" *New York Times,* November 27, 2008.

12   Stephen Fry, "Gee, One Bold Storm Coming Up . . . ," www.stephenfry.com, December 11, 2008, www.stephenfry.com/2008/12/11/gee-one-bold-storm-coming-up/.

13   Rory Cellan-Jones, "Can Stephen Fry Kill a Gadget?" dot.life blog, *BBC News*, November 27, 2008, www.bbc.co.uk/blogs/legacy/technology/2008/11/can_stephen_fry_kill_a_gadget.html.

14   Amol Sharma and Sara Silver, "BlackBerry Storm Is Off to Bit of a Bumpy Start," *Wall Street Journal,* January 26, 2009.

12 / OFFSIDE

1   Oral Ruling of the Ontario Securities Commission, "In the Matter of Research in Motion Limited, James Balsillie, Mike Lazaridis, Dennis Kavelman, Angelo Loberto, Kendall Cork, Douglas Wright, James Estill and Douglas Fregin," February 5, 2009, p. 2. www.osc.gov.on.ca/documents/en/Proceedings-RAD/rad_20090521_rim_set.pdf.

2   Two weeks later the Washington-based Securities and Exchange Commission unveiled a settlement requiring the RIM executives to pay an additional $1.4 million in penalties for the options backdating and disgorge an additional $843,415.

3   Janet McFarland, "OSC Slaps RIM Officials with $77-Million Payment," *Globe and Mail*, February 5, 2009.

4   United States Bankruptcy Court, District of Arizona, In re Dewey Ranch Hockey, LLC, Coyotes Holdings, LLC, Coyotes Hockey, LLC and Arena Management Group LLC, debtors, case no: 2:09-bk-09-09488-RTBP, "PSE Sports and Entertainment LP's position on August 5 sale hearing and August 3 NHL sale rescheduling motion," Doc. 533, filed July 31, 2009, p. 5.

5   Sinclair Stewart and Paul Waldie, "Beware Balsillie's Competitive Fever," *Globe and Mail*, June 15, 2007.

6   United States Bankruptcy Court, District of Arizona, In re Dewey Ranch Hockey, LLC, Coyotes Holdings, LLC, Coyotes Hockey, LLC and Arena Management Group LLC, debtors, case no: 2:09-bk-09-09488-RTBP, "Declaration of Craig Leipold," Doc. 585, filed August 7, 2009, p. 2.

7   Ibid., Exhibit A.

8   The Competition Bureau of Canada did make inquiries into NHL practices in 2007, but the file was closed within weeks.

9   United States Bankruptcy Court, District of Arizona, In re Dewey Ranch Hockey, LLC, Coyotes Holdings, LLC, Coyotes Hockey, LLC, and Arena Management Group, LLC, debtors, case no: 2:09-bk—09-09488-RTBP, "Declaration of Craig Leipold," Doc. 585, filed August 7, 2009, p. 5.

10 Ibid.

11 Reyes eventually sold his stake in the San Jose Sharks after a prolonged legal battle that saw his conviction overturned, then reinstated in 2010 after a second trial.

12 United States Bankruptcy Court, District of Arizona, In re Dewey Ranch Hockey, LLC, Coyotes Holdings, LLC, Coyotes Hockey, LLC, and Arena Management Group, LLC, debtors, case no: 2:09-bk—09-09488-RTBP, "Supplemental submission of the National Hockey League in support of motion for a determination

that debtors' NHL membership rights may not be transferred to PSE or an affiliate thereof," Doc. 879, filed September 1, 2009, p. 2.

13 Based on author search of Factiva online database. First mention of abbreviated Protiviti report was: Teresa Poletti, "Time for RIM Chiefs to Dial Back Their Roles," *MarketWatch,* July 11, 2011.

13 / DISCONNECT

1   Stephen H. Wildstrom, "How Apple's iPhone Reshaped the Industry," *Bloomberg Businessweek Magazine,* December 10, 2008.

2   Walter Isaacson, *Steve Jobs,* New York, Simon & Schuster, 2011, p. 502.

3   "BusinessWeek/Interbrand Release Annual Ranking of the 100 'Best Global Brands,'" press release, September 18, 2009.

4   Kate Solomon, "RIM: We Don't Need 200 Fart Apps for App World Success," *Recombu,* September 29, 2010, http://recombu.com/mobile/article/rim-we-dont -need-200-fart-apps-for-app-world-success_M12412.html.

5   Fred Vogelstein, *Dogfight: How Apple and Google Went to War and Started a Revolution,* New York, Penguin, 2013, pp. 92–93.

6   Ken Auletta, "Searching for Trouble," *New Yorker,* October 12, 2009.

7   Niraj Sheth and Jessica E. Vascellaro, "Google, Verizon Deepen Ties: CEOs Develop Friendship as They Look to Challenge Apple's iPhone," *Wall Street Journal,* November 10, 2009.

8   Fred Vogelstein, "How the Android Ecosystem Threatens the iPhone," *Wired,* April 14, 2011.

9   Wailin Wong, "'No Quick Fix' for Motorola Cell Unit; 3,000 Job Cuts, Sales Decline Expected; Company Posts Loss," *Chicago Tribune*, October 31 2008.

10 Sheth and Vascellaro, "Google, Verizon Deepen Ties."

11 Vogelstein, *Dogfight.*

12 Data for monthly U.S. smartphone subscriber market share published by comScore, Inc., at comscore.com.

13 Data released by market research firm Canalys at Canalys.com.

14 Transcript from interview with Mike Lazaridis conducted by Ron Milton in "The Laureate: Journal of the Computerworld Information Technology Awards Foundation," June 2008, pp. 8–17.

15 This anecdote was shared by Verizon's John Stratton with a RIM executive in 2014. A second RIM executive was told the Barcelona meeting "broke the camel's back" and permanently impaired the Verizon-RIM relationship.

14 / GOAT RODEO

1 "Heroes of Manufacturing," *Fortune Magazine*, March 17, 2003.

2 Dan Dodge, "Software Comes of Age," *ECN*, April 1, 2006.

3 Customers posted their complaints about Torch here: http://supportforums .blackberry.com/t5/BlackBerry-Torch/Button-panel-peeled-off-ATT-replaced -my-torch/td-p/569359.

4 By 2012 Heins would declare the quality improvement project successful after it meaningfully improved return rates and lessened customer complaints.

5 Other than confirming that he told Tobin he should be reporting to him, Lazaridis declined to comment on his relationship with Tobin.

6 www.rankingthebrands.com/Brand-detail.aspx?brandID=21.

15 / FAULT LINES

1 Ben Worthen, "Businesses Add iPads to Their Briefcases," *Wall Street Journal*, August 24, 2010.

2 Jobs claimed Adobe "screwed" him by refusing to make a Mac version of Adobe Premiere in 1999 and later attacked Flash, telling biographer Walter Isaacson that it was "a spaghetti-ball piece of technology that has lousy performance and really bad security problems." Isaacson, *Steve Jobs,* pp. 514–5.

3 Clayton Christensen, *The Innovator's Dilemma,* Boston, Harvard Business Publishing, 1997.

4 BlackBerry turned down interview requests with Dan Dodge for this book.

5 Chloe Albanesius, "Adobe Ditching Mobile Browser Flash Player Development," *PC Magazine*, November 9, 2011.

6 RIM's share of AT&T, which was lower to begin with because of the carrier's relationship with Apple, dipped to 15 percent in the fourth quarter of 2010, down from 18 percent a year earlier.

7 Mikael Ricknäs, "Samsung Becomes Biggest Smartphone Vendor, as Android's Market Share Grows," *PC World,* November 15, 2011.

8 Paul Christoper Webster and Iain Marlow, "Where the BlackBerry Still Reigns Supreme," *Report on Business Magazine*, November 29, 2012.

9 Susana Ferreira and Will Connors, "In These Countries, BlackBerry Is Still King—Of Pop Culture," *Wall Street Journal*, September 11, 2012.

10 "BlackBerry Babes," *The Economist*, December 8, 2012.

11   "BlackBerry Loses Top Spot to Apple at Home: Corporate Canada," *Bloomberg*, March 22, 2012.

12   Zahraa al Khalisi, "BlackBerry 'Pins' Are the New Licence Plates," *The National* (United Arab Emirates), September 19, 2009; author interview with Patrick Spence, 2014.

13   Sandeep Singh Grewal, "Comeback Vow by Journalist," *Gulf Daily News,* September 23, 2010; Yousef, "Blackberries, Breaking News and Bans," Flipcorp.com, September 25, 2011, www.flipcorp.com/en/read/blog/bahrain-blackberries.blog.

14   This information is based on a statement of defense and counterclaim filed in Canadian Federal Court by Kik Interactive against RIM in April 2011; it was not tested in court. Court filing case T-1996-10 was filed by RIM against Kik Interactive in November 2010 and settled out of court in September 2013. BlackBerry subsequently declined to comment on the case.

15   Sean Silcoff, "BlackBerry, Kik Interactive Settle Lawsuit over Instant Messaging App," *Globe and Mail*, October 7, 2013.

16   The lawsuit was settled out of court in 2013.

17   Stuart Weinberg and Roger Cheng, "RIM Tries to Push PlayBook Tablet," *Wall Street Journal*, April 15, 2011.

18   E. B. Boyd, "Jobs Takes a Swing at Android, BlackBerry," www.fastcompany.com, October 18, 2010, www.fastcompany.com/1696148/jobs-takes-swing-android-blackberry.

19   Clint Boulton, "RIM CEO: Apple Is Wrong for Having an App for That," *eWeek*, November 16, 2010.

20   Peter Kafka, "RIM Co-CEO Mike Lazaridis, Live at Dive into Mobile," *AllthingsD.com*, December 7, 2010. A video of the on-stage interview with Lazaridis is posted at: http://allthingsd.com/20101213/d-dive-into-mobile-the-full-interview-video-of-rims-mike-lazaridis/.

21   Adrian Cover, "Can You Figure Out WTF RIM's CEO Is Talking About?" *Gizmodo*, December 7, 2010.

16 / WATERLOO SPRING

1   Omar El Akkad, "Rim Slashes Profit Outlook as Wireless Competition Heats Up," *Globe and Mail*, April 28, 2011.

2   Martin Peers, "BlackBerry Maker's Slow-Motion Decline," *Wall Street Journal*, March 26, 2011.

3   Ian Austen, "Eyes on a Rebound," *New York Times*, April 11, 2011.

4   Jonathan S. Geller, "Open Letter to BlackBerry Bosses: Senior RIM Exec Tells All as Company Crumbles Around Him," *BGR*, June 30, 2011. http://bgr.com/2011/06/30/open-letter-to-blackberry-bosses-senior-rim-exec-tells-all-as-company-crumbles-around-him/.

5   Austen, "Eyes on a Rebound."

6   "RIM CEO Calls a Halt to BBC Click Interview," *BBC*, April 13, 2011, http://news.bbc.co.uk/2/hi/programmes/click_online/9456798.stm.

7   Stuart Weinberg and Roger Cheng, "RIM Tries to Push PlayBook Tablet," *Wall Street Journal*, April 15, 2011.

8   Jay Palmer, "The BlackBerry Strikes Back," *Barron's,* April 16, 2011.

9   Dean Bubley, "Joyn, a World of Delusion," posted at disruptivewireless.blogspot.ca, March 18, 2013.

17 / HANGING UP

1   Gordon Pitts, "Roger Martin: Defying RIM's Critics," *Globe and Mail,* February 10, 2012.

2   Caline Malek, "BlackBerry Cuts Made Roads Safer, Police Say," *The National* (United Arab Emirates), October 15, 2011.

3   Rolfe Winkler, "Heard on the Street/Financial Analysis and Commentary," *Wall Street Journal,* October 14, 2011.

4   Toby Shapshak, "Cracks Showing at BlackBerry," *The Sunday Times,* Oct. 16, 2011.

5   "BlackBerry Sorry, but Is It too Late," *Chicago Tribune,* October 14, 2011.

6   The *Kitchener-Waterloo Record* was renamed *The Waterloo Region Record* in March 2008.

EPILOGUE

1   Greg Mercer, "The New Heart of Quantum Valley," *Guelph Mercury,* September 22, 2012.

2   Harry McCracken, "The BlackBerry Passport's Weird Design Pays Off—But the App Situation Remains Bleak," *Fast Company,* September 24, 2014, www.fastcompany.com/3036124/blackberry-passport-review.

3   "Android Captures 84% Share of Global Smartphone Shipments in Q3 2014," posted by *Strategy Analytics*, October 31, 2014, http://blogs.strategyanalytics.com/WSS/author/nmawston.aspx.

/ / / INDEX